Evangelicals Adrift
Supplanting Scripture with Sacramentalism

Matthew E. Ferris

Paperback ISBN:	978-0-9965168-0-8
Mobipocket ISBN:	978-0-9965168-1-5
ePub ISBN:	978-0-9965168-2-2

Printed in the United States of America

Contents

"Religious conversion among Catholics and Protestants has generated a deluge of whitewater on the Tiber River. Some enjoy the thrill. Others drown. In the face of this tumult, Matt Ferris has written *Evangelicals Adrift* as a life preserver. Anyone considering conversion to Rome will find in these pages questions and arguments worth consideration."

- Chris Castaldo, PhD. Lead Pastor, New Covenant Church, Naperville, Illinois, and author, *Talking with Catholics about the Gospel.*

"Matt Ferris has done us a great service with this hard-hitting and courageous book. Alarmed by the trend of evangelicals leaving their faith for the sacramentalism of Roman Catholicism or Orthodoxy, Matt carefully and passionately lays out the key differences between these two approaches to God and to religious knowledge. May *Evangelicals Adrift* spark renewed conversation, reflection, prayer, and – most of all – Bible reading."

- Stan Guthrie, author, *God's Story in 66 Verses: Understand the Entire Bible by Focusing on Just One Verse in Each Book.* and *All That Jesus Asks: How His Questions Can Teach and Transform Us.*

Acknowledgements

My thanks are due to several friends who assisted me at various points in the writing of this book. Stan Guthrie provided suggestions on how to refine the text to widen its appeal. Anthony Gosling gave guidance and support, and Matt Tully was an early reader of the manuscript who gave encouragement, as did Chris Castaldo. Ted Pallock agreed to expand on his personal experience of coming to Christ, for which I am grateful. Jim and Sue Holmes of Great Writing have eyes for detail that time and again surprised me. Jim's suggestions and expertise have been immensely helpful throughout this project. Ken Miller taught me early in my Christian life to have respect for the Scriptures as they are written, put good books in my hands, and gave me a foundation that still pays rich dividends. My wife, Jane, read the manuscript through several times and provided feedback that proved essential. Without her this book would be a poorer offering.

1
An Evangelical Identity Crisis

If we could put forth one summarizing feature of evangelicalism today, it may be that diversity best captures its essence. Within the porous borders of the movement, one finds everything from Southern Baptists, Reformed Baptists, Anabaptist peace churches, to Pentecostal and charismatic groups, and seeker-sensitive mega-churches, as well as more traditional free churches and direct descendants of the Reformation. Evangelicalism is populist, decentralized, and eclectic. The shape of American evangelicalism today has deep roots in the history of the country, and in the character that developed in the American mind. Corwin E. Smidt refers to the "democratic revolution" in American Protestantism following the first and second Great Awakenings, and how this influenced popular religion: "During the First Great Awakening, it was the authority of those clergy who had not had a conversion experience that was brought into question, but during the Second Great Awakening, the authority of all clergymen was largely brought into question."[1]

As a byproduct of this democratization, the Bible was restored to a place of authority in the life of the individual rather than its being dependent on the mediation of the clergy. "This movement toward hearing the voice of the people in religion clearly encouraged a more literal interpretation of scripture."[2] The centrality of the Bible for the Christian life, though it would be opposed and redefined in subsequent decades, remains a primary feature of evangelicalism. This anti-clerical position of evangelicalism had a decidedly salutary effect on spreading the gospel through various missions' organizations devoted to Bible

---

[1] Corwin E. Smidt, *American Evangelicals Today* (Lanham, MD, Rowman & Littlefield Publications, 2013), p. 21.

[2] Smidt, p. 22.

translation, radio broadcasting, and the sending of missionaries. Evangelicals do not require the sanction of any church to undertake what they plainly read the Bible as telling them to do. Indeed, this has been one of the great strengths of the evangelical movement.

The fact that we can speak of no single "evangelical" denomination showcases the decentralized nature of evangelicalism. No headquarters or governing body exists to define doctrine or to administer discipline. This fact highlights two salient features of the movement. Firstly, the ultimate source of authority for evangelicals is the Scriptures, and secondly, ecclesiastical authority, to whatever extent it exists, is entirely subservient to the Bible and to the centrality of the gospel. Despite the distributed nature of the evangelical movement, cooperation among like-minded Christians has not been lacking. In the nineteenth century, organizations such as the China Inland Mission and D.L. Moody's Student Volunteer Movement were expressly founded to promote the gospel, quite apart form any ecclesiastical concern or structure. Here, too, cooperation among like-minded individuals, apart from confessional distinctions, has advanced the gospel. That some Christians today are clamoring for the kind of centralized authority evangelicalism has lacked does not argue that decentralization has been ineffective so much as that these believers may be looking to other traditions for different reasons.

Eclecticism has also been a distinction of evangelicalism. Denominational affiliations and labels are less important than advancing the kingdom of God. As it developed in the late twentieth century, American evangelicalism often resisted easy categorization. While placing an emphasis on individualism, evangelicals nevertheless place an enormous emphasis on personal accountability.[3] They tend to be hostile to institutions,

---

[3] Donald E. Miller, *Reinventing American Protestantism: Christianity in the New Millennium* (Berkeley, Univ. of California Press, 1997), p. 20.

bureaucracies, and routinized aspects of organized religion. On the other hand, they place an extremely high value on community, and, for many individuals, the church is the center of their lives.[4]

This diversity and eclecticism led to a crisis of identity for some. The traits that David Bebbington identified in his "Evangelical Quadrilateral" as distinctives: Biblicism, Crucicentrism, Conversionism and Activism[5], are now less important for some than they were for believers of a previous generation. As evangelicalism has constantly reinvented itself, have we arrived at a time when to describe someone as an "evangelical" is to say very little indeed about his or her core beliefs? Molly Worthen comments, "The term evangelical has produced more debate than agreement. The word is so mired in adjectives and qualifiers, contaminated by politicization and stereotype, that many commentators have suggested that it has outlived its usefulness."[6] For some who identify as evangelical, the strengths of the movement's diversity also contain the seeds of its weakness. Democratization can lead to an interpretive din where the voice of God is difficult to discern. These believers view decentralization as disunity and schism, and eclecticism can begin to look like chasing after the latest fad.

Perhaps because of their experience with evangelical diversity, some believers have sought to solve this identity crisis through conversion to Catholicism or Orthodoxy. If they are accustomed to accept truth where they find it, regardless of denomination, and if they have been empowered to interpret Scripture on their own, then such a switch is not as unlikely as it may at first appear. For many evangelicals who take this step, the change is often attended

---

[4] Donald E. Miller, p. 22.

[5] David W. Bebbington, *Evangelicalism in Modern Britain: A History from the 1730s to the 1980s* (London: Unwin Hyman, 1989), p. 2-3.

[6] Molly Worthen, *Apostles of Reason: The Crisis of Authority in American Evangelicalism* (Oxford University Press, USA. Kindle Edition, 2013), Kindle Locations 88-90.

by a great deal of angst and wrestling, and when they do decide to join the Catholic or Orthodox Church, it is frequently accompanied with statements of having finally "arrived." Titles such as Dwight Longenecker's *More Christianity: Finding the Fullness of the Faith*, Peter Gillquist's *Coming Home: Why Protestant Clergy are Becoming Orthodox*, and Thomas Howard's *Evangelical is Not Enough* demonstrate the attitude that while these believers knew the Lord in their evangelical years (a distinction that is critical to understand), they now view their former faith as deficient and incomplete.

For evangelicals, the believers who make this change pose an inherent challenge. Simply put, they are telling evangelicals they are wrong about their understanding of God and how human beings relate to Him. For them, evangelicalism is wrong about the Bible, wrong about the church, her nature, ministry, and ordinances, and wrong about her future. It may be ecumenically incorrect to state it in these terms, but it is nevertheless the crux of the matter when an evangelical converts to Catholicism or Orthodoxy.[7] They look upon those who remain evangelicals as part of an ersatz church, and the faith they practice as incomplete and substandard. Kristine L. Franklin typifies this attitude of the convert from evangelicalism, "During our long, circuitous journey home to the Catholic Church, we found that there is indeed only one gospel, the Catholic gospel. There is only one place where we can find the fullness of truth and the most personal of relationships with Jesus Christ – and that place isn't Protestantism."[8] This attitude, which might be called militant sacramentalism, is far

---

7 To some extent, this holds true for Anglicanism as well. As a kind of "sacramentalism-lite", Anglicanism embraces some, but not all of the doctrines found in Catholicism or Orthodoxy. To the degree that Anglicans hold to sacraments as vehicles of grace, and the authority of Scripture is replaced by ecclesiology, this discussion would also apply to Anglicanism.
8Patrick Madrid, *Surprised By Truth 2* (Manchester, Sophia Institute Press, 2000), p. 26.

more prevalent in converts than in cradle Catholics. Ironically, it is the latter who are more likely to affirm truth in other traditions.

What has changed within evangelicalism, or within the sacramental churches for that matter, to bring a consideration of these traditions as possible alternatives for evangelicals? In 2002, Professor Scot McKnight of North Park University researched the reasons behind what he termed "ERCs" (Evangelical Convert to Roman Catholicism): "The ERC came to a crisis of transcendence and that crisis had four manifestations: first, a crisis over the limits of human knowledge, seeking certainty; a crisis over temporality, seeking a continuous place in history; a crisis over division, seeking unity; and a crisis over interpretive opinion, seeking an authoritative arbiter of truth."[9] In other words, there is a desire to know for sure what is true, to maintain a connection with previous generations of believers, to be part of demonstrable union in the body, and to have a definitive voice to solve the question of interpretive diversity. These four categories identified by McKnight will inform my examination.

These concerns are not recent, but what is new is that evangelicals are willing to consider answers to these questions that they previously rejected. In subsequent chapters, I lay out the evidence of why the answers offered by sacramentalism are not the right answers, and why they do not represent historical Christianity in the sense of that which can be traced back to the apostles. Professor McKnight's identification of the reasons for conversion exposes the exceedingly diverse nature of evangelicalism, and also the challenges and responsibilities that accompany a movement that is highly decentralized. It is a loss of confidence in evangelical distinctives as much as an attraction to sacramentalism that lies behind many conversion decisions. Having come to the conclusion that the foundations of evangelicalism are not

---

[9] Scot McKnight, "From Wheaton to Rome: Why Evangelicals Convert to Roman Catholicism," *Journal of the Evangelical Theological Society*, September, 2002, p. 470.

trustworthy, converts instead choose the hierarchical church[10] and her sacramental rites. But is this a surer foundation than what they leave behind?

A Crisis of Certainty

In the quest for certainty and truth, what formerly characterized evangelicalism was Biblicism, "a particular regard for the Bible as the source of all spiritual truth." [11] This was, perhaps more than anything else, the distinctive feature of the evangelical ethos. The clarion call of the reformers was *sola scriptura*, Scripture alone as final and ultimate authority. Nor was this view of scriptural authority a Protestant or Reformational innovation. Regarding the scriptures as having unique and ultimate authority over the Christian was part of the church's charter. The apostles and first Christians already had a Bible – the Scriptures that we now know as the Old Testament – and their preaching and apologetics were drawn from these writings. The early church fathers were likewise committed to Scripture as the Word of God, the expression in written form of the message that the Logos, Jesus, had brought through the incarnation. In later centuries the authority of Scripture was to suffer demotion as a system of canon law developed in the institutional church, but this was not part of apostolic Christianity.

Scholars have written much about the struggles of Fundamentalism in the late nineteenth and early part of the twentieth century. These contentions with the surrounding culture are cast mainly as reactions against liberal views of Scripture and revelation that arose out of higher criticism and a relativizing of

---

[10] Throughout this book, I use the term hierarchical church to indicate the church organized around a head (pope or patriarch), archbishops, bishops, and priests. In essence it is the church structure considered apart from its members. This would encompass the Roman Catholic Church and the Orthodox Church, and in some cases, the Anglican Church.
[11] Bebbington, Loc. cit.

the Bible. But these struggles often took on an internecine nature through long decades of strife. On one side were theologians such as B.B. Warfield and J. Gresham Machen who held to the inerrancy of scripture and its authority over the believer and the church. Scholars have often viewed these definitions of inerrancy with eye-rolling skepticism, ascribing them to the deep-seated fears and insecurities of fundamentalists struggling to find their place in the modern world. But this is a facile analysis of their motives. As David Wells observes, "The assertion that the Bible should be read 'literally' not only signaled their intention to take the Bible seriously, but also, it would seem, to reject the whole raft of literary theory and critical chicanery that had made a mockery, in learned circles, of biblical inspiration."[12]

In the later years of the twentieth century these struggles within evangelicalism over inerrancy and authority of Scripture continued, with the pronouncements sometimes taking on an almost creedal structure. The Chicago Statement on Biblical Inerrancy came about in 1978 as just such an effort to define a robust view of the Bible in the evangelical mind. Creeds are as often used as winnowing agents to separate from one's theological opponents, as they are positive statements of faith. Here too, the Chicago Statement is notable as much for what it denies as for what it affirms: "WE AFFIRM that the Holy Scriptures are to be received as the authoritative Word of God. WE DENY that the Scriptures receive their authority from the Church, tradition, or any other human source. WE AFFIRM that the Scriptures are the supreme written norm by which God binds the conscience, and that the authority of the Church is subordinate to that of Scripture. WE DENY that Church creeds, councils, or declarations have authority greater than or equal to the authority of the Bible."[13]

---

[12] David F. Wells, *No Place for Truth: Whatever Happened to Evangelical Theology?* (Grand Rapids, Wm. B. Eerdmans, 1993), p. 128.
[13] Quoted in G.K. Beale, *The Erosion of Inerrancy in Evangelicalism* (Wheaton, Crossway, 2008), p. 270.

While sacramental churches make use of the Scriptures, they are clearly not in agreement with ecclesiastical authority being subordinate to that of the Bible.

On the other side of the inerrancy debate were those who argued for an accommodation to science and what they deemed to be the evidence of biblical criticism that the Scriptures should not be regarded as inerrant, yet should still be considered infallible in expressing the mind and will of God. "They had come to believe that while the Bible remained an 'infallible' guide on matters of doctrine, worship, and Christian life, it was not accurate in every scientific and historical fact."[14] Inevitably, these two viewpoints collided and spawned factions and division. It appeared to conservatives as just so much logomachy to suggest infallibility without inerrancy, or authority founded on no certain view of the Bible. As the experience of mainline Protestantism would demonstrate, it becomes difficult to hold to infallibility on matters of doctrine or moral teaching when we doubt the historicity and accuracy of the Scriptures. It is one of the startling facts of history that those churches that opted for biblical dilution saw decline in members and attendance. It was as if Christians determined that if God is not speaking inerrantly, then he doesn't have anything to say worth listening to.

The other factor of the sacramental equation is found in Orthodoxy, which, while similar to Catholicism in many ways, is distinct in others. The "smells and bells" qualities of Orthodox worship services are buttressed by claims of antiquity. More so than Catholicism, Orthodoxy prides itself on maintaining what was passed on. Indeed, to the Orthodox, to describe a theologian as "innovative" is to imply that he or she is heretical. This impression of stability and of not accommodating doctrine to culture appeals to many that have seen the leaders of their own churches become more marketers than ministers. In her study of American conversions to Eastern Orthodoxy, Amy Slagle interviews converts, one of

---

14 Worthen, Kindle Locations 873-874.

whom says, "I came [to Orthodoxy] because the doctrines that I read of the [church] fathers didn't match up with any other church on the *planet*. The closer you get your doctrines to match those of the early church, the closer you're going to get to the truth."[15] As I will show, however, antiquity does not always equal doctrinal integrity, and this is true in Orthodoxy as much as in Catholicism.

A Crisis of History

Converts often cite the crisis of temporality, or what the church of today has in common with the historical church, as what convinced them to make the decision to convert. A student at The King's College in New York City typifies this reasoning, when after a "crisis of spiritual authority," he questioned everything he had learned. "This questioning led him to study the historical origins of scripture and then of the Christian church itself. Eventually he concluded that Catholicism in its current form is the closest iteration of the early church fathers' intentions. He asks, 'If Saint Augustine showed up today, could we seriously think that he'd attend a Southern Baptist church in Houston?' The answer, [to this student,] is a resounding 'No'."[16] It is plain that selectivity and a parsing of the historical evidence have already taken place in this student's decision – if he was even aware of the earlier history.

Why ask the question of what Augustine would do? Augustine was active at the end of the fourth and beginning of the fifth century. He has less of a temporal connection to the apostolic church than contemporary Americans have to the founding fathers of the United States. Why not ask, rather, what earlier fathers

---

15 Amy Slagle, *The Eastern Church in the Spiritual Marketplace: American Conversions to Orthodox Christianity* (DeKalb, IL, NIU Press, 2011), p. 7.

16 Jonathan D. Fitzgerald, "Evangelicals Crossing the Tiber to Catholicism", *Religion Dispatches*, July 28, 2010, http://www.religiondispatches.org/archive/atheologies/2731/evangelicals_ crossing_the_tiber_to_catholicism/.

would do, or what the apostles themselves would do? And were Augustine to show up today, he would not recognize the Catholic Church any more than a Southern Baptist Church, for the practices of today are exceedingly different than what Augustine knew. There were no cardinals, curia, or pope in the sense of Rome having primacy over all of the church, none of the elaborate Marian dogma of subsequent centuries, and no seven sacraments. All of these things are later developments of history. The bishop of Hippo would no doubt be shocked to find himself declared a "doctor of the Church," as well as the patron saint of brewers.

As Everett Ferguson observed, when most people speak of the "early church," they usually mean the fourth and fifth centuries, but a different picture emerges if we look at evidence from still earlier epochs.[17] The historical evidence shows that, far from presenting a church that was unified in doctrine and practice, the early church fathers display an often heterogeneous set of views that speak to diversity of practice, and certainly do not support a hierarchical structure of authority.

Hierarchical traditions often chide evangelicals for casting aside the witness of history, of having no connection with the past. But here also, we need to ask the question of which past one wishes to choose? Scott Hahn has selected one interpretation of history when he says, "No wonder, as I discovered in my study, the Church practiced infant baptism from the beginning."[18] However, the evidence shows that infant baptism was not a practice of the apostolic church. History indicates that the doctrine of baptism gradually shifted away from being a sign of identification with Christ and instead moved towards removing

---

17 Paul Hartog, "The Complexity and Variety of Contemporary Church – Early Church Engagements," in *The Contemporary Church and the Early Church: Case Studies in Ressourcement*, Paul Hartog, ed. (Eugene, Wipf & Stock, 2010), p. 6.

18 Scott and Kimberly Hahn, *Rome Sweet Home: Our Journey to Catholicism* (San Francisco, Ignatius Press, 1993), p. 16.

original sin and initiating one into the institutional church. (Here too, the thought of Augustine, who looms so large in the Western Church, has proven imperious over other evidence of history.)[19]

If the institutional church has sometimes revised its history to fit current opinions, it is also true that evangelicalism has embraced a pragmatism that can leave one asking, to paraphrase Tertullian, "What has Madison Avenue to do with Jerusalem?" Throughout the mid-twentieth century, Evangelical leaders began to embrace tactics usually found in the social sciences in order to grow their congregations. Bill Hybels, founder of Willow Creek Community Church, gathered data on unchurched suburbanites through surveys, and then tailored his services to meet the needs that his respondents said the church had previously ignored. G.A. Pritchard writes, "The heart of Willow Creek's strategy centers on unchurched Harry (or Mary), the 'typical' unmotivated, unchurched individual."[20] Willow Creek has grown to be a sprawling suburban campus with multiple satellite locations throughout the region, and affiliated church plants around the country. The Willow Creek Association shares with pastors and leaders throughout the world the techniques that have grown the home church's numbers so dramatically. Willow Creek has profoundly shaped evangelicalism in the United States, but in ways that were not always anticipated.

Observers may not at first realize the sea change that the seeker-sensitive model represents when compared to the historical understanding of the church. Beginning in the book of Acts, the gathering of the church was, by definition, for believers alone. The

---

[19] Hans Küng writes that, "Anyone who wants to understand the Catholic Church has to understand Augustine. No other figure between Paul and Luther has had a greater influence on the Catholic Church and theology than this man." *A Short History of the Catholic Church*, trans. John Bowden (New York, Modern Library, 2003), p. 45.

[20] G.A. Pritchard, *Willow Creek Seeker Services, Evaluating A New Way of Doing Church* (Grand Rapids, Baker, 1996), p. 23.

word church is from the Greek *ekklesia*, which means "called out." The earliest Christians evangelized in the marketplace and in the world around them. The gathering of the church was where they met to worship, to remember Jesus through the Lord's Supper, and to be exhorted by the preaching and teaching of gifted men. In the later history of revivalism and evangelism, George Whitefield and Dwight Moody preached to unbelievers in meetings that were evangelistic in purpose and therefore, *ipso facto*, not a meeting of the church. Itinerant evangelists of a bygone era, such as Billy Sunday, or even those of our own day, such as Billy Graham, both held meetings that were evangelistic in purpose – not meetings of the local church.

The Willow Creek model upends this and reframes the primary purpose of the church gathering as evangelistic. What is good and commendable about Willow Creek is a desire to reach those with little to no exposure to the gospel – the unsaved. The danger of this is captured by Marshall McLuhan's well-known aphorism, "The Medium is the Message." Everything about a Willow Creek Sunday service is carefully crafted for its appeal to the unbeliever, and for its relevance to him or her. The music, the lighting, the use of drama – all is calculated as to how it will appeal to the unbeliever. "Willow Creek's use of marketing language and reasoning has been adopted wholesale from the marketplace. The problem is that the marketing perspective of needs, research, target markets, market share, target-audience profile, and product inevitably modifies any human endeavor to which it is applied."[21] For some evangelicals, this has raised questions of whether this is really what the church in her corporate life is supposed to be.

This reorientation of the corporate gathering of Christians away from worship and toward outreach has left many with the impression that their experience of worshiping God is lacking. One might say that the focus has turned from being theocentric to

---

[21] Ibid., p. 242.

anthropocentric. Many converts from evangelicalism to liturgical traditions cite this as one of their reasons for conversion. The questions this should raise, however, are not whether our worship is historically informed, but whether it is biblically informed? By making certain rites and rituals binding and mandatory, sacramentalism has frequently gone beyond apostolic testimony and entered the realm of mystery and speculation.

For the believers who regularly worship in seeker-sensitive churches, an ancillary question is what is there to nurture spiritual growth and maturity after they commit to Christ? If the primary emphasis is to preach the gospel to the unchurched, what is there for disciples? Warren Cole Smith refers to the Willow Creek model as a turning point in evangelicalism. "One of the unintended consequences of a church that is constantly focused more on outreach than spiritual formation is that this model all but ensures every generation will have to be reevangelized, since the current adult generation does not have the spiritual training or maturity to raise its own children in the nurture and admonition of the Lord."[22] Because the gatherings of some churches have focused so much on outreach, the careful and systematic teaching of doctrine has been diminished. This has left some evangelicals quite often unable to defend the distinctives of the movement from a biblical foundation.

The Emergent church[23] has also contributed to this drift in Evangelicalism. Somewhat allied with seeker-sensitive churches, (Brian D. McLaren, who is viewed by some as a founder of the Emergent church movement, is a member of the Willow Creek Association), it goes further in some areas. The emphasis within the Emergent church is on *relevance*. In his book *The Church on the Other Side*, McLaren offers a series of strategies for making the

---

[22] Warren Cole Smith, *A Lover's Quarrel with the Evangelical Church* (Colorado Springs, Authentic Publishing, 2008), p. 74.
[23] I use the term Emergent, but am aware that some draw a distinction with Emerging.

Church culturally relevant; among them are a series of questions we should ask, such as "If this message is credible, could I live with it, or would I want to? Would embracing it make me a better person or a worse one? Would this contribute to my happiness and health, or to my disintegration and dysfunction?"[24] Just as in the seeker-sensitive model, the common thread through all of these questions is that they are focused on the believer, rather than on God. Church growth models are part of the Emergent church as well, with the emphasis on what "works" to multiply a congregation.

Amidst the diversity I earlier noted, all of this variety occurred within the body of Christ. To deny basic and biblical doctrine was to put oneself outside the believing company. With the Emergent church, this is no longer so clear. Rob Bell's 2011 book, *Love Wins*, is an example. Taking a position that would historically be called universalism, Bell affirms that in the end all will be redeemed to God. It is thus a denial of Biblicism and Crucicentrism.[25] While there were many prominent evangelicals who roundly condemned Bell for heretical teaching, there were others who defended him. The fact that the latter came from (and still belong to) evangelicalism is the new reality of the frayed fabric that is this segment of the universal church.

A Crisis of Unity

In the previous fifty years or so, ecumenism and the desire to present a unified Christian witness to the world have assumed an increasingly important place in faith dialogue. The legacy of the Fundamentalist-Modernist controversies was often separation from

---

24 Brian D. McLaren, *The Church on the Other Side* (Grand Rapids, Zondervan, 2000), p. 80
25 Rob Bell, *Love Wins: A Book About Heaven, Hell, and the Fate of Every Person Who Ever Lived* (New York, HarperOne, 2011); see pages 103-119 in particular.

a perceived evil, or from those who didn't hold to the same views. Some evangelicals began asking whether the fragmenting was itself the problem. Converts from evangelicalism have frequently cited this as an animating force in their thought process. Paul C. Fox writes, "During the twenty years I had been a Christian, I had accepted the believers'-church approach. Yet now I could see that in the years since the Reformation, this approach had led to the splintering of Protestantism, making it impossible to identify Christ's church with any certainty. Instead, one was confronted with a myriad of sects, each claiming to be the believer's church and each with its unique vision of what to believe and how to act."[26] Convert Stephen K. Ray similarly says, "The petty disputes and rival interpretations of competing denominations had always grieved us and indicated something was very wrong. Without continuity with the early Church and the intervening centuries, Protestantism was like a branch without the tree, a wing without a bird."[27]

Several assumptions are behind these criticisms of the sectarianism found in evangelicalism, all of which I will expand on in later chapters. Briefly stated, the assumption that prior to the Reformation there wasn't division or schism is false. Without question there may be more plurality in the church of today, but when it is a question of unity, are repeated schisms any worse than one grand schism? For sheer duration, nothing in contemporary Christianity can compare with the Great Schism between East and West, now approaching nearly 1,000 years. Another assumption is that the Roman Catholic Church of today does not have the same problem of sectarianism found in Protestantism and evangelicalism. In fact, the same situation prevails there as in evangelicalism, but one of the chief differences is, no one need

---

26 Patrick Madrid, *Surprised By Truth 3* (Manchester, Sophia Institute Press, 2002), p. 97.
27 Stephen K. Ray, *Crossing The Tiber: Evangelical Protestants Discover the Historic Church* (San Francisco, Ignatius Press, 1997), p. 28.

leave the church to give full expression to their individualism, or sectarianism.

The final assumption of these converts is that there is unity between the sacramental churches of today and the early church. (This is a frequent claim of Orthodoxy.) Scholar after scholar, Catholic as well as Protestant, testifies that it is inaccurate and untenable to draw such connections between the hierarchical church of today and the earliest church. This spills over into the crisis of history that I discussed earlier. The entire question of doctrinal development (of which more in Chapter 5) is one that converts have been the most disingenuous in facing. Here, too, scholars without an apologetic agenda have admitted to the facts of doctrinal development in a way that acknowledges things now believed that were not at all part of the faith of the early church.

A Crisis of Interpretive Opinion

As I will demonstrate, the real issue any convert must confront is *ecclesiology*. To be sure, evangelicalism has frequently subjugated ecclesiology to other concerns to such an extent that many evangelicals cannot adequately articulate a biblical doctrine of the church. Lewis Sperry Chafer, the founder of Dallas Theological Seminary, wrote that whether it is Presbyterian, Episcopal, or Congregational, "every existing form of church rule will claim that its procedure is justified by the Scriptures. This fact serves to emphasize the truth that church government is a mere convenience which serves a limited purpose."[28] Chafer's view is that how the church is organized is not important. He would never have expressed such a thing regarding eschatology, believing that God's prophetic plan was exact and specific. Yet when it comes to ecclesiology, he is exceedingly flexible. Within sacramental doctrine, it is ecclesiology upon which virtually everything rests.

---

[28] Lewis Sperry Chafer, *Systematic Theology, Vol. 4* (Dallas, Dallas Seminary Press, 1948), p. 150.

Almost all parties agree that the doctrine of the church is the crux of any ecumenical discussion.

The conversionism emphasis of evangelicalism may have caused a focus on the individual's relationship to God, and stressed that the believer can and must have a relationship with Him that is personal, but this relationship sometimes comes at the expense of recognizing the importance of the church in God's plan for the individual. In sacramental thinking, a specific doctrine of the church is certainly not lacking, but the question is how it can be squared with the New Testament documents. If evangelicals have too often had a concept of the church that did not adequately appreciate the Spirit's operation and presence in the church, sacramentalism has swung to the other extreme by assigning an oversized importance to the church, and the hierarchical church in particular. If Christ is the head of the church, and she is his body, the sacramentalist concept of the church looks far more like the body leading the head. Through many centuries, the believer is confronted with a church that in essence tells him to pay little attention to what Christ has said in his Word, and instead to listen to the church. Where clear scriptural mandate for something exists, this is set aside on the authority of the church or her canons. Where no scriptural authority for certain doctrines and practices exist, believers are told to do and believe certain things because the church says so. The answer that sacramentalism has to interpretive diversity is not so much solving it as simply relocating authority. It represents an outsourcing of one's faith decisions to another entity but it's still something each person decides to do.

Evangelicals of today may look upon their forebears with some embarrassment as theological "crazy uncles" for insisting on an inerrant Bible, but we are now seeing the flowering of disregard for the primacy of Scripture within the whole of the Christian life. Research in recent years points out that within the Protestant and evangelical church there is a nascent biblical illiteracy. A 2010

Christianity Today report found that Christians themselves took a harsh view of their own familiarity with the Scriptures, 25 percent calling themselves not too mature or not at all mature in their Bible knowledge.[29] The Barna Group's assessment of its research states that the Christian Church is becoming less theologically literate: "The theological free-for-all that is encroaching in Protestant churches nationwide suggests the coming decade will be a time of unparalleled theological diversity and inconsistency."[30]

This is not to say that Catholics and Orthodox have a better handle on biblical truth, but the Scriptures have never been a primary source for them. When evangelicals do not maintain an intimate knowledge of the Scriptures, the Scriptures' importance to faith and practice becomes less critical. These evangelicals are thus more willing to consider other sources of authority when faced with the issues that Scot McKnight examines. The question remains whether abandoning what is distinctively biblical in favor of a different model of authority offers satisfactory answers to the questions McKnight poses.

The Essence of Sacramentalism

In *The New Faithful: Why Young Adults Are Embracing Christian Orthodoxy*, journalist Colleen Carroll writes about the resurgence in Christian commitment among young people across America. Published over a decade ago, the book describes a situation that has held true on college campuses and among young professionals. While there are references to this demographic embracing evangelicalism, the main thrust of the book is to chronicle those who have gravitated toward liturgical traditions,

---

[29] Collin Hansen, "Why Johnny Can't Read the Bible". *Christianity Today*, May 24, 2010.
[30] Barna Group, "Six Megathemes Emerge from Barna Group Research in 2010", https://www.barna. org/barna-update/culture/462-six-megathemes-emerge-from-2010.

chiefly Roman Catholicism. Carroll admits that the group is not monolithic, yet she strives to identify some hallmarks of these young adults and their faith journey. Reaction against a secular culture that acknowledges no authority or truth, a commitment to authenticity, and an increased integrity in their pursuit of personal holiness – these are among the features the new faithful display. The most important to note is this one: "They yearn for mystery and tend to trust their intuitive sense that what they have found is true, real, and worth living to the extreme."[31]

To be sure, the Bible speaks of mystery, but not as sacramentalism defines it. Paul calls the truth of Jews and Gentiles being part of one body "the mystery of Christ." This was hidden in previous ages, and so a mystery. But it has now been revealed, Paul says. It is no longer a mystery. He also writes to Timothy of the mystery of godliness, "God was manifest in the flesh." The incarnation is a mystery to be received, and accepted. Our worship is informed by this mystery because the Bible offers it for our wonder. This is not to say that the Christian does not acknowledge God to be transcendent, or to deny that our understanding of him is limited, because we are limited. As William Placher notes, "We can know the transcendent God not as an object within our intellectual grasp but only as a self-revealing subject, and even our knowledge of divine self-revelation must itself be God's doing."[32] God has chosen his abiding self-revelation to be the Scriptures. Though sacramental doctrine has shrouded the Bible, too, in mystery, the Scripture's own testimony is that the Bible was written "that you might know." Walter Kaiser counters the idea that God has not spoken plainly in giving a revelation of himself through the Bible. "To deny this is to say that

---

31 Colleen Carroll, *The New Faithful: Why Young Adults are Embracing Christian Orthodoxy* (Chicago, Loyola Press, 2002), p. 15.
32 William Placher, *The Domestication of Transcendence: How Modern Thinking About God Went Wrong* (Westminster John Knox Press, Louisville, 1996), p. 182.

God gave a revelation in which nothing is revealed or that the disclosure of God is also a concealment! God has deliberately decided to accommodate mankind by disclosing himself in our language and according to the mode to which we are accustomed in other literary productions."[33] In short, while we might not be able to fully *comprehend* God, yet because of his self-revelation in Scripture, we are able to *apprehend* him.

Sacramentalism takes mystery in a different direction. It is highly personal, difficult to define, and by its very nature, amorphous. The irony is that this kind of mystery manifests the same tendency that sacramental traditions often accuse evangelicals of embracing: excessive individualism. Yet there is an important difference. The mysteries embraced by sacramentalism are not informed by Scripture, nor constrained by the Bible. As Carroll notes, these seekers trust their intuitive sense of what is valid and right. Such mystery cannot be contradicted, because who is to say whether the experience I have had, the emotions I have felt, are not real? When mystery is elevated to an authoritative level, the Bible and its authority are left behind. When the rites and acts so infused with mystery begin to take on an authority of their own such that they supplant the revelation of God and the person of Christ, the believer is no longer on apostolic ground.

Some may ask whether these are simply questions of personal devotion or of worship style. If some Christians feel closer to God by contemplative prayer, or by Eucharistic adoration, is this really so objectionable? Is it in fact different than what evangelicals may feel and experience in their worship? I consider it is fundamentally different in this way: In sacramentalism, the grace of God becomes a substance independent of the person of Christ. It is made the currency of our relationship with him, and in the apex of

---

33 Walter C. Kaiser, Jr., "Legitimate Hermeneutics", in *A Guide to Contemporary Hermeneutics: Major Trends in Biblical Interpretation*, Donald K. McKim, ed. (Grand Rapids, Wm. B. Eerdmans, 1986), p. 114.

sacramentalism, grace was quite literally monetized. The buying and selling of forgiveness through indulgences that Luther inveighed against was in a sense almost inevitable, for if we turn our relationship with God into one of barter, we will quite naturally strive to do whatever we can to increase the balance in our account. The sacramental churches are no longer so brazen as to suggest that with a donation of some sort one can purchase God's grace, but the sacramental principle remains in full force. The believer experiences God and his grace through the rites and rituals defined by the Church. She stands as a grand market maker in between the believer and God to mediate and parcel out this grace. Nothing happens outside of the sacraments, and in this way the Lord himself is sidelined in the life of the Christian. Sacramentalism paraphrases Jesus' words to his disciples to instead say, "Abide in the Church, for apart from her, you can do nothing."

Among those who embrace sacramentalism, many will strive to locate its doctrine and practice in the Bible, no matter how tenuous or thin the evidence. Apologists such as Scott Hahn would fit this category.[34] These efforts come with a set of challenges all their own, which I will explore. An evangelical making the move to Roman Catholicism or Orthodoxy must recognize such a decision is based on far more than seeing certain passages of Scripture differently than one did in the past. It is instead a radically different way of engaging with theological truth claims. In his book *How to Go From Being A Good Evangelical to a Committed Catholic in Ninety-Five Difficult Steps*, sociologist Christian Smith (adapting Thomas Kuhn's idea) is at least willing to admit that for an evangelical to become a Catholic requires a

---

34 Cf. Scott Hahn, *Signs of Life: 40 Catholic Customs and Their Biblical Roots* (New York, Doubleday Religion, 2009).

"paradigm shift."[35] Smith, himself a convert from evangelicalism, describes in part wrestling with theological issues, but often the book is just as much a depiction of adopting the Catholic culture and mindset. His "Did you ever notice?" approach to the evangelical paradigm is thus highly personal. Some of his 95 steps include "4. Start to grow weary of 'meaningful' worship services.[36] 19. Start noticing that Evangelicalism seems to thrive on external threats and alarmist claims.[37] 35. Take note of sub-standard preaching."[38] These are the things that bothered him; the questions *he* was asking about evangelicalism. One might ask what criteria are applied to arrive at meaning versus meaninglessness in worship, or how Smith evaluates preaching to deem evangelicalism's normal fare as substandard, as compared to the brief homily one hears at a Mass. It is easy to see that these are preferences and subjective assessments of an individual. The irony is that Smith seems not to have noticed that his move to Catholicism was predicated on individual, private judgment – again the very thing for which sacramentalists often cry foul against evangelicals. The combined weight of all of his questions left him apparently unable to reconcile with the evangelical paradigm, and thus he felt that switching to Catholicism made more sense. He does not address the anomalies that come with the Catholic paradigm.

Of course, this paradigm shift goes the other way too. Many Catholics, including priests and nuns, have asked some of the corollary questions, and have arrived at exactly the opposite

---

[35] Christian Smith, *How to Go From Being A Good Evangelical to a Committed Catholic in Ninety-Five Difficult Steps* (Eugene, Cascade Books, 2011), p. 6.
[36] Smith, p. 32.
[37] Smith, p. 50.
[38] Smith, p. 70.

answers.[39] When faced with the biblical teaching on salvation and faith, and the nature of the church, many determined that what the Church was teaching them could not be reconciled with Scripture.[40] For others, it was the hierarchy and claims of authority

---

[39] For the personal stories of Catholics who found church teaching incompatible with Scripture and decided to leave the Church, see James G. McCarthy, *Conversations with Catholics* (Eugene, Harvest House, 1997); Mary Ann Collins, *Is Catholicism Biblical? A Former Nun Looks at the Evidence*, (N.p.: Createspace, 2010); Richard Bennett, *Far from Rome, Near to God: The Testimonies of Fifty Converted Roman Catholic Priests*, (Carlisle, Banner of Truth, 2009); Chris Castaldo, *Holy Ground: Walking with Jesus as a Former Catholic*, (Grand Rapids, Zondervan, 2009); Bartholomew F. Brewer, *Pilgrimage From Rome*, (Greenville, Bob Jones Univ. Press, 1982); Tony Coffey, *Once A Catholic*, (Eugene, Harvest House, 1993); Mary Hertel, Richard Bennett, ed., *The Truth Set Us Free: Twenty Former Nuns Tell Their Stories*, (N.p.: WinePress Publishing, 1997); Scott McKnight, Hauna Ondrey, *Finding Faith, Losing Faith: Stories of Conversion and Apostasy*, (Waco, Baylor University Press, 2008); and Joanna H. Meehl, *The Recovering Catholic*, (Amherst, Prometheus Books, 1995).

[40] Father Thomas Reese notes, "One out of every 10 Americans is an ex-Catholic. If they were a separate denomination, they would be the third-largest denomination in the United States, after Catholics and Baptists." For those who end up in Evangelical churches, the Bible is a more important factor than for those who end up in Mainline churches. "Catholic scripture scholars have had decades to produce the best thinking on scripture in the world. That Catholics are leaving to join evangelical churches because of the church teaching on the Bible is a disgrace. Too few homilists explain the scriptures to their people. Few Catholics read the Bible. The church needs a massive Bible education program. The church needs to acknowledge that understanding the Bible is more important than memorizing the catechism. If we could get Catholics to read the Sunday scripture readings each week before they come to Mass, it would be revolutionary. If you do not read and pray the scriptures, you are not an adult Christian. Catholics who become evangelicals understand this." (Thomas Reese, "The Hidden Exodus: Catholics Becoming Protestants", *The National Catholic Reporter*, April 18, 2011).

23

that they could not square with the Bible. Their stories are interspersed in the following chapters, as a demonstration of the life-giving word that is the gospel. It is sometimes the case that the truth can become mundane to those who are closest to it. Someone looking out his back window every day at the Rocky Mountains might lose the wonder of that. A visitor who has never seen these peaks is likely struck by their majesty and beauty. So it is with those raised in evangelicalism. We need to recover the majesty and beauty of the gospel in God's Word.

Individuals have their own epistemic assumptions, and for evangelicals the one at the base of all others is that doctrine and practice must be rooted in Scripture. For sacramentalists, the basic epistemic assumption is that the Church is the final authoritative source of truth. How the Church has historically developed tells them what is true. But these two assumptions converge on this: both of them reach a point where they affirm a self-evident, self-attesting authority. We come to a question that does not admit of further proof. It must be taken at face value.

Any evangelical considering joining a sacramentalist church, Roman Catholic or Orthodox, must honestly contend with the stubborn facts of history. If he is looking for an engagement with "the apostolic church," he will not find it in either the Roman or Orthodox communions of today. John Henry Newman famously said that to be deep in history is to cease to be Protestant. However, examining the historical record will show that to be *deeper* in history is to cease to be Roman Catholic or Orthodox. That said, this book is not an apology for Protestantism. Roman Catholic and Orthodox Christians have frequently (and often rightly) pointed out the weaknesses of Protestantism. And this simply demonstrates the point that no movement or organization has the guarantee of the abiding blessing of God, nor of remaining firmly moored to the truth of the gospel. An organism – a body – this alone has such a guarantee as the bride of Christ, but only so far is it remains faithful to its constitution as laid out in the New

Testament. My task is to show that the definition of the bride of Christ put forth by sacramentalism is an erroneous one, and that Scripture is the only sure guide for the way forward in the Christian life.

The audience for this discussion is evangelicals who are considering such a move toward sacramentalism. That is, those whose ecumenism has led them to conclude that there are no fundamental differences between evangelical beliefs and those of sacramentalism, or who are dissatisfied with the answers to their questions that evangelicalism has provided. The most frequent reason for this dissatisfaction is that they have not actually examined the evidence for things such as canon formation, historical continuity in doctrine, and the fact that the early church was, similar to evangelicalism, quite diverse. Those who are presented with evidence for a practice or belief that putatively goes back to the very beginning of the Church may not have done the research to demonstrate that it is not so. My hope is that such a reader will find here the other side of these questions that often goes unexplored and unheard.

For evangelicals who make the move to sacramentalism, it is almost always the case that a *relationship* is pivotal in their decision. They may have met someone of exemplary life or profound kindness, and this caused them to consider, "Well, if she's a Catholic, maybe there is something to it." The importance of relationships in the body of Christ is significant, but it is vital to remember that these can never be a source of authority for faith. To invest relationships with authority or weight in doctrinal decisions is but another avenue of making experience the arbiter of what is true.

While not a defense of Protestantism, this book is decidedly not a screed against Roman Catholic or Orthodox believers. I am not writing as "anti-Catholic" or "anti-Orthodox", but rather as pro-Scripture. My desire is to see others transformed by the truths found in the Bible, as they present Jesus alone as our salvation.

Some of what I write will of necessity be polemical, but I have tried to do so without ad hominem attacks. I don't doubt the sincerity or motives of those within sacramentalism; rather, the foundations of the sacramental system are what I examine.

I do not subscribe to the cynicism that says a full-throated defense of what Scripture clearly teaches, of the settled truths that come with redemption, and of standing for the authority of Scripture above all others is an attack on any particular denomination or communion. Any church that claims to be the only true representation of Christ's body on earth (as both Catholicism and Orthodoxy do) by such a claim invites close scrutiny, and I am engaging with the historical doctrines and practices of these communions rather than the behavior of individuals that belong to them. The believers whose stories punctuate the following chapters likewise recorded their experiences precisely because they have a deep love for family and friends still in these churches. They want to see them brought to life in Christ and to experience the freedom they have found.

I am not suggesting there is no value in ecumenical dialogue, or that Christians of different traditions cannot learn from one another. Nor am I making statements about who is or is not a Christian because of the church they are part of. I am suggesting rather that evangelicals should understand that adopting the epistemic assumptions of sacramentalism is not simply changing churches. It is a wholesale shift in what they believe about God and our relationship to him, and evangelicals need to admit that one cannot hold dual citizenship in evangelicalism and sacramentalism. I consider in certain areas the sacramental position is stating things to be true of God that are actually false. Evangelicals investigating sacramentalism have often been given a truncated or sanitized view of history for evidence of the "true church". This view of history has yielded spurious conclusions. I believe the evidence most strongly supports a faith that checks everything by Scripture, and this is the practice that adheres to the truth of God.

2
I Will Build My Church

Participants in ecumenical dialogue report an astounding level of progress since Vatican II, but their enthusiasm is tempered by the reality of still pervasive and fundamental disagreements. As I noted in the previous chapter, those making a clear-eyed assessment see ecclesiology as the sticking point. Near the end of a favorable appraisal of today's Catholic Church, Mark Noll and Carolyn Nystrom acknowledge, "The most serious disagreements continue to exist between Catholics and evangelicals over questions of the church."[1] Whatever changes or restatements came out of Vatican II, the view of the nature and identity of the Church did not change from previous decades. To be sure, Catholic ecclesiology has undergone much change through the centuries, but Vatican II did not alter fundamental claims about the Church in her organization, power, or prerogatives.

When we search for the foundation of the church, our focal point must be the New Testament. Jesus himself predicts its inception in Matthew 16:18, saying, "I will build my church, and the gates of hell shall not prevail against it." Jesus does not expand upon this brief promise. The nature of the church, its organization, its order; these are not addressed in the gospels at all. The only other reference by Jesus is the matter of confronting a sinning brother; if the offender does not listen to the overture of two or three witnesses, the matter is to be brought before the church. Yet here, too, no explanation of the nature or composition of the church is given. The full explanation of this is reserved for the apostolic doctrine, and the apostle Paul most especially.

There is variation among the traditions regarding the church's

---

[1] Mark A. Noll, Carolyn Nystrom, *Is the Reformation Over? An Evangelical Assessment of Contemporary Roman Catholicism* (Grand Rapids, Baker Academic, 2005), p. 233.

beginning. Orthodox priest John Meyendorff refers to Pentecost[2] as the time when the Church was founded, which matches the evangelical view: "On that day the Spirit was poured out upon the disciples to form the body of Christ, the church."[3]

In the Roman Catholic view, there is no defined point in time when the Church as the body of Christ began: "Jesus inaugurated his church by preaching the Good News. The origin and growth of the church are symbolized by the blood and water which flowed from the open side of the crucified Jesus." [4] This is in keeping with the emphasis on mystery that is ingrained in Roman Catholic theology. Yet one must ask, without the Holy Spirit, how can we say the church is formed? The Roman Catholic Church does acknowledge that the Spirit has a role: "The Holy Spirit was sent on the day of Pentecost in order that he might continually sanctify the Church."[5] But whether the Church had a formal beginning at Pentecost is unclear, and other statements in the Catechism do not elucidate, but rather obfuscate the point: "As Eve was formed from the sleeping Adam's side, so the Church was born from the pierced heart of Christ hanging dead on the cross."[6] To be fair, these are the not sum total of statements about the Church in the Catechism. There is much that discusses the founding of the Church as maintaining continuity with Israel, the people of God in the Old Testament. This has profound implications, and will be explored further in this chapter, and later.

---

2 John Meyendorff, *The Orthodox Church, Its Past and its Role in the World Today* (New York, Pantheon Books, 1962), p. 7.

3 Robert L. Saucy, *The Church in God's Program* (Chicago, Moody Press, 1972), p. 64.

4 *Catechism of the Catholic Church* (New York, Image Books, 1995), p. 219.

5 *Catechism of the Catholic Church*, p. 220.

6 *Catechism of the Catholic Church*, loc. cit.

The Nature of the Church

When we leave the question of foundation and turn to the nature of the church, there emerges a wide divergence between the sacramentalist and the evangelical understandings. The Roman Catholic view of the church, organized around a hierarchical structure of bishops with a more institutional polity, is of later origin, as we shall see further in this chapter. In current Roman Catholic teaching, the understanding of this hierarchy is that "When Christ instituted the twelve, he constituted them in the form of a college or permanent assembly, at the head of which he placed Peter, chosen from among them."[7]

The Orthodox assessment of this is quite different. Meyendorff states that "The College of the Twelve ceased to exist: Herod caused 'James, the brother of John, to be beheaded' (Acts xii: 2), and no one thought of replacing him by electing a successor in order to keep up the symbolical number of Twelve, as they had in the case of Judas."[8] That said, the Orthodox certainly adhere to the apostolic succession of bishops, but have always had a more collegial view than Rome. The evangelical understanding is different still; because the church is the body of Christ, she acknowledges no earthly head, and, "authority among the followers of Jesus is the moral authority of those who show the most interest in and the most in the way of loving service for others."[9] To be sure, there are definite qualifications established for those serving in leadership, but "if the word 'office' is to be used in the church, it is not to be thought of as 'official' in the sense of government or military officials, but as referring to function: 'whoever aspires to the episcopate desires a good work' (1 Tim. 3:1)."[10]

---

7 *Catechism of the Catholic Church*, p. 233.

8 Meyendorff, p. 8.

9 Everett Ferguson, *The Church of Christ, a Biblical Ecclesiology for Today* (Grand Rapids, Wm. B. Eerdmans, 1996), p. 296.

10 Ibid., p. 297.

The hierarchical understanding of church structure informs virtually every aspect of sacramentalism. Indeed, one can say that, in the Catholic view, the Church exists apart from the believers who form the body of Christ. Cardinal Avery Dulles speaks of the powers and functions of the Church, defined by Vatican I, as threefold: "Teaching, sanctifying, and governing. The division of powers leads to further distinctions between the Church teaching, and the Church taught, the Church sanctifying and the Church sanctified, the Church governing, and the Church governed. In each case, the Church as institution is on the giving end. So these authors say: The Church teaches, sanctifies, and commands, in each case identifying the Church itself with the governing body or hierarchy."[11]

This bifurcation of the Church is vital not only to ecclesiastical function, but how the Church has historically developed. *Lumen Gentium*, the Dogmatic Constitution of the Church, affirms that "just as the office granted individually to Peter, the first among the apostles, is permanent and is to be transmitted to his successors, so also the apostles' office of nurturing the Church is permanent, and is to be exercised without interruption by the sacred order of bishops."[12] The encyclical goes on to state, "Episcopal consecration, together with the office of sanctifying, also confers the office of teaching and of governing, which, however, of its very nature, can be exercised only in hierarchical communion with the head and the members of the college."[13] (The head here, of course, refers to the pope.) Orthodoxy rejects the authority of the pope as supreme pontiff over all the faithful, yet agrees with Rome as to the doctrine of apostolic succession: "The apostolic succession of the hierarchy is the unbroken continuity of authority within the Church, originating with Jesus Christ, passing to the

---

[11] Avery Dulles, *Models of the Church* (New York, Image Books, 1987), p. 37.

[12] *Lumen Gentium*, 3:20.

[13] *Lumen Gentium*, Loc. cit.

apostles, and continuing to the present time by the laying on of hands of bishops. The Church is apostolic, because the root and foundational source of her entire hierarchical structure lies in the apostles themselves."[14] Yet the evidence does not sustain this concept of permanence surrounding the apostolic *office*. Hans von Campenhausen speaks of the "once-for-all" character of apostolic function, and that "the rank and authority of the apostolate are restricted to the first 'apostolic' generation, and can neither be continued nor renewed once this time has come to an end."[15]

When we look at both the biblical record, and the history of the church, it becomes clear that apostolicity is neither found in men, nor in succession to a particular office, but in the teaching of the apostles. In the very earliest days of the church, the disciples were devoted to the apostles' teachings, rather than to the men themselves. (Acts 2:42). When Paul calls the bishops of the Ephesian church together to bid them farewell, he presents them with a charge and a warning: "Pay careful attention to yourselves and to all the flock, in which the Holy Spirit has made you overseers, to care for the church of God, which he obtained with his own blood. I know that after my departure, fierce wolves will come in among you, not sparing the flock; *and from among your own selves* will arise men speaking twisted things, to draw away the disciples after them" (Acts 20:28-30).

Paul avows that within the plurality of bishops itself, men will err from the truth and teach what is false. Sacramental tradition holds that the charism is transferred from bishop to bishop in an unbroken succession of apostolic consecration. If this is so, where does the error that Paul plainly predicts originate? The sacramental church has never been able to adequately explain an infallible

---

14 Gregory Afonsky, *Christ and the Church* (Crestwood, NY, St. Vladimir's Seminary Press, 2001), p. 80.

15 Hans von Campenhausen, *Ecclesiastical Authority and Spiritual Power in the Church of the First Three Centuries* (Stanford, Stanford University Press, 1969), p. 23.

church in the face of clear evidence of episcopal error.

The true apostolic witness and inheritance of the church is the body of doctrine that the apostles taught and committed to the next generation: "The church is apostolic, and is to be apostolic because it is founded on and is faithful to the Word of God given through the apostles. From the apostles until the present day, the gospel that they preached has been handed down. There has been a succession of apostolic teaching based on the Word of God. Writing to the Galatians, Paul stressed that their allegiance to the gospel message he had already given them superseded any allegiance to him personally (see Gal. 1:6-9)."[16] The New Testament itself "became the real heir of the apostles' authority."[17] To insist on apostolic succession as proof of the presence of the Spirit is to subjugate the gospel to the church. This is consistent with the sacramental ecclesiology, but inconsistent with the biblical record. Paul ascribes salvific power not to the church and her apostles, but to the gospel message, calling it the power of God for salvation (Rom. 1:16).

Apostolicity rests in the gospel, not in the office. Paul himself dismisses any sort of hierarchy within the apostolic community: "And from those who seemed to be influential (what they were makes no difference to me; God shows no partiality)—those, I say, who seemed influential added nothing to me" (Gal. 2:6). "And when James and Cephas and John, who seemed to be pillars, perceived the grace that was given to me, they gave the right hand of fellowship to Barnabas and me, that we should go to the Gentiles and they to the circumcised" (Gal. 2:9). For Paul, there is no partiality with God – he certainly does not identify Peter as preeminent among the apostles. In the sub-apostolic era as well, the gospel itself remains primary. Commenting on Irenaeus' presentation of truth in *Adversus Haereses*, Hall notes that

---

[16] Mark Dever, *The Church: The Gospel Made Visible* (Nashville, B&H Publishing Group, 2012), p. 18-19.
[17] Von Campenhausen, p. 24.

"Irenaeus is concerned with the succession of true doctrine, and its transmission in the public teaching of the bishops. 'Apostolic succession' may have included for him some idea of a sacramental grace exclusively passed to bishops from apostles; but if so he never refers to it. This is in fact a later idea."[18]

The Organization of the Apostolic Church

The organization of the church that the New Testament describes has several identifiable features. Firstly, bishops or presbyters are those who shepherd local congregations. While some claim that these represent two distinct offices, this cannot be sustained from the New Testament. The qualifications for bishops are given in 1 Timothy 3 and Titus 1. In 1 Timothy, Paul uses the Greek word ἐπίσκοπος, commonly translated as bishop, but literally meaning overseer. In Titus, he uses both ἐπίσκοπος and πρεσβύτερος, or presbyter. The latter is sometimes translated as elder, as in the Acts 20 passage cited above. Paul calls for the elders (presbyters) of the church and tells them that the Holy Spirit has made them bishops (episcopos). Benjamin L. Merkle affirms that "Almost all scholars agree that a three-tiered ecclesiastical system (overseer, elder, and deacon) is a later development and therefore foreign to the New Testament documents. There is simply not enough evidence to maintain a distinction between the terms elder and overseer."[19] Anglican Roger Beckwith agrees with this: "Earlier in the apostolic age, as is well known, the presbyter-bishop seems to have been one and the same person. Because of the original identity of the presbyter and the bishop, we find the two-fold expression 'bishops and deacons' in Philippians 1:1, and the qualifications are listed in 1 Timothy 3 for those to be

---

18 Stuart G. Hall, *Doctrine and Practice in the Early Church* (Grand Rapids, Eerdmans, 1991) p. 61.
19 Benjamin L. Merkle, *The Elder and Overseer, One Office in the Early Church* (New York, Peter Lang, 2003), p. 160.

appointed to the two offices of 'bishop' and 'deacon', but not to any third office."[20] Roman Catholic historian Robert Louis Wilken also has written, "the terms 'elder' (presbyter) and 'overseer' (episcopos) are used interchangeably."[21] Walter Schmithals likewise agrees, "It is not a question of a different office; rather, a presbyter is designated as a 'bishop' when this reflects the duties of his office and ministry. Thus monepiscopacy is still foreign to the pastoral epistles."[22] It is clear that in the apostolic congregations, bishop and presbyter refer to one office.

Where then did the division of the one office of bishop into two offices of bishop and presbyter (priest) originate? The answer is, of course, that it is a later development, an innovation. Catholic historians acknowledge the divergence from the original model: "the one office, which in apostolic times bore the double designation of episcop or presbyter, was divided into two and the term overseer or bishop reserved exclusively for the holder of the highest office in the congregation."[23] We are thus confronted with the perennial question of authority. The division of bishop and presbyter may be of an old tradition, but it is clearly not the oldest. For those who insist on an apostolic faith, the apostles left a model of only two offices in the church. The justification for setting aside the apostolic model is, of course, tradition. The argument is that the church was in the early days primitive, and, as time passed, the division of office into bishop and priest came into being. But this is to beg the question: Will the Holy Spirit lead the church in a direction wholly contrary to the New Testament? Stated differently, do we believe the apostles to be the inspired witnesses of

---

20 Roger Beckwith, *Elders in Every City, The Origin and Role of the Ordained Ministry* (Carlisle, Cumbria, Paternoster Press, 2003), p. 11-12.
21 Robert Louis Wilken, *The First Thousand Years: A Global History of Christianity* (New Haven, Yale University Press, 2012), p. 31.
22 Walter Schmithals, O.C. Dean, Jr., trans., *The Theology of the First Christians* (Louisville, Westminster John Knox Press, 1997), p. 177.
23 Karl Baus, Hubert Jedin, and John Dolan, eds., *From the Apostolic Community to Constantine* (New York: Herder and Herder, 1965), p. 148.

God speaking through their writings? Are the New Testament documents indeed authoritative for the church today? The final arbiter of authority for sacramentalism returns once more, not to the Scriptures, but to the church.

If the sacramentalist view on bishops is inconsistent with the biblical record, what does this say about apostolic succession? That is, are the bishops the legitimate successors of the apostles themselves, and do they carry apostolic authority? *Lumen Gentium* plainly affirms this: "among those various ministries which, according to tradition, were exercised in the Church from the earliest times, the chief place belongs to the office of those who, appointed to the episcopate, by a succession running from the beginning, are passers-on of the apostolic seed."[24] That this idea is founded in tradition rather than revelation is plain from the text of the document. Examining the biblical record, Catholic exegete Raymond E. Brown notes that "The affirmation that all bishops of the early Christian Church could trace their appointments to the apostles is simply without proof – it is impossible to trace with assurance any of the presbyter-bishops to the Twelve and it is possible to trace only some of them to apostles like Paul."[25]

Brown similarly doubts that the locus of apostolic authority is found in Peter, despite the statements of *Lumen Gentium* (see note 12): "The claims of various sees to descend from particular members of the Twelve are highly dubious. It is interesting the most serious of these is the claim of the bishops of Rome to descend from Peter, the one member of the Twelve who was almost a missionary apostle in the Pauline sense – a confirmation that whatever succession there was from apostleship to episcopate, it was primarily in reference to the Pauline type of apostleship, not that of the Twelve."[26] Father Francis Sullivan agrees "with the

---

[24] *Lumen Gentium*, 20.

[25] Raymond E. Brown, *Priest and Bishop: Biblical Reflections* (Paramus, Paulist Press, 1970), p. 73.

[26] Brown, p. 72.

consensus of scholars that the available evidence indicates that the church of Rome was led by a college of presbyters, rather than by a single bishop, for at least several decades of the second century."[27] Thus, even Catholic scholars draw the conclusion that the historical evidence is not consistent with the understanding of succession that the magisterium affirms. What does this say about the implications of this model? For Brown, it is ultimately unimportant that Peter cannot be traced back as the first bishop of Rome. He is comfortable with the fact that the Papacy, being identified with the Roman bishop, is only a later understanding of history.[28] This is one of the hallmarks of the paradigm shift to sacramentalism. A need to justify from Scripture, or even from the earliest decades of church history, is simply not relevant for the validity of a doctrinal stance. Those who convert from evangelicalism feel more of a burden to prove that the tenets of the church extend back to the apostles and the New Testament. For this latter group, this proves problematic when scholars of their new communion put forth conclusions that contradict these positions.

The oversight of the apostolic congregations was also plural. A sole bishop presiding over the church or all the churches in a city was only introduced later. Again, the Ephesian example shows that there were multiple elders in the congregation. The epistle to the Philippians is the only one of Paul's letters where he addresses any church leaders, and he begins, "To all the saints in Christ Jesus who are at Philippi, with the overseers and deacons" (Phil. 1:1). He addresses not the bishop, but the bishops. Merkle notes, "In every case the term 'elders' is used in the New Testament it is found in the plural (except 1 Tim. 5:19). This strongly suggests that the New Testament Church was governed by a group of qualified

---

27 Francis A. Sullivan, S.J., *From Apostles to Bishops: The Development of the Episcopacy in the Early Church* (Mahwah, The Newman Press, 2001), p. 221-222.
28 Brown, p. 54.

leaders and not by one individual."[29] Wayne Grudem affirms, "There is quite a consistent pattern of plural elders as the main governing group in New Testament churches. No passage suggests that any church, no matter how small, had only one elder. The consistent New Testament pattern is a plurality of elders 'in every church' (Acts 14:23) and 'in every town' (Titus 1:5)." [30] Merkle elaborates, "The local church should not be structured in such a way that one leader has sole authority within the church. The model of Scripture is that a group of qualified leaders are needed which provides accountability, balance, and the sharing of responsibilities."[31] The sacramentalist tradition rejects this; both the Roman Catholic and Orthodox Church maintain a hierarchical order where a single bishop holds jurisdiction over a defined geographical area. Once again, this is a tradition that cannot be traced to the apostles.

The rise of the monarchical bishop, also known as the monepiscopate, is found in Ignatius of Antioch, who first argues for unswerving obedience to the bishop. He enjoins that "we should look upon the bishop even as we would look upon the Lord Himself."[32] He also tells the Magnesians to do nothing without the bishop and presbyters.[33] This is quite obviously a novelty from what the New Testament enjoins, and thus leads to the question, in what sense can the Church be apostolic if it runs counter to the model the apostles themselves left us? F.F. Bruce believes that "the vehemence of Ignatius's protestations, indeed, is the plainest evidence that his view of the indispensable and supremely authoritative character of the office was far from being

---

29 Merkle, p. 160.

30 Wayne Grudem, *Systematic Theology, An Introduction to Biblical Doctrine* (Grand Rapids, Zondervan, 1994), p. 912-913.

31 Merkle, p.161.

32 *Epistle to the Ephesians*, ch. 6.50.

33 *Epistle to the Magnesians*, ch. 7.

universally shared."[34] In other words, if the authoritative nature of the single bishop were common practice from the start, why would there be any need to insist upon what already prevailed? Sullivan concurs that "The very urgency with which he [Ignatius] exhorted the Christian communities to unity with their bishops can be seen as an indication that the episcopal structure was not so firmly established so he wanted it to be."[35] Historian David Rankin agrees with this: "We might also note that the evidence of the letters of Ignatius of Antioch, while substantial and important, is largely uncorroborated by other contemporary sources. [Ignatius's] letter to the church at Rome, unlike those to other churches, reflects the governing of that church not by a single bishop but by the presbyterate."[36] Josef Lössl believes that Ignatius's view stands apart from his fellows, and assigns its origin to the surrounding culture: "The witness of Ignatius of Antioch went further than any of his contemporaries when, following pagan Hellenistic traditions, he constructed the episkopos as a 'quasi-monarchical' presider at the liturgy, resembling God the Father." [37]

Even as we witness the move away from a plurality of bishops to a single man, the change to authority did not take place all at once. Chadwick writes that even after the emergence of the monarchical bishop, he was still elected by the congregation rather than being appointed by any hierarchy: "Originally, a bishop was freely elected by his people, and the voice of the laity was substantially more than a mere assent or testimony to fitness. By 381 there appear clear beginnings of a concentration of power

---

34 F.F. Bruce, *The Growing Day: The Progress Of Christianity from the Fall of Jerusalem to the Accession of Constantine (A.D. 70-313)* (Grand Rapids, Wm. B. Eerdmans, 1954), p. 67.

35 Sullivan, *loc. cit.*

36 David Rankin, *Tertullian and the Church* (Cambridge, Cambridge University Press, 1995), p. 2.

37 Josef Lössl, *The Early Church: History and Memory* (London; New York, T & T Clark, 2010), p. 195.

at a yet higher level than that of the metropolitan."[38] The pattern begins to manifest of the Church taking its cues from the state in government and administration. This tendency was to have spiritually harmful effects in later centuries.

Finally, the office and work of a bishop/elder applies to a local congregation. When Paul calls the elders of Ephesus, he calls them as responsible for the congregation of that city. There is no indication that there was more than a single gathering of Christians in Ephesus. He likewise tells Titus to appoint elders in every city. The implication is that those elders would be overseers of the congregation in the city of their appointment. The idea of a bishop having authority over multiple congregations of Christians is not found in the New Testament, nor is the idea of an archbishop. Cyprian of Carthage, (a canonized saint in both Catholic and Orthodox tradition) rejects this notion of an archbishop in his letter on the seventh council of Carthage: "For neither does any of us set himself up as a bishop of bishops, nor by tyrannical terror does any compel his colleague to the necessity of obedience; since every bishop, according to the allowance of his liberty and power, has his own proper right of judgment, and can no more be judged by another than he himself can judge another."[39] In later centuries, the idea of collegiality within sacramentalism was to ebb and flow, until Pius IX finally stamped it out for the Western church with his declaration of papal infallibility. This, too, has proven to be one of the major areas of disagreement between Orthodoxy and Catholicism. Orthodoxy has never fully abandoned the conciliar and collegial model of its bishops, even if it did adopt a view of the episcopate that is not sustainable by the New Testament.

---

[38] Henry Chadwick, *The Penguin History of the Church, Volume I: The Early Church*, Rev. Edition (London, Penguin Books, 1993), p. 165.

[39] *Ante-Nicene Fathers, Vol. 5*, Philip Schaff, ed. (Grand Rapids, Christian Classics Ethereal Library, n.d.), p. 1387-1388.

Clerical Powers and Prerogatives

What did the overseers of these apostolic congregations do? As I earlier noted, Paul only addresses the overseers directly in a single epistle. Recognizing this, along with the qualifications listed in 1 Timothy 3, and Titus 1, it is clear that the ministry of overseers did not dominate congregational life, but had primarily a pastoral role. They were shepherds, guiding the local flock, and demonstrating by their lives what a follower of Jesus does and says. In both 1 Timothy and Titus, it is not an office that is described, but rather the character of the man who would aspire to be an overseer:

"Therefore an overseer must be above reproach, the husband of one wife, sober-minded, self-controlled, respectable, hospitable, able to teach, not a drunkard, not violent but gentle, not quarrelsome, not a lover of money. He must manage his own household well, with all dignity keeping his children submissive, for if someone does not know how to manage his own household, how will he care for God's church? He must not be a recent convert, or he may become puffed up with conceit and fall into the condemnation of the devil. Moreover, he must be well thought of by outsiders, so that he may not fall into disgrace, into a snare of the devil." (1 Tim. 3:2-7)

"For an overseer, as God's steward, must be above reproach. He must not be arrogant or quick-tempered or a drunkard or violent or greedy for gain, but hospitable, a lover of good, self-controlled, upright, holy, and disciplined. He must hold firm to the trustworthy word as taught, so that he may be able to give instruction in sound doctrine and also to rebuke those who contradict it." (Titus 1:7-9)

It is evident that notions of preeminence, or of controlling the church, are completely at odds with the shepherding metaphors used in the New Testament, and with the characteristics described in these passages. The bishop is not an administrator, but an example. Without question, administrative duties later came to belong to bishops, but this is just the point we have seen repeatedly – this is an innovation. Turning the office into an administrative position belongs to later years, and not to the New Testament description of the overseer's duties. Bishops did not preside at the Lord's Table, nor is there any hint that their presence ratified or legitimized the celebration of the Lord's Supper. No bishop presided at any confirmation or chrismation, because such things were not in existence during the apostolic era. Nothing in the epistles of the New Testament gives an indication that the bishop's role and purpose is anything other than a humble leader of God's people. In fact, Peter cautions against the opposite tendency, exhorting the elders in 1 Peter 5:3 to "not [be] domineering over those in your charge, but [be] examples to the flock." An elder also had a teaching responsibility. He must be able to both exhort Christians in their lives, instructing them with solid teaching, and to likewise gently correct those who oppose sound doctrine.

Whatever view one has of pastors in the evangelical sense, few would claim that they possess any special power that sets them apart from the congregation. Gifts are another matter, and it is of course the case that some are very able expositors of the Bible. But an expository gift does not mean a clerical superiority, or that no one else may also ably preach. Evangelical pastors likewise have the responsibility to shepherd and guide the flock, but as themselves under the chief shepherd, Jesus.

If the division of the office of bishop and presbyter (priest) came later, so too did the attachment of unique prerogatives to the clergy. Roman Catholic Alexandre Faivre notes this in a chapter called "The wonderful time when there was neither clergy nor laity": "In his epistle to the Colossians, Paul speaks of the '*kleros* [i.e., called, clergy] of the saints' and in Acts he uses the expression 'inheritance' (*kleronomia*) among (all) those who are sanctified. And what justifies this belonging to this particular lot is neither a function of government or direction, nor a more advanced level of holiness or any special merit, but membership of the people. By whom is the *kleros* constituted in the first epistle of Peter? Not by the elders appointed to oversee the flock, but by the flock itself."[40] 'Called,' or 'clergy,' is an adjective that the New Testament applies to every Christian.

Brown also questions the idea that ordination confers any particular enablement on a priest: "The theory about passing on powers through ordination faces the serious obstacle that the NT does not show the Twelve laying hands on bishops either as successors or as auxiliaries in administering sacraments."[41] Meyer agrees, "Apart from the case of Christ and the people of God as a whole, the New Testament does not attribute the priestly charism to anyone or any group. In the course of time the priestly charism of the Church began to be personified in the office holders, in particular the offices of supervisor (bishop), elder (priest) and deacon."[42] The key is, as Meyer says, that this view of priesthood developed over time. Dunn comments on this change. "Increasing institutionalization is the clearest mark of early catholicism – when church becomes increasingly identified with institution, when authority becomes increasingly coterminous with office, when a basic distinction between clergy and laity becomes increasingly self-evident, when grace becomes increasingly narrowed to well-defined ritual acts."[43]

Along with this, the Church began to look toward the Old Testament for guidance in regard to office, as well as rights and

[40] Alexandre Faivre, David Smith, trans., *The Emergence of the Laity in the Early Church* (Mahwah, NJ, Paulist Press, 1990), p. 6.
[41] Raymond E. Brown, *Priest and Bishop: Biblical Reflections* (Paramus, Paulist Press, 1970), p. 55.
[42] Charles R. Meyer, *Man of God: A Study of the Priesthood* (Eugene, Wipf and Stock, 2002), p. 45-46.
[43] James D.G. Dunn, *Unity and Diversity in the New Testament: An Enquiry into the Character of Earliest Christianity*, 2nd Ed. (London, SCM Press, 1990), p. 351.

powers. Rahner readily ascribes this viewpoint to the example of Israel: "In the light of the old testament the catholic priest is a unity of cultic-levitical priesthood."[44] In discussing the role of the sacraments, I will further explore the tendency of the hierarchical church to look to the Old Testament as the justification for the sacramental system. In embracing the Old Testament for this, the fundamentally Christian truths of the New Testament – the once and for all finished work of Christ, the priesthood of all believers, and the freedom for every single Christian to approach God without a mediator – are obscured, and in some cases denied, by a system which puts the priest as a necessary intermediary between the worshipper and God.

Summary

Much is made in sacramental tradition of the Nicene marks of the Church as one, holy, catholic, and apostolic. I have here chiefly examined the last of these, and found that, while the apostles left a definite pattern of church order and government, this is not the order that prevails in contemporary sacramentalism. Churches that have cast aside the New Testament pattern can assert no credible claim to apostolicity.

Richard Peter Bennett learned through reading the scriptures for himself that they are sufficient for every aspect of the Christian life, even how we know what the Church is. Bennett, an Irishman raised near Dublin, was ordained to the Roman Catholic priesthood in 1963. He describes a youth that was happy, and a devout family atmosphere. "By the time I was about five or six years of age, Jesus Christ was a very real person to me, but so also were Mary and the saints. I can identify easily with others in traditional Roman Catholic nations of Europe and with Hispanics and Filipinos who put Jesus, Mary, Joseph, and other saints on a

---

[44] Karl Rahner, Edward Quinn, trans., *The Priesthood* (New York: Seabury Press, 1973), p. 104.

par with one another."[45] Yet the subsequent years of serving as a priest left Bennett feeling empty and distanced from God. Serving as a missionary in Trinidad found him getting people to come to Mass, but not necessarily to Jesus. An accident laid him aside for an extended period of recuperation. "In the suffering that I went through in the weeks after the accident, I began to find some comfort in direct personal prayer. I stopped saying the breviary (the Church's official prayer for the use of the clergy) and the rosary, and began to pray using parts of the Bible itself. This was a very slow process. I did not know my way through the Bible and the little I had learned over the years had taught me more to distrust it than to trust it. My training in philosophy and in the theology of Thomas Aquinas left me helpless, so that coming into the Bible now to find the Lord was like going into a huge dark wood without a map."[46]

"First, I discovered that God's Word, the Bible, is absolute, and without error. I had been taught that the Word is relative and that its truthfulness in many areas is to be questioned. Now I began to understand that the Bible could, in fact, be trusted. I discovered that the Bible teaches clearly that it is from God and is absolute in what it says. It is true in its history, in the promises God has made, in its prophecies, in the moral commands it gives, and in its instructions as to how to live the Christian life."[47]

Bennett calls the ensuing years "Tug of War" years, as he sought to reconcile what he read in the Bible with what the Church was telling him was true. The clash brought personal anguish and struggle. He tells of the turning point when he at last submitted to God's Word.

---

[45] Richard Peter Bennett, *Far from Rome, Near to God*, Richard Peter Bennett, Martin Buckingham, eds. (Carlisle: Banner of Truth Trust, 1994), p. 343-344.
[46] Bennett, p. 347-348.
[47] Bennett, p. 349.

In October 1985 God's grace was greater than the lie that I was trying to live. I went to Barbados to pray over the compromise that I was forcing myself to live. I felt truly trapped. The Word of God is absolute indeed. I ought to obey it alone; yet to the very same God I had vowed obedience to the supreme authority of the Roman Catholic Church. In Barbados I read a book in which was explained the biblical meaning of the church as 'the fellowship of believers'. In the New Testament there is no hint of a hierarchy; the 'clergy' lording it over the laity is unknown. Rather, as the Lord himself declared, one is your master, even Christ; and all ye are brethren (Matt. 23:8). Now to see and to understand the meaning of 'church' as fellowship left me free to let go of the Roman Catholic Church as supreme authority and to depend on Jesus Christ as Lord. It began to dawn on me that in biblical terms the bishops I knew in the Roman Catholic Church were not believers. They were for the most part pious men taken up with devotion to Mary and the rosary and loyal to Rome, but not one had any idea of the finished work of salvation, that Christ's work is done, that salvation is personal and complete. I left the Roman Catholic Church when I saw that life in Jesus Christ was not possible while remaining true to Roman Catholic doctrine. Finally, at age forty-eight, on the authority of God's Word alone, by grace alone, I accepted Christ's substitutionary death on the cross alone. To him alone be the glory.[48]

Through centuries of theological and ecclesiastical accretions, very fundamental differences between the apostolic organization of the church and the contemporary church have arisen. Sacramental traditions may state that the church order of today's hierarchical church is the one that the apostles provided, but the evidence of the New Testament shows that claim to be spurious. Yet even in the hierarchical tradition, there were flickering hopes of a return to a more biblical model. Charles de Guise, one of the

---

[48] Bennett, p. 352-353.

fathers at the Council of Trent, presented a plea to do away with the clerical system that had developed through custom. "For three hours de Guise held the attention of his audience as he developed his theme: the church had to break with contemporary practices, especially nomination [of bishops] by secular rulers, and let itself be guided by principles found in the early church. He proposed a radical program that espoused election of bishops by people and clergy. He met immediate resistance."[49]

To choose sacramentalism is to choose a later interpretation of church polity – neither the oldest nor the most biblical. Because sacramentalism puts so much weight on the doctrine of the Church it is not simply a question of practicality or organization, but instead influences every other area of faith and practice. The development of sacramentalism depends very heavily on this definition of organization and hierarchy; thus ecclesiology is not a mere convenience, or a utilitarian doctrine that provides expediency. It is rather the rationale behind so much of the power claimed for sacramental theology. It became the locus for the tradition that competed with, and indeed overcame, scriptural revelation as the authority for Christendom. This is something that is too little examined by evangelicals adopting sacramentalism, but it is a question that everyone needs to ask. Is this the church the apostles left us?

---

[49] John W. O'Malley, *Trent: What Happened at the Council* (Cambridge, The Belknap Press Of Harvard University, 2013), p. 215.

3

The Pillar and Ground of Truth:
The Church as Authority

Romania is a country where the Orthodox Church has been deeply embedded in the culture of the people, even when the government was communist. To be Romanian was to be Orthodox. In rare cases, the truth of the gospel overcame the authority of the Church in the lives of the people. One such case is John, a believer who had an encounter with the Word of God that convinced him of its authority as greater than the church. His story was told in an interview with Trevin Wax.

"Though the church building was just four houses down the street from his, John rarely attended. 'I usually went to the midnight Easter vigil,' he recalls. 'A few days before Easter, I would go confess my sins to the local priest. But this had no effect on me. When I walked out of a church service, I was the same as before.' In his early twenties, John became active in the Communist party in Romania. One evening, he was on an assignment to visit one of the Baptist churches and to see how many of the 'repenters' (as they were derogatorily called) were present. He was also told to ask the Baptists questions about why they were attending churches other than the Orthodox Church. 'I had no intention of converting to evangelicalism,' he says. 'But when I heard the Word of God preached for the first time, and the concept of repentance and being 'born again,' I was touched. I realized that I had never truly repented of my sins. Here I would go to the Orthodox Church, cross myself, kiss an icon one moment and despise God the next. I realized that the Orthodox church was a societal organization that had taught me nothing.' So John decided to 'follow Jesus' and turn away from his sinful past.'[1]

Despite strenuous opposition from his family, John did not waver in his new life, and the transformation effected by Christ could not be denied.

"How did your family get over their condemnation of your newfound faith?" I wonder aloud. John smiles and begins to get visibly excited. He tells me how his family could deny his new beliefs, but none could deny the visible change in his lifestyle. 'I stopped getting drunk, stopped smoking, stopped cursing. I began reading my Bible, going to church, praying. I had been born again,' he says. Within months, his wife, parents, and even his 80-year-old grandmother who had been a mainstay of the village Orthodox church, had all converted, as a direct result of his testimony. "I have pleaded for the past thirty years with my Orthodox friends to come to Christ and know Him personally," John says, with tears in his eyes. "My Orthodox friends confess Christ with their mouths, but they do not know Him in their hearts. Religiosity does not mean salvation.... People can be sincere and still be sincerely wrong. The Orthodox Church feeds on tradition, not on Scripture. If Orthodox believers would read Scripture without it being interpreted for them by the Church, they would discover the truth."[2]

John has had the experience of hearing the gospel preached, of being called to repentance, and of responding in faith to that call. Living his life in Christ means submission to the scriptures as his authority, despite opposition, or what the Church may say. For this Romanian Christian, the test of authority is whether something is found in the Bible.

---

[1] "John's Story: Why I left Eastern Orthodoxy for Evangelicalism", http://thegospelcoalition.org/blogs/trevinwax/2006/11/09/johns-story-why-i-left-eastern-orthodoxy-for-evangelicalism/
[2] Ibid.

The manner in which the church is authoritative for the Christian has been in contention, not just in recent years, but also for many centuries. Throughout history, one can find multiple examples of those who contradicted the church hierarchy, and who also questioned how it developed. We have seen how in the earliest decades of the church, she adhered to the apostolic pattern of elders and deacons, but that before too long, different ideas began to intrude on the simplicity of the New Testament model, leading to an organization of the Church that was patterned more on the imperial government than on any biblical outline. Bruce writes, "It is fairly clear that when one reads between the lines of Ignatius's letter to the Roman Church that the monarchical episcopate did not yet exist in that church."[3] The *Shepherd of Hermas* also mentions a plural oversight of the congregation. Corinth, Philippi, and Alexandria were all known to have a college of presbyters.[4] Hall observes that with Cyprian, several new features make their appearance: "Thus a bureaucracy parallel to that by which the Empire was run, managing dossiers of letters and documents had grown up, and for Cyprian only those recognized in the system belong to it. His own training in public affairs made him take this for granted."[5] When this bureaucracy became combined with the monepiscopacy that originated with Ignatius, the organized church moved into a new era.

All scholars affirm that with the declaration by Constantine legitimizing Christianity within the Empire, a fundamental change took place in the relationship between the church and society. The Christian faith went from being persecuted by some emperors and grudgingly tolerated by others to being made official. With the

---

[3] F.F. Bruce, *New Testament History* (Garden City: Anchor Books, 1972), p. 418.

[4] Ibid., p. 419.

[5] Stuart G. Hall, *Doctrine and Practice in the Early Church* (Grand Rapids, Eerdmans, 1991) p. 90.

Constantinian shift, the government and the church entered into a changed relationship. We see the hierarchical church engaged with believers in an essentially different way than previously. To deviate in any detail from the official church teaching was not simply to be heterodox, it was to be a disloyal subject of the emperor. From this time begins that long and grim history of violence against those outside the mainstream. The persecution of those with different views that culminated in the Inquisition began in these earlier centuries due to the desire on the part of the emperor to have a single unified faith throughout the Empire. The motivation for right doctrine was not necessarily spiritual, but social. The *modus operandi* became to threaten, excommunicate, and, in some cases, put to death those who differed.

Those who encourage evangelicals to more fully engage with the historical church (of which there is more in Chapter 5), need to strongly deny the "Constantinian Fall" of the church, or when the church, allied with the Empire, entered into a period of apostasy that prevailed until the Reformation. D. H. Williams believes this interpretation to be revisionist history, and to be animated chiefly by Reformational polemics that require this view to justify a restitutionist mindset of going back to the earlier, pristine era of the church: "The Constantinian [Fall] model has come to indict all fourth-century Christianity and subsequent ages as seriously flawed and having abandoned their biblical moorings. Those who would walk the path of Christian faithfulness must therefore go around it to stay on the path."[6] For others, the Constantinian Fall suggests that the promise of Jesus that the gates of hell would not prevail against his church has failed if she has indeed been so thoroughly compromised by Constantinian apostasy.[7] In one

---

[6] D.H. Williams, *Retrieving the Tradition and Renewing Evangelicalism: A Primer for Suspicious Protestants* (Grand Rapids, Wm. B. Eerdmans, 1999), p. 124.

[7] Darryl G. Hart, "The Use and Abuse of the Christian Past. Mercersburg, the Ancient Church, and American Evangelicalism," in *Evangelicals and the*

sense, the Constantinian Fall is too optimistic. If we draw a line at a given point in history and say that prior to this the church was pure, yet her association with the Empire from this time is the root of apostasy, we ignore the evidence, and the biblical record as well. With the exception of Corinthians, all of the second epistles of the New Testament – Thessalonians, Timothy, John, Peter – are apostasy epistles. They each warn of a departure from the faith that was *already* happening. Departure and apostasy did not suddenly arrive with Constantine, or with any other event. These elements were present from the beginning, and the apostles themselves were quick to identify error in the church.

Critics of the Constantinian Fall view of church history dismiss it as justification for a radical and naïve agenda of returning to the earliest Christian witness. They claim that Jesus was leading his church, even in the patristic era, and to suggest a sudden and sharp departure at the Edict of Toleration is ridiculous. I submit that both of these views are correct. Jesus has promised his presence to the church throughout history, because she is his bride, but the New Testament likewise predicts sure and certain apostasy, and that which originates *within* the church. How should these be reconciled? The example of Israel provides a pattern. Israel as the chosen nation, the people that God selected as his own, the congregation in the wilderness, was put into a special covenant relationship with him. Yet there was apostasy, idolatry and departure from the faithfulness that God had called them to. Did God abandon his people? By no means, but we are told that faithfulness was preserved in a remnant. Not in the whole, but in the part were the promises maintained.

When Jesus expounds on the mysteries of the Kingdom of Heaven in Matthew 13, it is evident that there are wheat and tares, good seed and bad seed growing together. What is clear as well is that Jesus does not refer to the church in this passage. Rather, he

---

Early Church: Recovery, Reform, Renewal, George Kalantzis, Andrew Tooley, eds. (Eugene, Cascade Books, 2012), p. 94-95.

discusses the wider concept of the Kingdom, where his rule is known and assented to, but where there has not necessarily been an experience of new birth, or he presents the Kingdom in its eschatological sense. Jewish-Christian commentator Alfred Edersheim says, "We must dismiss the notion that the [Kingdom] expression refers to the Church, whether visible (according to the Roman Catholic view), or invisible (according to certain Protestant writers). It is difficult to conceive, how the idea of the identity of the Kingdom of God with the Church could have originated."[8] Doubtless there is an eschatological element to the parables of the kingdom as well, when Jesus refers to the close of the age, and the angels separating the good from the evil. Jesus says, until then, let the wheat and the tares grow together. This is in contrast to the church, where there is to be discipline for sin, and a coexistence of evil alongside good, is decidedly not to be tolerated when known. Paul counsels the Corinthians very differently from what Jesus says in Matthew 13: "Let him who has done this be removed from among you. You are to deliver this man to Satan for the destruction of the flesh, so that his spirit may be saved in the day of the Lord." (1 Cor. 5:2, 5) In this way, the parables of Matthew 13 present a picture of what we see in Christendom, but not necessarily Christianity. Such an understanding accounts for the sovereign working of God in history, but does not deny the presence of evil as well. In short, simply because Jesus promised that he would not forsake his church does not mean that everything the church will do has his blessing and endorsement. Skeptics of the Constantinian Fall do not accept every development of history as divinely ordained. If not all of fourth-century Christianity stands indicted, neither is all of it wholly approved. Advocates of patristic engagement are in the same position as skeptics of the hierarchical church, weighing and parsing the evidence to come to a conclusion about what is legitimate.

---

8 Alfred Edersheim, *The Life and Times of Jesus the Messiah* (Grand Rapids, Wm. B. Eerdmans, 1962), vol. 1, p. 269.

Is the Church Necessary for Salvation?

For evangelicals who embrace sacramentalism, there is a further frontier that is necessary to cross, a doctrine of ecclesiology wholly different than that of evangelicalism. We earlier examined the view that conceives of the church as a separate entity from believers themselves. One of the prime manifestations of this is the belief that the church is necessary for salvation. Cyprian of Carthage is famous for his much-quoted statement; "He cannot have God for his father, who has not the Church for his mother." This may be a clever parallel to the biological necessity of children requiring both a father and a mother, but is it biblical? The metaphors and pictures used for the church in the New Testament are many, but several are dominant. The church is the body of Christ, it is a holy temple, and it is the bride of Christ. Of the 96 pictures of the church found in Paul Minear's exhaustive study *Images of the Church in the New Testament*, none of them refers to the church as the mother of believers. Styling the church as the mother of Christians fits into the hierarchical paradigm of the church as existing apart from the body of believers, and directing the members of the body, yet there is simply no biblical data to support the idea of the church as our mother. Catholic dogma teaches that apart from the church there is no salvation. The witness of the New Testament is that upon believing one is made a member of the church. The church then is not the *conduit* of salvation, but the *result* of it. Those who put their faith in Jesus are by that fact instantly made members of the church. Insisting that the church in any way grants salvation is an *a priori* assumption of sacramentalism that puts the body in place of the head, and redefines the purpose and fundamental nature of the church.

What Cyprian said after his famous remark shows that he conflates things that are not the same: "If you could escape outside Noah's ark, you could escape outside the Church. The Lord warns us, saying: 'He that is not with me is against me, and he that

53

gathereth not with me scattereth'. To break the peace and concord of Christ is to go against Christ."[9] Cyprian's quick pivot to the references to scattering and gathering is curious. The salvific work that redeems us belongs to Christ alone, not to his Church. There are many types of Christ in the Old Testament, often explained as such in the New Testament. Where in the New Testament is the ark identified with the church? The ark is far more explicable as a picture of Jesus than that of the church. Cyprian also falls into the same sectarianism that Jesus warned the disciples of. The passage he references from Matthew 12 about not gathering with Jesus needs to be understood with Mark 9:38-41. The disciples tell Jesus of finding someone who was casting out demons in Jesus' name, but they hindered him, "because he was not following us." Jesus says, "Do not stop him, for no one who does a mighty work *in my name* will be able soon afterward to speak evil of me. For the one who is not against us is for us." In both instances, identification with Christ is the key. He who does not gather with *me*, scatters. The ones the disciples sought to stop were doing these things in Jesus' name, and thus Jesus says, do not hinder him. The fact that they were not identified with the disciples was not determinative; it is identification with Jesus himself that is.

Sacramental teaching clearly mishandles the scriptural record on the point of the necessity of the church. Ott says, "The apostles teach the necessity of the Church for salvation. Peter confesses before the High Council: 'Neither is there salvation in any other' (Acts 4:12)."[10] That Peter teaches the exclusivity of salvation is certain, but where does one find mention of the church in this passage? The full context of Peter's address makes plain that he has Jesus himself in view: "Let it be known to all of you and to all the people of Israel that by the name of Jesus Christ of Nazareth,

---

[9] Cyprian, "The Unity of the Catholic Church," in *Early Latin Theology*, S. L. Greenslade, ed., (Louisville, Westminster Press, 1956), p. 128.

[10] Ludwig Ott, Patrick Lynch, trans., James Bastible, ed., *Fundamentals of Catholic Dogma* (Rockford, IL, Tan Books and Publishers, 1955), p. 312.

whom you crucified, whom God raised from the dead – by him this man is standing before you well. This Jesus is the stone that was rejected by you, the builders, which has become the cornerstone. And there is salvation in no one else, for there is no other name under heaven given among men by which we must be saved" (Acts 4:10-12). Ott's own presuppositions about Catholic ecclesiology make him substitute the church for Jesus himself. It is an exegetical fallacy to find the church here where it speaks clearly of Jesus. To the one mediator between God and man – Christ Jesus – Catholic dogma has added another mediator between man and Christ – the church. While one can find this in post-apostolic writers such as Cyprian, one cannot find it in the apostolic teaching. In later centuries, this mediation is often assigned to Mary, but this too is found only in tradition, rather than the biblical record.

Much later, alongside the necessity of the Church for salvation, the doctrine of the infallibility of the Church was added. Yves Congar says, "Considered in this way according to its constituent principles (not only such as they exist *in* God, but as they are *given* and exist *within the church* as its formal principles), the church is impeccable, infallible, and virginal, with the impeccability and the virginity of God himself and of Jesus Christ."[11] In this broad definition of infallibility, which says nothing other than that Jesus has founded the church and in that he is God incarnate, the principles he imparted to her are infallible. No one would argue with this abstract definition, but the implementation and application of these things is another matter, which Congar also acknowledges: "We are looking here at the use that human beings make of these gifts – humans with all their freedom, their weakness, their instability, and their essential fallibility. This is the doorway through which sin and various other weaknesses penetrate into the church. This is the 'material cause' of the

---

[11] Yves Congar, Paul Philibert, O.P., trans., *True and False Reform in the Church* (Collegeville, Liturgical Press, 2011), p. 93.

church, the human beings who make up the people of God who are vulnerable to these weaknesses."[12]

The division we noted earlier between the church as institution and the church as the people of God is very much evidenced here. The sacramental church points to the divinely established institution that Jesus founded as the church that cannot fail. The sinners who comprise it are very much prone to failure. Discerning the difference between these two is of course the challenge. But what possible manifestation of the church on the earth can there be apart from the sinners who make up the church? During long years of corruption, the institutional church had as its leaders men who were often morally bereft, and who treated the church as a personal fiefdom. Was she preserved from error in these years? If the definition of infallibility remains in the realm of theory as Congar first describes, then there is no practical sense in which we can speak of it at work in the church. If the claim is that infallibility is very much at work in practice within the institutional church, we are right to ask, how is this shown? To consider the church as Jesus founded it as a divinely chartered organization that cannot err is nothing other than the principle of *sola ecclesia*: The church cannot err because it is founded by Jesus. If it appears that she has erred, this cannot be, because she is the divinely founded church. All evidence that the church has erred must be rejected because the principle underlying everything is that she cannot.

Outside the Mainstream

The claim is often repeated that before the Reformation, there was but one church, i.e., only a single ecclesial manifestation, and if anyone believed something different from the hierarchical church, where is the evidence? But prior to the Reformation itself, there were those who objected to what the Church was teaching,

---

[12] Congar, p. 95.

and what she was claiming for the sacraments. Given the definition of the necessity of the Church for salvation, it is clear why there was such vehement opposition to those believers who did not adhere to the sacramental principle in all aspects and why they were cast as heretical and schismatic. Strayer summarizes the motivation behind this conflict: "The Church, and the Church alone, could put men on the path to salvation. Only by believing the eternal truths taught by the Church, only by receiving the sacraments administered by the Church, could men be saved. Anyone who denied these truths, anyone who repudiated the sacraments, anyone who sought to destroy the Church was an enemy of mankind, a murderer who sought to kill the immortal soul rather than the earthly body. No weakness in the Church could excuse such a crime."[13] The Church made disagreements over the sacraments equally heretical with something as grave as denying the deity of Christ. In short, there were no secondary or minor issues; any deviation was a challenge to the Church.

It is at times difficult to discern what the so-called heretics were in fact guilty of. An eleventh-century monk, Heribert, warns his co-religionists of heretics in the region of Perigord, France. His letter, notes Michael Frassetto, "was written by one of the victors in the great struggle between orthodoxy and heresy in the Middle Ages and bears the mark of the biases held by the established clergy. It was the clergy who possessed the truth; the doctrines and dogmas sanctioned by the Church were the only true teachings, and those perceived as offering something different, even if it were based on the Gospels, were deemed to be in error."[14] The profile that emerges is that the term "heretic" was applied not necessarily to one who was heterodox in his views on the person of Christ, or on the Christian life, but whose offense was quite often simply to

---

[13] Joseph R. Strayer, *The Albigensian Crusades* (New York, The Dial Press, 1971), p. 23.

[14] Michael Frassetto, *The Great Medieval Heretics: Five Centuries of Religious Dissent* (New York, BlueBridge, 2008), p. 3.

be outside of the hierarchical church. The evidence for their views was "in all likelihood based on a stock collection of beliefs drawn from St. Augustine, and earlier writers, who had outlined what the heretics were *supposed* to believe."[15]

The Church often went to great lengths to destroy any documents or evidence of these groups whom they judged to be heretical, and, in large measure, this effort succeeded. The surviving documents are not nearly as numerous as those of the hierarchical church. Along with the destruction of any documents was a concerted effort to portray these believers in the most execrable light possible, or to paint a picture of gross sin and immorality, one that would color the perception of any enquirer into their doctrines and practices. E.H. Broadbent echoes this caution: "The true histories of these have been obliterated as far as possible; their writings, sharing the fate of the writers, have been destroyed to the full extent of power allowed to their persecutors. Not only so, but histories of them have been promulgated by those to whose interest it was to disseminate the worst inventions against them to justify their own cruelties."[16] We should therefore be cautious and suspect when we read the depictions by their enemies as to what these groups outside the mainstream actually believed and taught.

Who were these Christians who were outside the mainstream, who taught something other than what the hierarchical church was teaching? A first case is Tertullian, the irascible Carthaginian. Here is an example of how history has been molded to tell the story from the viewpoint of the hierarchical church. His doctrine on baptism and on leadership in the Church (both of which we will examine later) were not hierarchical church teachings. For polemicists of the official position, it is convenient to place someone such as Tertullian outside of the Church. Father Edward

---

[15] Frassetto, Loc. cit.

[16] E.H. Broadbent, *The Pilgrim Church* (London, Pickering & Inglis, 1931), p. 42.

Gratsch says that "after he went over to Montanism, Tertullian rejected the Church of the bishops and extolled the Church of the Spirit."[17] Locating him outside the official Church allows Tertullian to be cast as a schismatic, rather than the representative of a different tradition within the Church. Yet David Rankin affirms that "there are a number of passages from his later works – his 'Montanist' period – which will support a contention contrary to that traditionally adopted; namely that Tertullian never left the Catholic church, but rather continued his fight for a more vigorous and disciplined Christian discipleship from within the Catholic church itself."[18]

The narrative of a single, unified tradition through the centuries is of course undermined if Tertullian is viewed in this latter fashion. Rankin further notes that even when Tertullian uses the Latin pronoun "nos" to refer to himself and his Montanist brethren, as opposed to "vos" when referring to the Catholics, this does not represent schism, but rather "the flavour of a select group within the church – an 'ecclesiola in ecclesia' – undertaking the self-appointed task of 'saving' the orthodox from the dangers of heterodoxy."[19] Tertullian's posture fits more logically into the category of a remnant. "Tertullian no longer regards himself as 'at one' with that element of the church which, in his renewed desire for greater discipline and rigour in the life of the church, he now brands (in the language of the New Prophecy) as 'Psychici' or 'carnally minded.'"[20]

Tertullian and Cyprian were representatives of the rigorist strain of faith that was typical of the Christianity of North Africa. These men taught that the morality of the clergy was not unimportant or

---

[17] Edward J. Gratsch, *Where Peter Is: A Survey of Ecclesiology* (New York, Alba House, 1975), p. 31.

[18] David Rankin, *Tertullian and the Church* (Cambridge, Cambridge University Press, 1995), p. 28.

[19] Ibid, p. 30.

[20] Ibid, p. 31.

incidental to their ministry, but in fact was vital. While the sacramentalist likes to quote Cyprian for his insistence on the Church as the mother of believers, they are less inclined to adopt his view on the sinfulness of a priest contaminating those who receive the Eucharist from him. In his epistle *To the Clergy and People Abiding in Spain, Concerning Basilides and Martial,* Cyprian fulminates against the idea later to be known as *ex opere operato*: "Nor let the people flatter themselves that they can be free from the contagion of sin, while communicating with a priest who is a sinner, and yielding their consent to the unjust and unlawful episcopacy of their overseer, when the divine reproof by Hosea the prophet threatens, and says, 'Their sacrifices shall be as the bread of mourning; all that eat thereof shall be polluted' (Hos. 9:4) teaching manifestly and showing that all are absolutely bound to the sin who have been contaminated by the sacrifice of a profane and unrighteous priest."[21] Both Cyprian and Tertullian adhere to beliefs that were outside of what was later defined as official dogma.

In the mid-seventh century, an Armenian named Constantine began to examine the four gospels and the fourteen epistles of Paul (counting Hebrews as among them). He received these manuscripts as the gift of a fellow Armenian who had been the captive of Saracens and who had stayed in the house of Constantine on his journey home after his release.[22] The effect of reading these on Constantine was the repudiation of what he found in the institutional church as antithetical to the New Testament witness. "Testifying to new life he had received, he soon found fellowship with groups of people of a like experience who rejected the idolatry and superstition of the organized church, and met together in accordance with what he had learned from his

---

21 *Ante-Nicene Fathers, Vol. 5*, ed. Philip Schaff (Grand Rapids, Christian Classics Ethereal Library, n.d.), p. 893.
22 Broadbent, p. 45.

study of the scriptures."[23]Apparently in imitation of Paul, who changed his name upon conversion, Constantine took the name of Silvanus. For reasons that are not clear, the believers who gathered with Silvanus came to be called Paulicians. In 684, the Byzantine emperor sent a delegation to enforce an edict against the Paulicians, and to kill Silvanus. The officer in charge of the delegation, Simeon, himself became a disciple in a few short years. Changing his name to Titus, he too suffered a martyr's death.

The imperial edict failed to eradicate the Paulicians, for they were still in existence some 200 years after Silvanus. The emperor again sent a representative in 870, Peter Siculus, who later wrote a history of the Paulicians, *Historia Manichaeorum qui Pauliciani Dicuntur*. Faber sarcastically reports of Siculus' account of Constantine that "nothing can be more clear and more certain, than, that, from the study of the New Testament, whence he had learned the catholic doctrines of the Trinity and of Christ's godhead and incarnation, the man rose a hardened and inveterate Manichean!"[24] How the study of the New Testament led Constantine to embrace Manicheism is not explained. Indeed, Siculus could find nothing to condemn in the lives of the Paulicians; his conclusion is that their piety is but a veil of hypocrisy. Faber counters, "The Paulicians, though perpetually by their enemies charged with the Manichean heresy, uniformly denied the justice of the accusation; and always rejected, with strong expressions of abhorrence, both Manes and Manicheism. They held the allied doctrines of the Trinity and the Incarnation: but they renounced the worship of the Cross and of the Virgin and of the Saints; while they evidently disbelieved that material

---

23 John W. Kennedy, *The Torch of the Testimony*, (Beaumont, TX, The Seed Sowers, 1965), p. 112.

24 G.S. Faber, (2014-01-18). *The History of the Ancient Vallenses and Albigenses* (Kindle Edition, Delmarva Publications, 2014), Kindle Location 2206-2212.

presence of the Lord's body and blood in the consecrated elements which finally received the name of Transubstantiation."[25] Here, too, we find an early witness of those who sought to order their lives by the New Testament, and for doing so were labeled as heretics.

Moving a few centuries into the future, and further west, we encounter the Waldensians, a group named after an early leader, Peter Waldo, alternately known as Valdès or Vaudès. The Waldensians (or the Poor of Lyons) were first known around the year 1170. Vaudès was apparently a merchant who renounced his life for three things: poverty, preaching, and the Bible. Vaudès sought to emulate in his life what he read in the Scriptures, and to endeavor to spread the message of the gospel. "To Vaudès' mind, the duty to spread the good news was therefore imperative. The merchant from Lyons and the group that formed around him, following him and doing as he did, were, however, laymen. In the Roman Church, only clergymen could preach, as they had been trained for that mission. By challenging the clergy's monopoly of the Word, the poor of Lyons provoked first astonishment, then reprobation and finally the condemnation of the Church hierarchy."[26]

What was it that caused the Church to oppose the Waldensians? "They held that there had been no true Pope since the days of Sylvester; that temporal offices and dignities were not meet for preachers of the Gospel; that the Pope's pardons were a cheat; that purgatory was a fable; that relics were simply rotten bones which had belonged to one knew not whom; that to go on pilgrimage served no end, save to empty one's purse; that flesh might be eaten any day if one's appetite served him; that holy water was not a whit more efficacious than rain-water; and that

---

25 Faber, Kindle Locations 2524-2535.
26 Gabriel Audisio, Claire Davison, trans., *The Waldensian Dissent: Persecution and Survival, c. 1170- c. 1570* (Cambridge, Cambridge University Press, 1999), p. 12.

prayer in a barn was just as effectual as if offered in a church. They were accused, moreover, of having scoffed at the doctrine of transubstantiation, and of having spoken blasphemously of Rome as the harlot of the Apocalypse."[27] Their offenses are to have rejected the teachings of the institutional and hierarchical church, but not those of the Scriptures. Strayer expands on Waldo's views: "With the help of some telling examples from the early church, he argued that all true Christians could preach the gospel. Waldo had been driven to deny any basic distinction between layman and cleric. Such a doctrine obviously attacked the validity of ordination, the authority of the Church, and the significance of the apostolic succession. By implication it weakened the value of the sacraments, since, in case of necessity, they could be administered by laymen."[28] From this two things are clear; the Waldensians represent a pre-Reformation example of a group that held to the priesthood of all believers, and denied any special powers to clergymen. Second, the Scriptures were the source of Waldo's teaching. This put Waldo at odds with the Church of his day, but recalling the crisis of temporality – to seek a link with the historical – in this regard, Waldo found just such a link by going back to the apostles and their doctrine.

Among the Waldensians, we also find one of the earliest examples of the Bible being translated into the vernacular. Vaudès himself commissioned two clergymen from Lyons to translate the Scriptures into the common tongue, one who translated it, and the other who wrote the translation down.[29] Preaching by laymen, and reading in the vernacular were too much for the established Church, which excommunicated Vaudès and his poor preachers. They refused to stop their preaching, and were eventually driven from Lyons and ultimately anathemized by the Fourth Lateran Council in 1215. Though persecuted, the Waldensians were not

---

[27] J.A. Wylie, *The History of the Waldenses* (Kindle Edition, 2011), p. 14.

[28] Strayer, p. 37.

[29] Audisio, p. 11.

conquered by the established Church, but joined with the Protestant Reformation centuries later. Their beliefs and simplicity of faith are a rebuke to the idea that in prior centuries there was simply no other Church but the hierarchical. "Apart from the Holy Scriptures, they had no special confession of faith or religion, nor any rules, nor any authority of any man, however eminent, was allowed to set aside the authority of Scripture."[30] In tracing these movements of previous eras, the point is not to suggest that these were somehow proto-evangelicals, but rather that there were Christians outside the authority of the hierarchical church who took their *raison d'être* for their faith not from ecclesiastical pronouncements, but from the Scriptures.

The Conciliar Tradition

One way of confronting division and enforcing unanimity in the church was to convene a council of the bishops to resolve their theological differences. For Constantine and his successors, theological diversity was as much a political problem as an ecclesiastical one. The calling of church councils is of old tradition, but not all traditions agree on the authority they carry. Catholicism and Orthodoxy differ on what represents an ecumenical council. The list of those councils that are considered ecumenical (and thus universal and authoritative for the Church as a whole) is limited to the first seven councils for Orthodoxy. Protestant reformers considered the first four to be authoritative. In Catholicism, the list of ecumenical councils now stands at twenty-one. Concerning the appellation of "ecumenical" to any council, Ramsay MacMullan notes, "Anything so described was 'of the whole civilized world'. Yet what a preposterous boast! first made for ecclesiastical matters in the AD 330s and subsequently competed for and valorously claimed for themselves by councils

---

[30] Broadbent, p. 98.

which certainly should have known better."[31] Catholicism's definition of what constitutes an ecumenical council is anachronistic and revisionist. All of the first seven councils were convened not by any pope or patriarch, but by the emperor. Catholic historians themselves affirm concerning Nicaea, perhaps of first importance among the councils, "It is certain that Constantine neither had negotiations with Rome on an eventual convocation of the great synod, nor did he ask the consent of the Roman Bishop."[32] Indeed, in the early centuries, Rome and the West were of decidedly secondary importance: "The East was still the most numerous, the best educated, and the richest part of Christendom. It was still the source of learning and civilization; and it continued to be the scene of the most important definitions of Christian orthodoxy."[33] Each of the first seven councils was held in the East.

It is clear that councils were every bit as much political events as they were theological ones. From the histories of the councils one can see that consolidation of power, while not always overtly stated, was often high on the agenda of participating bishops. The various sees that became known as the pentarchy – Jerusalem, Antioch, Rome, Alexandria, and Constantinople – contended for theological preeminence within the Empire. This, it seems, is what was behind much of Cyril of Alexandria's fulminations against Nestorius. Alexandria did not want to cede any authority to Constantinople, and to the upstart bishop that Cyril felt Nestorius to be. At least one Orthodox writer has re-examined the

---

31 Ramsay MacMullen, *Voting About God in Early Church Councils* (New Haven, Yale University Press, 2006), p. 68.

32 Karl Baus, Hans-Georg Beck, Eugen Ewig, Hermann Josef Vogt; Anslem Biggs, trans., *The Imperial Church from Constantine to the Early Middle Ages* (New York, Seabury Press, 1980), p. 22.

33 R.W. Southern, *The Penguin History of the Church, Volume II: Western Society and the Church in the Middle Ages*, (London, Penguin Books, 1970), p. 61.

documents surrounding the Council of Chalcedon, where Nestorius was condemned, and concluded that Cyril and Nestorius were affirming largely the same thing, but quite often talking past one another.[34] When Nestorius heard the term "Mother of God," he feared that this was opening the door to the view that somehow Mary was connected with Christ's deity, rather than his humanity, and it was a suggestion that his deity had a beginning. In other words, Nestorius was keen to protect the full deity of Christ in any creedal definitions. None of the bishops of the day was stating what Nestorius feared, but in an atmosphere of tension and kneejerk reactions, the party of Cyril prevailed in condemning Nestorius as heretical at the first Council of Ephesus in 431. Anastos counters: "My own thesis is that Nestorius was not only thoroughly and indubitably orthodox, but also in many respects the profoundest and most brilliant theologian of the fifth century."[35] The differences in word usage, as well as theological presuppositions and inferences, kept the bishops from agreement, and affected the course of ecclesiastical history. How much authority, then, is it proper to ascribe to councils when their purposes were always tinged with political machinations?

The question every Christian faces is whether conciliar decisions are in fact authoritative in defining what it is that we believe, or practice. Some affirm that the only reason we believe in the deity of Christ is because Nicaea defined it. But is this so? Is it the case that the deity of Christ is known and believed only because of the creed?

The council wrestled with the how to express the relationship of the Logos (Jesus) to the Father. Was he *homoousios* (of the same substance) or *homoiousios* (of like substance)? The latter term was rejected as not adequately closing the door on the Arian position of the Son as a created being. As happened with most of the

---

[34] See Milton V. Anastos, "Nestorius Was Orthodox" in *Dumbarton Oaks Papers, Vol. 16,* (1962), p. 117-140.
[35] Anastos, p. 123.

ecumenical councils, the matter was not finally settled. *Homoousios*, though included in the creed, was "a notoriously slippery word"[36] not at all definite in the exclusivity of its meaning. In the years following Nicaea, there were councils called which alternately affirmed Nicene orthodoxy (Rome in 340, Rimini in 359) or Arianism (Tyre in 335, Sirmium in 357). Athanasius was repeatedly exiled and recalled during his long episcopate, as orthodoxy within the empire waxed and waned. Apparently growing impatient with the esoteric theological wrangling of the bishops, the emperor Constantius finally forced a compromise at Seleucia (359), "the holdouts being browbeaten by the emperor personally far into the night of Dec. 31, 359."[37] The council of Constantinople (381) was called as an attempt to make explicit anything that was left implicit at Nicaea.

When modern day Arians come knocking on the door, evangelicals who know their Bibles show Christ's deity from the New Testament, rather than appealing to conciliar decisions or creeds. There is evidence also that the later church did in fact judge Nicaea afresh, and accepted only part of its conclusions. Canon 20 from Nicaea stipulates, "For as much as there are certain persons who kneel on the Lord's Day and in the days of Pentecost, therefore, to the intent that all things may be uniformly observed everywhere (in every parish), it seems good to the holy Synod that prayer be made to God standing." Here is an example of a conciliar canon that has been set aside, for every Sunday today multitudes kneel to pray.

Just prior to the Council of Chalcedon in 451, where Nestorius was condemned for the second time, the so-called "Robber Council" of 449 was held at Ephesus. The true business of the council is difficult to determine due to the overt personal

---

[36] Leo Donald Davis, S.J., *The First Seven Ecumenical Councils (325-787): Their History and Theology* (Collegeville, MN, The Liturgical Press, 1983), p. 61.

[37] Davis, p. 98.

animosities of the principals. Dioscurus, who presided at the council, had military police to help encourage bishops to sign the official acts of the council. "For greater convenience, some of the bishops were induced to sign blank sheets to be filled in later by Dioscurus' notaries."[38] The tactics used at the Robber Council were patently coercive and its results did not stand. What this demonstrates is that not all councils are equal or legitimate. There is common agreement that the Robber Council was illegitimate, but disagreement about later councils. Conciliar authority provides no sure or certain foundation.

On the historical development of infallibility, whether of the church itself, ecumenical councils, or the pope, Father Francis Sullivan writes:

In approaching this question, it is sobering to recall the following facts: that explicit belief in the infallibility of ecumenical councils does not appear in Christian literature until the ninth century; that the infallibility of the pope has never been a matter of faith for Christians of the Eastern Orthodox tradition; that explicit belief in the infallibility of the pope appears in western Christianity only in the last quarter of the thirteenth century and that the doctrine of infallibility of the pope was much contested in the West from the thirteenth to the nineteenth century, and became universally accepted in the Roman Catholic Church only when it had been defined by the First Vatican Council in 1870.

These facts suggest that the doctrine of conciliar and papal infallibility cannot be very clear and obvious in Scripture or early Christian tradition. In view of this history, it can hardly be claimed that the scriptural texts usually cited in favour of the infallibility of the magisterium provide a simple and easily convincing proof of the thesis. The texts are convincing, it would seem, only to those who are disposed to accept the doctrine. Therefore one must be realistic and

---

[38] Davis, p. 178.

not expect that there is scriptural 'proof' of conciliar and papal infallibility that will convince everyone 'of good will' who hears it.[39]

As Scot McKnight found in his research, converts from Evangelicalism to Roman Catholicism have a desire to connect with history: "So the crisis becomes one of temporality. How can we be connected with the entire history of the church, and how is it right for so many Christians to live in small, disengaged splinter groups?"[40] The irony of this is that, rather than engaging with the entire history of the church, these converts are encountering only certain centuries, certain writers. Augustine and Aquinas are favorites, but what of the Renaissance popes? Are the profligates embraced alongside the prophets? Father Sullivan points out the challenge of trying to assert a connection with history where one clearly does not exist. The Orthodox as well go back not to the apostolic doctrine, but to that finally settled on in 787 at the seventh ecumenical council. This view of history – stability or change – has proven a contentious point even within sacramental- ism. Those who insist on what was previously defined as dog- matic, or what was held by an earlier era of Christians as normative frequently clash with those who argue for a contin- uously evolving understanding. Against the view of the normative value of tradition, Henri de Lubac writes that a faithful son of the Church "will of course never take it into his head to appeal from the present teaching of the magisterium to some past situation, doctrinal or institutional, or invoke such things in order to apply to that teaching an interpretation which would in fact be an evasion, for he will always accept the teaching of the magisterium as the

---

39 Francis A. Sullivan, S.J., *Magesterium: The Teaching Authority in the Catholic Church* (Ramsey, NJ, Paulist Press, 1983), p. 82-83.
40 Scot McKnight and Hauna Ondrey, *Finding Faith, Losing Faith: Stories of Conversion and Apostasy* (Waco, Baylor Univ. Press, 2008), p. 209.

absolute norm."[41]   In other words, what previous councils may have decreed, what previous fathers may have said, is not in any way to be set against the current position of the magisterium. Several historians, doubtless considering themselves good Catholics, do just that when they point out the conciliar versus papal strife of the medieval ages that ultimately came to be termed Gallicanism vs. Ultramontanism. For adherents of the former position, ecumenical councils were the supreme authority, and even a pope was bound to obey their decrees. *Haec Sancta*, the encyclical promulgated at the Council of Constance in 1415, at a time when there were three simultaneous popes, declared:

All persons of whatever rank or dignity, even a Pope, are bound to obey it in matters relating to faith and the end of the schism and the general reformation of the Church of God in head and members. Further, it declares that any person of whatever position, rank, or dignity, even a Pope, who contumaciously refuses to obey the mandates, statutes, ordinances, or regulations enacted or to be enacted by this holy synod, or by any other general council lawfully assembled, relating to matters aforesaid or to other matters involved with them, shall, unless he repents, be subject to condign penalty and duly punished.[42]

Conciliarism vs. papal power was a point of strife that would surface again and again in the following centuries. Subsequent to Constance, Father John. W. O'Malley notes that, "The Council of Basel had in 1432 and 1434 declared that general councils were the supreme authority in the church. Then on May 16, 1439, it declared that doctrine a matter of faith, so that rejection of it was

---

[41] Henri de Lubac, trans. Michael Mason, *The Splendor of the Church* (San Francisco, Ignatius Press, 1956), p 244-245.

[42] Cited in Frank Welsh, *The Battle For Christendom: The Council of Constance, the East-West Conflict, and the Dawn of Modern Europe* (Woodstock, NY, The Overlook Press, 2008), p. 141-142.

heresy."[43] Pius II apparently did not get the memo. A few decades later, in his bull *Execrabilis*, he condemned conciliarism and the final authority of councils over popes. Francis Beckwith claims, "The pope is constrained by settled doctrine, including scripture, ecumenical councils, and prior ex cathedra papal pronounce-ments."[44], but clearly the pope and a legitimately convoked council were saying two opposing things. No amount of theological creativity or casuistry can reconcile the fact of "the Church" coming down on opposite sides of this question. *Haec Sancta* was not the only declaration to emerge from the Council of Constance that would in later years be pushed aside. *Frequens* called for the convocation of a council at regular intervals of a decade. O'Malley says that while Constance preserved the papacy by solving the issue of three simultaneous popes, "The Schism had inflicted almost irreparable damage on the belief that the popes could be counted on to handle properly their own affairs and the affairs of the church. The decree *Frequens* was a massive vote of no confidence."[45] In the spirit of his eponymous predecessor, Pius IX sought to wipe out conciliarism once and for all with the declaration of papal infallibility at Vatican I, yet it remains alive and well in some quarters of the Western Church.

In the East especially, there has been a kind of *stare decisis*, where previous council decisions could never be overturned, only received. The West felt no such compunction. The fact that papal infallibility was not found in history, even in the weakest foreshadowing, proved no barrier. Brian Tierney says much the same as Father Sullivan in the opening remarks of his *Origins of Papal Infallibility, 1150-1350*. Tierney observes that, regarding the question of papal infallibility, "Real issues of ecclesiastical power

---

[43] John W. O'Malley, *Trent: What Happened at the Council* (Cambridge, The Belknap Press Of Harvard University, 2013), p. 30.

[44] Francis J. Beckwith, *Return to Rome: Confessions of an Evangelical Catholic* (Grand Rapids, Brazos Press, 2009), p. 126.

[45] O'Malley, Op. Cit., p. 26.

are involved. If popes have always been infallible in any meaningful sense of the word – if their official pronouncements as heads of the church on matters of faith and morals have always been unerring and so irreformable – then all kinds of dubious consequences ensue. Most obviously, twentieth century popes would be bound by a whole array of past papal decrees reflecting the responses of the Roman church to the religious and moral problems of former ages. As Acton put it, 'The responsibility for the acts of the buried and repented past would come back at once and for ever.' To defend religious liberty would be 'insane' and to persecute heretics commendable. Judicial torture would be licit and taking of interest on loans a mortal sin. The pope would rule by divine right 'not only the universal church but the whole world.' Unbaptized babies would be punished in Hell for all eternity. Maybe the sun would still be going round the earth."[46]

One may wonder about the purpose of examining seemingly recondite details of church history such as the Council of Constance or long-forgotten papal bulls, but the point is that those who desire a connection with history frequently pick and choose from the historical record, dismissing what may be inconvenient to their arguments. The hierarchical church of today is but a contemporary interpretation of the historical church. The Catholic Church, moreover, has stated that it has the right to expand, revise, and change what is believed and taught as Christian truth. But this view creates a fissure with history. Cyril of Jerusalem writes, "For concerning the divine and holy mysteries of the faith, not even a casual statement must be delivered without the Holy Scriptures; nor must we be drawn aside by mere plausibility and artifices of speech. Even to me, who tells you these things, give not absolute credence, unless you receive the proof of the things which I

---

[46] Brian Tierney, *Origins of Papal Infallibility, 1150-1350* (Leiden, E.J. Brill, 1972), p. 2.

announce from the Divine Scriptures."[47] Echoing Cyril a few years later, we find the bishop of Hippo in his treatise *On the Trinity* saying, "Do not be willing to yield to my writings as to the canonical Scriptures; but in these, when you have discovered even what you did not previously believe, believe it unhesitatingly."[48]

Summary

In 1 Tim. 3:15, Paul writes to Timothy: "If I delay, you may know how one ought to behave in the household of God, which is the church of the living God, a pillar and ground of the truth." Whether it is a gloss on this text, or he is engaging in interpretation and application, or simply recalling the verse inaccurately, it is interesting to find Irenaeus in his *Adversus Haereses,* applying this not to the church, but to the Scriptures: "We have learned from none others the plan of our salvation, than from those through whom the Gospel has come down to us, which they did at one time proclaim in public, and, at a later period, by the will of God, handed down to us in the Scriptures, to be the ground and pillar of our faith."[49] Later, he notes that the number of four gospel records is of divine origin: "It is not possible that the Gospels can be either more or fewer in number than they are. For, since there are four zones of the world in which we live, and four principal winds, while the Church is scattered throughout all the world, and the 'pillar and ground' of the Church is the Gospel and the spirit of life."[50] It is evident that Irenaeus is not talking about any oral

---

[47] Cyril of Jerusalem, *Catechetical Lectures,* IV.17 in *Nicene and Post-Nicene Fathers, Series 2, Vol. 7,* ed. Philip Schaff (Grand Rapids, Christian Classics Ethereal Library, n.d.), p. 136.

[48] Augustine, *On the Trinity,* III.2, in *Nicene and Post-Nicene Fathers, Series 1, Vol. 3,* ed. Philip Schaff (Grand Rapids, Christian Classics Ethereal Library, n.d.), p. 102.

[49] *Ante-Nicene Fathers, Vol. 1,* ed. Philip Schaff (Grand Rapids, Christian Classics Ethereal Library, n.d.), p. 1059.

[50] Ibid., p. 1088.

gospel tradition, but about the written records of the four evangelists.

The tradition of later centuries would put the Church itself in the central place of authority in the life of the Christian. The Church is the pillar and ground of the truth only in that she upholds and defends it; she does not originate truth. Even in this brief survey of history, we see not stability but change in how succeeding ages understood the Church and its authority, whether it is conciliarism or papal primacy. It is chimerical to assert, however, that in joining oneself to sacramentalism, one is aligning with the historical church. This concept of the Church as the mediator of grace, withholding or granting forgiveness through the sacerdotal prerogatives of a priest, is an understanding of what the Church is, and what she can do, that dates not from the apostolic era, but from subsequent ages. As part of the paradigm shift to sacramentalism, one must accept that the Church is able to define doctrine, if even retroactively and anachronistically, to resolve the cognitive dissonances that inevitably result from a deeper look into history. It may be a serviceable paradigm, but is it defensible?

4
"These Things Are Written": Scripture and Authority

Joseph Mizzi is a pediatrician born and raised on the island of Malta. Though Malta is overwhelmingly Roman Catholic, Dr. Mizzi now proclaims the truth of being born again by faith in Christ, convinced of this through his reading of the Scriptures. "I was raised in a Roman Catholic home, and my parents and teachers taught me the fear of God, for which I will always be grateful. My country, Malta, is intensely Roman Catholic, with well over 95% of the population being Catholic. I was thoroughly indoctrinated in the Catholic religion since infancy. Sunday mass and daily rosary were obligatory in my family, and I happily attended mass on most days of the week before school. I was proud and sure of my religion. All that was about to change unexpectedly when I was completing my secondary education in the Catholic seminary."

"One day my brother came home and told me that we are justified by faith and not by works. Later on I found out that he had met some Evangelical Irish tourists earlier that week and that they had convinced him about their religion. I defended the Catholic teaching with much zeal. I remember arguing that faith must be accompanied by good works, the solid evidence of true faith. (Little did I know at the time that that was not what the Catholic Church teaches, but that good works actually increase and preserve the person's righteousness on the basis of which he would be justified at the end). For two years I studied the Catholic Bible because I wanted to bring my brother back to 'the true Church.' I also sought the assistance of my spiritual director and several priests. I wanted to show [my brother] that the Catholic teaching is biblical. Slowly however, I began to realize that many of the Catholic dogmas are not clearly taught in the Bible, or even worse, some seemed to contradict Scripture."[1] "There was no doubt about whether the scriptures were trustworthy or not because they are the Word of God. The problem is of course with me, my own fallibility, for I could easily misunderstand the scriptures. There was also the mammoth question to face: How could the Church be wrong? As I became more and more familiar with the scriptures, I simply could not reconcile what I was reading in the Book with what I had been taught. The Bible's message was not penance, human merit and the fire of purgatory, but Christ alone, his cross, his grace. Ultimately it was the Holy Spirit that gave me the courage to walk away from my religious comfort zone and embrace Christ as my Lord and Saviour."[2] "Of course I already 'believed' in Jesus. But I also believed in Mary, in the sacrifice of the Mass, in confession to a priest and penance, in purgatory, in myself and my good works by which I was expected to merit eternal life. By God's grace I realized that salvation is not what I do, or what the church does for me, or what Mary or the saints do. Salvation is of the Lord ALONE. I tossed away all these clutches, and I rested by faith on the Rock of my Salvation, the Lord Jesus Christ. Now I know what it means to believe on the Son. And I know that I have eternal life. Praise God!"

"Eventually I reluctantly left the Roman Catholic Church because I could not remain a member of an institution that teaches a different way of salvation than what is taught in the Scriptures. In a very real sense my heart remains with Roman Catholics because I am a debtor to them. My desire is to share the Gospel of the Scriptures – let us keep what is holy and true in the Catholic religion, but let us not be afraid to clean the house of the erroneous traditions that have accumulated through the years."[3]

1 Joseph Mizzi, "Why I Left the Catholic Church",
http://www.justforcatholics.org/a30.htm.
2 Joseph Mizzi, personal correspondence.
3 Joseph Mizzi, "Why I Left the Catholic Church",
http://www.justforcatholics.org/a30.htm.

All Christian traditions claim to base their faith and practice on the Scriptures. Whether liturgical or evangelical, all affirm that the Bible is the basis of authority, but to what degree, or whether in combination with other sources – this is where divisions are found. To what extent is any ecclesiastical authority a norm for the faith and practice of Christians today? Does the combination of a teaching authority alongside Scripture, as hierarchical traditions affirm, solve the problem of how the Scriptures are read? Is an oral tradition to be regarded equally with the written records of the New Testament? These questions are presented to anyone pondering a move from the evangelical understanding to the sacramental traditions. Without question, the earliest gospel witness was oral, and the preaching of the apostles rested on their authority as having been with Jesus and seen and heard the message from the Lord himself. Yet, as decades passed, there was a definite transition from the purely oral to the written. By looking at the history of Israel, we can see a similar pattern recorded there.

As Jews, the apostles were doing nothing that was not embedded in the history of Israel. The nation of Israel as a distinct people, chosen by God, preceded their documents. The call of Abraham was not predicated on written texts, but upon the voice of God speaking with Abraham, and subsequently Isaac and Jacob experiencing similar interactions with Yahweh. The law was given long after the founding of the nation, yet when the law did come in, the people were guided by it, and subject to it. Its provenance as chronologically later than the nation itself did not diminish its authority over the people. Nor is it proper to speak of Israel as the source of the law. Moses recorded the words of God as spoken to him, but they were no more Moses' words than a mailman is the author of a letter he delivers. From the time of the Exodus out of Egypt, a written record begins to be formed, and to acquire an authority that is considered that of God himself.

From Orality to Text in the Old Covenant

Orality was certainly important in Israel, but there came a time in the nation's history when written testimony assumed preeminence. "At the heart of biblical theology is the idea of a divinely revealed covenant at Sinai, physically represented by the Ten Commandments engraved on two tablets of stone."[4] The Decalogue was placed in the Ark of the Covenant as a sacrosanct record, an inscribed testimony of God's will for the nation. Later, the Pentateuch constitutes a written authority for the people of God who are in a covenant relationship with him. This covenant "and its fuller exposition in the Tora scroll (see Deut. 31:24-26) became central to Israel's faith."[5]

In speaking of the transition from Moses to Joshua, Brevard Childs describes the scene in Deuteronomy where "Moses enters into a series of crucial actions. He ends his sermon, fixes it in written form (31.9), commissions Joshua as his successor, and deposits the Law to be read at set periods in order that succeeding generations may hear and do the Law (31.12). This written law is to serve as a witness against any future generations who rebel. Indeed according to 31.22ff. Moses actually reckons with certain disobedience of the generation which follows. The central theological emphasis is that Moses, the mediator of the covenant, transfers his unique role to a written record."[6] Whether the nation was faithful to that law is another question. For much of their history they were not, but at those times when they did return to God, it was a return to this written law that marked their

---

[4] Aaron Demsky, "Writing in Ancient Israel," in *Mikra, Text, Translation, Reading and Interpretation of the Hebrew Bible in Ancient Judaism & Early Christianity*, ed. Martin J. Mulder and Harry Sysling (Peabody, MA: Hendrickson, 2004), p. 18.

[5] Ibid, p 19.

[6] Brevard S. Childs, *Old Testament Theology in a Canonical Context* (Philadelphia, Fortress Press, 1985), p. 110-111.

repentance. "In the time of Josiah a lawbook was found in the Temple. The lawbook was believed to have divine authority and to express God's will for the nation."[7] For the Jewish nation, then, this written law became the highest authority and standard for their practice and faith.

In the post-exilic return, Ezra was the leader God used to bring the people back to himself, but he did so through the instrumentality of the written law. "So Ezra the priest brought the Law before the assembly, both men and women and all who could understand what they heard, on the first day of the seventh month. And he read from it facing the square before the Water Gate from early morning until midday, in the presence of the men and the women and those who could understand. And the ears of all the people were attentive to the Book of the Law" (Neh. 8:2-3). Roger Beckwith affirms the importance of this transition in authority, and asserts that, while orality was important, writing was recognized to be more durable and reliable:[8] "The narrative of the Law-book found by Hilkiah (2 Ki. 22-23; 2 Ch. 34) is only intelligible if the unreliability of oral transmission was recognized."[9]

All of this demonstrates that the Jews had a high regard for the written word, and for the law as a final authority. The people viewed the law as the expression of God's will for the nation, as invested with the power of God himself. The five books of Moses form the bedrock upon which all else in Judaism is built. Secondly, the period of composition for these books covers a much greater period of time than the New Testament writings. The Jewish Scriptures were many centuries in the making, whereas the New Testament Scriptures were all penned within a period of fifty

---

[7] H.H. Rowley, *The Faith of Israel* (London, SCM Press, Ltd., 1956), p. 35.
[8] Roger Beckwith, *The Old Testament Canon of the New Testament Church* (Grand Rapids, Eerdmans, 1985), p. 66.
[9] Idem.

to sixty years.[10] Though the writing of the Old Testament occurred over many centuries, still this period came to an end.[11] The prophetic witness of later generations is a ministry of calling the nation back to the covenant they made with God, a covenant that is delineated in the Torah.

When the earliest Christians begin to preach that Jesus is the Messiah, their appeal was to these Jewish Scriptures. As ethnic Jews, they did not conceive of the gospel as a departure from their Jewish identity and faith, but as the fulfillment of the hope of Messiah. Jesus himself engages in this activity of pointing back to the Scriptures when he meets the disciples on the Emmaus road: "And beginning with Moses and all the Prophets, he interpreted to them in all the Scriptures the things concerning himself" (Luke 24:27). Early in the book of Acts, Peter quotes from Joel and the Psalms, arguing that what all in Jerusalem were witnessing was the fulfillment of Scripture. The statement punctuates Stephen's discourse in Acts 7, "as it is written in the book of the prophets" (Acts 7:42). At the Jerusalem council, James quotes the prophet Amos, and says, "[Moses] is read every Sabbath in the synagogues" (Acts 15:21). Paul begins his letter to the Romans with the explanation that the gospel of God was "promised beforehand through his prophets in the Holy Scriptures" (Rom 1:2).

The apostles came to the task of proclaiming Jesus with the conviction that God had revealed himself in the Scriptures, writings that were authoritative. Their proof of Jesus as the promised Messiah was contained in these very Scriptures. Father Denis Farkasfalvy summarizes the apostolic method: "Hence Paul does not speak only of *some* scriptural anticipation of Jesus' life-mission. He does what in preaching and in catechesis the

---

[10] Some scholars do not accept the Petrine authorship of 2 Peter, placing it later, after the apostle's death. Even if this were true, it would not greatly extend the time period over which the NT writings were composed.
[11] Sid Z. Leiman, *The Canonization of Hebrew Scripture, the Talmudic and Mishradic Evidence* (Hamden, Archon Books, 1976), p. 130.

apostolic Church generally did: he presupposes the faith which the people of Israel have put in their sacred writings and regards these writings as the authentic word of God."[12]

In such a milieu, it was natural that a written record of the newly-born church would be forthcoming. Farkasfalvy again notes, "One could even say that born with books in one hand, Christianity soon had to produce new books with the other."[13] Arthur Patzia cites at least four reasons why the gospel tradition moved from oral to written, including the expansion of the church, the passing away of eyewitnesses from the scene, a response to new challenges (i.e., confrontations with heresy), and the need for standard instruction.[14] While these were reasons for the early church to begin writing down what they knew of Jesus, it is also true that, as Jews, they had an expectation of a new covenant, and covenants came with documents. Andreas Köstenberger and Michael Kruger trace the features of covenants in the ancient Near East, and show how God's covenant with Israel followed this outline, culminating in the "deposit of written text of the covenant."[15] Far from expecting only an oral agreement between God and his people, the first Christians knew the covenantal soil from which they grew. "There would have been clear expectations that this new covenant, like the old covenant, would be accompanied by the appropriate written texts to testify to the terms of the new arrangement that God was establishing with His people."[16]

---

12 Denis Farkasfalvy, O. Cist, *Inspiration and Interpretation. A Theological Introduction to Sacred Scripture* (Washington, The Catholic University of America Press, 2010), p. 15.

13 Farkasfalvy, p. 10.

14 Arthur G. Patzia, *The Making of the New Testament* (Downers Grove, Inter-Varsity Press, 1995), p. 47-48.

15 Andreas Köstenberger and Michael Kruger, *The Heresy of Orthodoxy: How Contemporary Culture's Fascination with Diversity Has Reshaped Our Understanding of Early Christianity* (Wheaton, Crossway, 2010), p. 111.

16 Ibid, p. 112.

Is Scripture Ultimately Authoritative?

Sacramentalists often put forth the view that *sola scriptura* is not taught in the Bible itself. Many writers have stated this, but Phillip Blosser's position in *Not By Scripture Alone: A Catholic Critique of the Protestant Doctrine of Sola Scriptura* is emblematic of the hierarchical church view, and thus will serve as the position I will examine. "Why is it unbiblical? It [*Sola Scriptura*] is unbiblical because the Bible (a) nowhere teaches or assumes it; rather, the Bible assumes (b) a larger context of delegated ecclesiastical authority and normative tradition; (c) the continued normativity of extrabiblical traditions of divine instruction; and (d) the liturgical context of the worshipping community."[17]

Blosser's first point is somewhat of a straw man. Herbert Lockyer has pointed out that, "it never occurred to any prophet or apostle to prove the existence of God, as all writers presupposed God's existence with their writings being the product of His influence. Everywhere in the Bible, the existence of God is assumed as a fact."[18] Because we can point to no statements in Scripture that set out to prove God's existence, we would not thereby assume that the Bible does not teach this. It is an *a priori* assumption. We need not have a particular verse to point to in order to state, in effect, "these Scriptures will be the final authority in all matters of faith and practice" to affirm the preeminence and authority of the Bible. Rather, how the Scriptures are used, and the apostolic treatment of them, is indicative of their inherent authority. We likewise have no statement in Scripture that says, "The correct interpretation of the Bible shall be that which is

---

[17] Philip Blosser, "What are the Philosophical and Practical Problems of *Sola Scriptura*?", in *Not By Scripture Alone: A Catholic Critique of the Protestant Doctrine of* Sola Scriptura (Santa Barbara, Queenship Publishing, 1997), p. 43.

[18] Herbert Lockyer, *All The Doctrines of the Bible* (Grand Rapids, Zondervan, 1964), p. 11.

located in the hierarchical church", yet this is the argument that sacramentalists make. If no such statement is found in Scripture regarding this view of interpretation, why is it necessary to find such a statement about the authority of Scripture?

There are other ways the Bible demonstrates its authority aside from an explicit statement that the sacramentalist says is missing. In the apostolic use of Scripture, we see this superiority and authority demonstrated again and again. Even though the apostles were invested with authority from Jesus himself, in their preaching of the gospel we see them repeatedly make their appeal to the scriptures. Peter's first sermon in Acts 2 was a reference to what Joel had prophesied. In the following chapter, he tells the Jews that they are the sons of the prophets and of the covenant that God made with their fathers. That covenant was recorded in the Torah. When Peter is preaching to Gentiles in Acts 10, he likewise tells them concerning Jesus: "To him all the prophets bear witness." The prophetic witness was recorded in the Jewish Scriptures. Paul makes his appeal to the Pisidian Jews in Acts 13 by noting that the authorities carried out [against Jesus] all that was *written of him* (Act 13:29). At Thessalonica, Paul reasoned with them *from the Scriptures* (Acts 17:2). And at Berea, the new believers are found to be checking the apostle himself, *examining the Scriptures* daily (Acts 17:11).

This pattern continues with those who are apostolic associates or delegates. The Alexandrian Jew Apollos is described as a man competent in the Scriptures (Acts 18:24). His preaching method was to show *"by the Scriptures* that the Christ was Jesus" (Acts 18:28). In his defense before King Agrippa, Paul notes that his testimony is *"saying nothing but what the prophets and Moses said would come to pass."* (Acts 26:22). This is notable, for Paul affirms that his message is contained in and can be demonstrated by the Jewish Scriptures. All of these are just the examples that Blosser claims are missing. Paul's appeal is to the Scripture as final authority. The record in Acts is important because it is a demonstration of not only *what* the apostles taught, but *how* they taught.

When we turn to the epistles, the message is much the same. Paul begins his letter to the Romans by stating that the gospel was promised by God *"in the holy Scriptures"* (Rom. 1:2). When demonstrating that Abraham himself was justified by faith, Paul begins with the question, *"For what does the scripture say?"* (Rom. 4:3). His appeal is ever and always to the written testimony of God. Indeed, over ten times in the Roman epistle, Paul bolsters his argument with the phrase "It is written" (8:36, 9:13, 9:33, 11:8, 11:26, 12:19, 14:11, 15:3, 15:9, 15:21). The apostolic posture toward the Scriptures was to regard them as having paramount authority. Even though Paul had himself seen the risen Lord, it is to the Scriptures that his appeal is repeatedly made. The entire tenor of apostolic teaching is that it rested upon Scripture, because Scripture bore witness to the messianic promises. To suggest that the New Testament does not teach a final appeal to the Scriptures is to misrepresent the apostolic methods. Neil R. Lightfoot summarizes, "It was inevitable that these written instructions would become normative, for Christians could not have less respect for them, than for their Christ."[19]

Moreover, Blosser defines *sola scriptura* in a way that the Reformers did not, and which evangelicals of today need not. Both Martin Luther and John Calvin regarded the councils of the early church as explaining the biblical faith, not adding to it. They also both had a high regard for the church fathers and their readings of Scripture. Indeed, some evangelicals may insist that *sola scriptura* means that they are not informed by history and take no cues from what the early church taught or how they explained Scripture. But this is a fairly recent development, and stems less from an insistence on *sola scriptura* and more on a simple ignorance of history. It is a sad fact that, for many evangelicals and Protestants, their knowledge of church history goes back only as far as the

19 Neil R. Lightfoot, *How We Got The Bible*, 3rd Ed. (New York, MJF Books, 2003), p 156-157.

Reformation. The corrective to this is not to substitute an untenable authority for one that is God-ordained, but rather to study history.

Blosser's second point is that the Bible assumes a larger context of ecclesiastical authority and normative tradition. "Scripture is always found, rather, within a community in which God has conferred authority upon lawfully ordained human leaders."[20] He summons the example of Moses to show that it was only after his appointment by God to lead the people that his ministry actually began. He also notes that at the time of Ezra, only those priests who could prove their family lineage were accepted as valid priests. One assumes that Blosser is making a case for apostolic succession by this claim, as he goes on to say that "nowhere in Scripture is any member of the laity – or those who lacked lawful authority of Jesus, the apostles, prophets, or priests – ever praised for rebelling against the lawfully ordained authority on the basis of his private reading of Scripture."[21]

It is clear that Blosser takes his cues from the Old Testament for the priestly order and sacerdotalism that prevails in Roman Catholic dogma. I earlier noted that, owing to their Jewish heritage, the first Christians had an expectation of a covenant; it is likewise true that the content and terms of the new covenant are vastly different from the old. Dietary laws, Sabbath observance, and Temple worship were all succeeded by distinctively Christian worship. Because the old covenant has been set aside by the new, so has its priesthood. The ministers of the new covenant are in no way the equivalent of the Levitical priests. Blosser is guilty of an anachronistic reading of the New Testament to locate there what is only imposed later through sacramentalist tradition. The onus is on sacramentalists to prove that there is any such thing as "the laity." As I demonstrated in Chapter 2, the idea of a "clergy" is not found in the New Testament. In his introductory remarks to the Romans,

---

20 Blosser, p. 44.
21 Blosser, p. 45.

Paul uses the term *kleros* (clergy) as an adjective for all believers. Literally translated, "You are the *called* of Jesus Christ." (Rom. 1:6). The scenario of a member of the laity rebelling against authority by means of a "private interpretation" of Scripture is an argument from silence. Where does one find the New Testament recording rebellion of *any* kind based on *any* reading of Scripture?

The ecclesiastical authority that Blosser refers to is, for Catholics, summarized in the Catechism. "The Church, to whom transmission and interpretation of Revelation is entrusted, 'does not derive her certainty about all revealed truths from the holy Scriptures alone. Both Scripture and Tradition must be accepted and honored with equal sentiments of devotion and reverence.'"[22] When tradition proposes what is contrary to Scripture, then of course a determination must be made. Though sacramental tradition posits this as an impossibility, it is simply naïve and dishonest to suggest that throughout history tradition and Scripture have always been in perfect accord.

Oscar Cullmann observes that if this equality between tradition and Scripture exists, then the relationship of the church to Scripture is not clarified, but rather made more difficult: "If the fixing of the canon had been carried out by the Church on the tacit assumption that its teaching-office, that is, the *subsequent* traditions, should be set alongside this canon with an *equal normative authority*, the reason for the creation of the canon would be unintelligible. If after as well as before its creation the teaching-office of the Church continued to be a *supreme* norm of equal value, the Church could on its own authority alone always judge afresh as a last resort on the conformity of the teaching of its scholars with the apostolic tradition. In this case the fixing of a canon would have been superfluous."[23] As Cullmann points out, there is no need for a canon at all if the ultimate arbiter of truth is the Church and its magisterium. It can always tell the faithful what

---

[22] *Catechism of the Catholic Church*, p. 31.

[23] Oscar Cullmann, *The Early Church* (London, SCM Press, Ltd., 1956), p. 92.

is true and what to believe, regardless of any writings. For the evangelical, the reality that tradition is at times unbiblical is one reason for Scripture's ultimate authority. John R. Franke summarizes, "the significance of sola scriptura as establishing the principle that canonical Scripture is the *norma normans non normata* (the norm with no norm over it)."[24] The sacramental Church would not agree with this, and for all the attempts at explaining the place of tradition in Catholic or Orthodox doctrine as functioning alongside Scripture, in practice it works out that Scripture is of lesser authority than tradition. The only argument put forth as to why this dual authority of tradition as on a par with Scripture should be believed is because the Church says so.

The third of Blosser's claims is for a continued normativity of extrabiblical traditions of divine instruction. This is perhaps the weakest point of the argument against the sufficiency of Scripture. Blosser says that "the position of sola scriptura is self-defeating because it rests on a presupposition that cannot be proved from Scripture (let alone from history) – namely that *whole content* of God's revealed will for the ongoing instruction of His church was committed 'wholly to writing', so that *no unwritten residue* of divinely inspired instruction survived from the oral teachings of Jesus and His apostles that remained binding on God's people after the New Testament (NT) was written."[25] In similar fashion to Blosser, Scott Hahn claims that Jesus "never mentions a thing about writing to his apostles anywhere in the gospels"[26] – ironically arguing against writing from the written record itself.

---

[24] John R. Franke, "Scripture, Tradition, and Authority, Reconstructing the Evangelical Conception of Sola Scriptura," in *Evangelicals & Scripture: Tradition, Authority, and Hermeneutics,* Vincent E. Bacote, Laura C. Miguélez, Dennis L. Okholm (Eds.), (Downers Grove, IVP Academic, 2004), p. 192-193.

[25] Blosser, p. 45-46.

[26] Scott and Kimberly Hahn, *Rome Sweet Home: Our Journey to Catholicism* (San Francisco, Ignatius Press, 1993), p. 74.

The topic of tradition is exceedingly broad and will be more fully explored in Chapter 5, but a few remarks are in order here. Paul tells the Ephesians upon his departure that he has declared to them the *"whole counsel of God"* (Acts 20:27). Tertullian likewise ridiculed the idea that the apostles held something back in their doctrine. The argument of an unwritten, divinely inspired body of doctrine for ecclesiastical authority is not new with contemporary apologists. In fact it was encountered, and roundly condemned, by the early church. This is the argument put forth by the Gnostics, that they possessed a secret, unwritten tradition that was authoritative. Basil of Caesarea contended that there was a secret, unwritten tradition that supported such things as making the sign of the cross, or turning to the East in prayer. "These we derive from unwritten tradition."[27] R.P.C. Hanson notes that, "Basil's doctrine of secret tradition is a startling innovation. He is not content to say that the Scriptures must be interpreted by the mind of the Church and in accordance with the Church's traditional way of interpreting them, as all Christian writers had claimed since Irenaeus."[28] To claim an unwritten or extrabiblical tradition is to make the same argument the gnostic heretics made.

Jesuit scholar Joseph Mitros has written of the implications of such an extrabiblical tradition as Blosser suggests:

"A Catholic scholar, however, is faced with a special difficulty. Within the last hundred years several dogmas have been proclaimed in the Catholic Church. Now, according to the customary interpretation, a dogma is a doctrine solemnly proclaimed as divinely revealed by a pope or a general council. Thus the definition of the Assumption of Mary has created particular difficulties (to take only

---

[27] Schaff and Henry Wace, eds., Basil of Caesarea, *De Spiritu Sanctu*, in *Nicene and Post-Nicene Fathers*, vol. 8 (Peabody, MA, Hendrickson, 1995), p. 42.
[28] R.P.C. Hanson, "Basil's Doctrine of Tradition in Relation to the Holy Spirit", in *Vigiliae Christianae*, Vol. 22, No. 4 (Dec., 1968), p 251.

one example), since neither scientific exegesis nor a history of the first centuries of the Church has been able to discover even traces of this doctrine. To get out of the impasse, some theologians such as Benoit and R. Brown have defended the so-called fuller sense of Scripture, which would explain the appearance of the new dogmas. Some theologians-historians, e.g., Congar, have tried to introduce a new concept of tradition, some kind of Christian midrash, i.e., a constantly developing understanding of Scripture in the Church and by the Church. The objections leveled against these two attempts are serious, and no one seems to have proposed a sufficient solution. The fuller sense seems to reintroduce into exegesis the highly subjective and arbitrary method of the school of Alexandria, which has wrought such havoc in Christian biblical scholarship. The expansion of the concept of tradition seems to admit the emergence of a new revelation – another ominous phenomenon which may lead to the divinization of the papacy as it did towards the end of the Middle Ages."[29]

Mitros rightly sees where such an approach would lead. If doctrines that have no trace in Scripture are accepted and promulgated, how is the church to avoid the case of a continually developing revelation? This has in fact created a situation where the faith of the contemporary church affirms a body of doctrine that the early church knew nothing about, and would not recognize. If the church of today shares only a subset of doctrine with the apostolic and sub-apostolic church, where is the historical continuity that McKnight says converts long for? To cite one example, for the past few decades there has been a segment of Roman Catholics who have argued for the declaration of Mary as "co-redemptrix" along with Jesus. In 2008, five cardinals sent a petition to Pope Benedict XVI asking him to proclaim Mary as "the Spiritual Mother of All Humanity, the co-redemptrix with Jesus the redeemer, mediatrix of all graces with Jesus the one mediator, and

---

[29] Joseph Mitros, S.J, "The Norm of Faith in the Patristic Age", in *Theological Studies*, 29.3, (1968), p. 469.

advocate with Jesus Christ on behalf of the human race."[30] That such a doctrine is found in neither Scripture nor history presents no difficulty for the church. The hierarchy has shown great creativity in finding whispers and shadows of what they later declared dogma. But as Father Mitros points out, because there are no real boundaries as to what can be doctrinally defined, claims of apostolic origins are impossible to defend. No pope has yet proclaimed the dogma of Mary as co-redemptrix, but there is nothing in the Roman Catholic understanding of the basis of truth that would prevent him from doing so.

It is significant that Father Mitros ascribes a good bit of responsibility for these doctrinal difficulties to the Alexandrian school of interpretation. I will look at this in more detail in Chapter 6, but the notable aspect is that Mitros terms this hermeneutical method to be "highly subjective and arbitrary." Built on such a foundation of allegory as the Alexandrian school represents, it calls into question the basic tenets of the sacramental system.

Rather than an unwritten residue of teaching, we see a clearly emerging pattern of the early church preferring written testimony to oral. "The second century saw a growing awareness of the value of Christian writings, and largely with Justin and Irenaeus the center of authority moved away from oral traditions to a fixed normative text, even though the prompting for such a move in the orthodox community *may* have started earlier with Marcion."[31]

Within the New Testament itself, we see evidence of the inchoate authority of texts. In 1 Timothy 5:18, Paul joins two

---

[30] "Cardinals Hoping for a 5th Marian Dogma,"
http://www.ewtn.com/library/MARY/z5mardogm.htm.
[31] Lee Martin McDonald, *The Biblical Canon: Its Origin, Transmission, and Authority*, 3rd Ed. (Peabody, MA, Hendrickson, 2007), p. 248. (Emphasis his). The view that Marcion and his teachings forced the early church to define their Canonical Scriptures is one that is most famously expounded by Adolph Harnack, and later by Hans von Campenhausen. Not all scholars accept this position, and even if it is granted, it has no bearing on the question at hand – that of the authority granted to written documents.

phrases, prefacing the whole of it with "For the Scripture says: "You shall not muzzle an ox when it treads out the grain," and "The laborer deserves his wages." The passage about the ox is found in Deuteronomy 25, but the second phrase is found in Luke 10:7. The interesting fact is that they are both referred to as Scripture. It makes no sense to refer to scripture if Paul is simply echoing an oral tradition. Guthrie says that Paul "may be citing from a collection of the words of Jesus, and if so it is clear the such a collection was placed on an equality of authority with the Old Testament, at least as far as the authority of each was concerned."[32] That Paul is referring to an oral collection makes no sense, for "Paul here classes it as Scripture, which he could never have confused with a proverbial saying."[33] Moreover, the Greek of Luke 10:7 is verbatim that of 1 Timothy. Catholic exegete George Montague affirms this: "The text corresponds exactly, though, to Luke 10:7 (see also Matt. 10:10). This, then, would be the first witness in the New Testament quoting a word of Jesus as Scripture. If this letter is as late as some scholars think, it could well be that the writer has in front of him the very text of Luke."[34]

Another well-known passage is found in 2 Peter 3:15-16 where the apostle refers to the writings of Paul as Scripture. "Just as our beloved brother Paul also wrote to you according to the wisdom given him, as he does in all his letters when he speaks in them of these matters. There are some things in them that are hard to understand, which the ignorant and unstable twist to their own destruction, as they do the other Scriptures." Very early, then, we have testimony that the letters of Paul are regarded as authoritative, and are put in the same category as "the Scriptures." "By scripture, Peter refers to those writings that are seen as

---

[32] Donald Guthrie, *The Pastoral Epistles, an Introduction and Commentary* (Grand Rapids, Eerdmans, 1957), p. 105.

[33] Ibid, p. 106.

[34] George T. Montague, S.M., *First and Second Timothy, Titus* (Grand Rapids, Baker Academic, 2008), p. 114.

authoritative for the community. In this context, Peter is referring to Paul's letters in an authoritative manner and affirming that they should be read as such."[35] "The phrase in verse 16 'in all his letters' implies the existence of a nascent Pauline collection, known to the author and the audience. It is likely that the author is referring not to a formal, organized corpus, but to a small collection that was beginning to achieve authoritative status."[36] Whether we refer to these writings that became part of the New Testament as "canonical" at this point in history is entirely unimportant. They are authoritative, and the pattern is being set that written documents would be the final court of appeal in matters of doctrine.

Blosser goes on to ask, "But what is the Protestant partisan to do with instructions and practices that claim to be apostolic but were never put in writing in the NT?"[37] He cites no examples, but this is just the objection evangelicals have with teachings that find no basis in Scripture. It is difficult to see what Blosser hopes to demonstrate with this. Any number of doctrines and practices may claim apostolic origin, but in fact possess no such thing. The primary way to judge if an instruction is apostolic is whether it is evidenced in the New Testament. The scenario Blosser presents is to beg the question, and presents no problem for the evangelical. What can be shown as scriptural is defensible. What cannot be thus shown is a candidate for removal from practice and faith.

The fourth argument Blosser makes is that the context of the liturgical community argues against the authority of Scripture as absolute: "The Word of God was heard when it was proclaimed in the authoritatively-summoned assembly of God's people. The Bible is by design a text intended to be publicly read and heard.

35 Ruth Anne Reese, *2 Peter and Jude* (Grand Rapids, Eerdmans, 2007), p. 174.
36 Steven J. Kraftchick, *Jude, 2 Peter* (Nashville, Abingdon Press, 2002), p.172.
37 Blosser, p. 47-48.

We lose something when all we do is read it on our own. This privatized and bookish view is anachronistic and contrary to both the primary intended use of the Biblical texts to the historical milieu of Scripture itself."[38] It is a false dichotomy to suggest that the Scriptures are read in either a communal setting or privately. It is in fact both. This is akin to telling a musician not to practice his part alone, but only when the whole orchestra gathers for rehearsal. Evangelicalism has a far stronger heritage of public reading and preaching of the Bible than sacramentalism, so this is a curious line of reasoning for Blosser to follow. The evangelical argument for the authority of Scripture is in no way a call to remove the Bible from the public worship or preaching of the church. On the contrary, let us bring Scripture to bear on how we worship and our form of worship. One wonders at the apparent suggestion that there should be *less* reading of the Scriptures by Christians outside of corporate worship.

In its struggle with Protestantism during the Counter-Reformation, the Catholic Church was to adopt what today would be shocking attitudes toward the Scriptures: "Pope Paul V was perfectly serious when in 1606 he furiously confronted the Venetian ambassador with the rhetorical question, 'Do you not know that so much reading of Scripture ruins the Catholic religion?' One of the tasks of the 1564 Tridentine Index had been to keep vernacular Bibles away from the faithful; anyone wanting to read the Bible in a modern language required permission from the local bishop, and in the 1596 Roman Index the ban became complete and without exception. In Italy, the Index's ban was enforced. Bibles were publicly and ceremonially burned."[39]

---

38 Blosser, p 49.

39 Diarmaid MacCulloch, *The Reformation: A History* (New York, Penguin Books, 2003), p. 406.

The Definition of the Canon

The other aspect of the paradigm shift to sacramentalism concerning Scripture is to say that the only way we know today what the Scriptures *are* is because the hierarchical church has defined the canon. Peter Kreeft says, "The Church produced the Bible. The Church (apostles and saints) wrote the New Testament, and the Church (subsequent bishops) defined its canon."[40] Kreeft makes the leap one so frequently finds in sacramentalist thinking, that "the Church" means a hierarchical structure of bishops rather than the whole people of God. To be sure, men inspired by God wrote the books of the Bible that we now have. Yet these men were not acting as "The Church" in their writing. The Holy Spirit moved the men God chose as his vessels for the writing of Scripture, but it is not accurate to say they were writing in the context of the hierarchical church, for there was no such thing.

The Church is important with regard to the canon, but chiefly in the reception of the books as Scripture. To acknowledge a role for the people of God in producing and accepting Scripture is far different than assigning the definitive place to the Church as the *source* of these writings. What Kreeft argues for has been called the extrinsic model of canon. This theory holds that we don't know what the Bible is unless there is some external authority to tell us which books belong in it. The extrinsic model rests on several faulty assumptions. The first of these is that a closed list of authoritative books is required before we can speak of scriptural authority. Scholars are divided on when we can speak of a final, "closed canon." Some put this in the fourth century with Athanasius' 39th Festal Letter. Written in 367, it contains a list of the same 27 books of the New Testament we have today.[41] Others

---

[40] Peter Kreeft, *Catholic Christianity* (San Francisco, Ignatius Press, 2001), p. 20.
[41] The work of A.C. Sundberg has been influential in this debate. Sundberg argued that we cannot speak of canon until we have just such a closed,

point to such evidence as the Muratorian Fragment, by most accounts an earlier document, perhaps as early as the second century, for evidence that lists of books were in circulation from an early time. Despite evidence of the use of these writings as Scripture, exponents of the extrinsic view say that it is anachronistic to speak of the canon before such time as a definitive pronouncement, as Athanasius may provide. This assumption rests on the sharp distinction between Scripture and canon but as Michael J. Kruger has pointed out, "At best this is obscurant, and at worst misleading. Moreover, it feeds the notion that the canon was somehow the result of 'a great and meritorious act of the church.' And this is why this definition is a core tenet of the extrinsic model – it implies there was no (and could be no) canon until the church officially acted."[42] To assume that the writings we now know as the New Testament had no authority until there was an official pronouncement of them as 'canonical' is simply false and ahistorical. Authority must precede canonicity, or it makes no sense to canonize a book. Canonizing a book does not give it authority; rather, a book is canonized because it already has authority.

Some point to the councils of Hippo (393) or Carthage (397) as the conciliar evidence that the church acted in just such a manner as the extrinsic model requires. These two councils published among their canons lists of the books that were in use by the churches. Yet we should note that even those who favor a conciliar model of church leadership would admit that these were

---

authoritative list as the extrinsic definition requires. It must therefore be only at the end of this entire process that we can speak of a canonical, authoritative Bible. For counterarguments to Sundberg's thesis, see Michael J. Kruger, *Canon Revisited: Establishing the Origins and Authority of the New Testament Books* and John Barton, *Holy Writings, Sacred Text: The Canon in Early Christianity.*

[42] Michael J. Kruger, *The Question of Canon: Challenging the Status Quo in the New Testament Debate* (p. 33) (InterVarsity Press, Kindle Edition, 2013).

but provincial councils, rather than ecumenical. By the definition in church tradition, their authority is thus limited. But even were we to grant that these councils had universal authority for the church of their day, we would ask whether Christians only began to regard the writings of the New Testament as authoritative *after* these councils? Is there any evidence that pervasive confusion on the part of the church prevailed as to which books were in, which were out, and that this confusion was only eliminated when these councils were held? James O'Donnell writes, "Before translocal hierarchies of bishops and eventual popes and patriarchs ever evolved to have any doctrinal authority, Christians had come to agree, without noticing it, without debate, without anybody planning it, that scriptural texts, gathered in collections of apostolic authority, would prevail."[43]

Augustine, like Jerome, inherited the Canon of scripture as a 'given.'"[44] Writing in *On Christian Doctrine*, Augustine weighs the various churches in their reception of books: "If, however, he [the reader] finds some books held by the greater number of churches, and others by the churches of greater authority (although this is not a very likely thing to happen), I think that in such a case, the authority of the two sides is to be considered equal."[45] The salient feature, as Bruce notes, is this: "It is plain from this that when Augustine wrote, no ecclesiastical council had made a pronouncement on the canon which could be recognized as the voice of the church".[46] Augustine first wrote this work in 397, (adding a fourth book in 426) several years after the Council of Hippo in 393. If the canons of Hippo were deemed authoritative (where he himself served as bishop), it is noteworthy that

---

[43] James J. O'Donnell, *Augustine: A New Biography* (New York, Harper Collins, 2005), p. 277.

[44] F. F. Bruce, *The Canon of Scripture* (Downers Grove, Inter-Varsity Press, 1988), p. 230.

[45] Augustine, *On Christian Doctrine* 2.12.

[46] Bruce, p. 231.

Augustine does not cite this as his proof of what is canonical. Donald Guthrie agrees, "The canon may have been recognized by the bishops and theologians, but it was not initiated by them."[47]

If no church council or hierarchical pronouncement gave us the Canon, how then did the books come to be regarded as authoritative, and later as canonical? Most scholars cite several criteria that the church applied in its view of these writings. These are apostolicity, orthodoxy, use, and reception by the church as a whole. The role and office of apostle was unique, and as the apostles were those who had kept company with Jesus, or who had seen a vision of the risen Christ as Paul had, their writings had credibility and authority. Bruce states, "If a writing was the work of an apostle or of someone closely associated with an apostle, it must belong to the apostolic age. Writings of later date, whatever their merit, could not be included among the apostolic or canonical books."[48] Books of later provenance are, *ipso facto*, not candidates for inclusion in the authoritative list of books used by the church. Matthew and John were themselves apostles, but Mark and Luke were not. Yet they were associated with apostles: Mark with Peter, and Luke with Paul. A book such as Hebrews, written anonymously, was to prove contentious for a time, precisely because its authorship was disputed. Eventually it was accepted in both East and West, though interestingly, upon his visit to the city, Athanasius had to urge the Roman Church to accept it.

There is early testimony to the use and authority of the apostolic writings as Scripture. According to Westcott, "From the close of the second century, the history of the Canon is simple and its proof clear. It is allowed even by those who have reduced the genuine Apostolic works to the narrowest limits, that from the time of Irenaeus the New Testament was composed of essentially the same books which we receive at present, and that they were

---

[47] Donald Guthrie, *New Testament Theology* (Downers Grove, Inter-Varsity Press, 1981), p. 41.
[48] Bruce, p. 259.

regarded with the same reverence as is now shewn to them."[49] Westcott is saying two important things here. Firstly, that the time from which we could speak of a collection of authoritative books is quite early, and, secondly, that these writings enjoyed a position of authority that other writings did not. Other scholars locate this authority even earlier. Theodore Zahn believes that, because of the pattern of usage for the books we would later know as the New Testament, "there was already a Christian canon by the end of the first century."[50] Barton further says that, "astonishingly early, the great central core of the present New Testament was already being treated as the main authoritative source for Christians."[51]

We earlier saw how the apostles themselves appealed to the Hebrew Scriptures for proof of the Messianic identity of Jesus. The apostolic fathers continued this use of the Old Testament, but also accorded an authority to the New Testament documents at an early date. Polycarp's epistle to the Philippians, written circa 150, quotes from several of Paul's epistles, including 1 Corinthians, Ephesians, 1 and 2 Thessalonians, and 1 and 2 Timothy. He quotes extensively from 1 Peter. Among the gospel writers, he is familiar with Matthew and Luke, and quotes them. Polycarp considers these writings as having a special authority because they were apostolic in origin.[52] Robert M. Grant agrees, "It is clear enough that Polycarp regards the statements to which he refers as authoritative."[53]

The Epistle of Barnabas is another early witness to the emerging authority of the New Testament texts. Barnabas was thought to be

---

[49] Brooke Foss Westcott, *A General Survey of the History of the Canon of the New Testament*, 5th ed. (Cambridge, Macmillan and Co., 1881), p. 6.

[50] John Barton, *Holy Writings, Sacred Text: The Canon in Early Christianity* (Louisville, Wesminster John Knox Press, 1997), p. 3.

[51] Ibid, p. 18.

[52] Paul Hartog, *Polycarp and the New Testament* (Tübingen, Mohr Siebeck, 2002), p. 207.

[53] Robert M. Grant, *The Formation of the New Testament* (New York, Harper and Row, 1965), p. 105.

an Alexandrian Jew (not Paul's companion, however), who became a Christian. His hortatory epistle is full of Old Testament quotations, but also quotes Matthew 22:14, "Many are called, but few are chosen." Papias is another early witness to the esteem the apostolic writings were given. Metzger notes, "Papias stands as a kind of bridge between the oral and written stages in the transmission of the gospel tradition. Although he professes to have a preference for the oral tradition, one nevertheless sees at work that form of tradition in favor of written gospels."[54]

Ignatius is another early father whose familiarity with the apostolic writings demonstrates that he regarded them as authoritative. "Among the Pauline corpus his knowledge of 1 Corinthians is assured and he seems to be able to cite large portions of this text from memory. Among the other Pauline epistles a strong case can be made for Ignatius' use of Ephesians and 1 and 2 Timothy."[55] There is also strong evidence that he knew Matthew's Gospel.[56] The apologists likewise testify to the use and esteem of the New Testament writings. Justin Martyr, "in the *Apology* (I,28,I)...says that 'from our writings' (i.e., those of the Christians) readers can learn that Christians call the chief of the demons by the names 'serpent', 'Satan', and 'devil'. The same point is made with greater precision in the *Dialogue* (103,5). Moses (i.e., in Genesis) calls him 'serpent', Job and Zechariah call him 'devil', and Jesus calls him 'Satan'. Thus it becomes clear that Justin has in mind the synoptic gospels, where Jesus uses this name. Again in the *Apology*, (66,3; 67,3) Justin twice refers to the 'memoranda' or 'reminiscences' of the apostles, which he

---

54 Bruce M. Metzger, *The Canon of the New Testament, Its Origin, Development, and Significance* (Oxford, Clarendon Press, 1987), p. 55-56.
55 Paul Foster, "The Epistles of Ignatius of Antioch and the Writings that Later Formed the New Testament," in *The Reception of the New Testament in the Apostolic Fathers*, Andrew F. Gregory, Christopher M. Tuckett, eds. (Oxford, Oxford University Press, 2005), p. 185.
56 Foster, Loc. Cit.

identifies, in the latter passage, by the Christian name 'gospels.'"[57] Henning Graf Reventlow observes that in Irenaeus, "we find approximately twice as many citations from the New Testament as from the Old. The only texts he does not seem to know are 3 John, Philemon, and Jude. Although the thought of a New Testament canon is still not developed in him, it is nonetheless clear that he concedes first place in the witness of the Scripture to the 'writings of the apostles' and the 'words of the Lord.'"[58]

Orthodoxy was likewise a critical facet of any writing that the church would consider as useful to its collection. There were numerous writings that circulated in the early years of the church, many of them claiming apostolic authorship, such as the *Gospel of Peter, Apocalypse of Peter,* and the *Gospel of Thomas,* yet these were ultimately rejected by the church, largely due to the fact that they were doctrinally unsound. The so-called New Testament Apocrypha has never been a contention between sacramental traditions and evangelicalism. Both reject these writings as spurious, so they need not command much attention in this discussion. The only differences are in the Old Testament Apochrypha. Here we note that there was disagreement among the fathers as to the authority of these books. Augustine accepted them, but Jerome rejected them. Athanasius also assigned to the Old Testament Apochryphal books a secondary status, "reckoning them suitable only for devotional reading."[59]

The place of the Apochrypha in the early church is to a large extent traceable to the cultural and linguistic differences that arose between Jews and Hellenistic believers. In what we now call the

57 Grant, p. 133.

58 Henning Graf Reventlow, Leo G. Purdue, trans., *History of Biblical Interpretation, Vol. 1: From the Old Testament to Origen* (Atlanta, Society of Biblical Literature, 2009), p. 157.

59 Richard A. Norris, Jr., "Augustine and the Close of the Ancient Period," in Alan J. Hauser, Duane F. Watson, eds., *A History of Biblical Interpretation, Vol. 1* (Grand Rapids, Eerdmans, 2003), p. 397.

inter-testamental period, seventy or so scholars in Alexandria, Egypt translated the Jewish Scriptures from Hebrew to Greek. From the number 70, this translation is called the Septuagint. Among the Jewish canonical books, the books of the Apocrypha are interspersed. The esteemed New Testament scholar Bruce Metzger comments that, "from this fact, some have leaped to the conclusion that the Jews of Alexandria, who used Greek, regarded these books as being inspired in the same sense as the Law, the Prophets, and the Writings. For several reasons, such a conclusion appears to be unfounded."[60] Metzger goes on to note that the various manuscripts of the Septuagint differ in which apochryphal books they include or exclude, and that Philo, the greatest of the Jewish Hellenists of Alexandria, never once quotes from them. "It is extremely difficult, therefore, to believe that the Jews received these books as authoritative in the same sense as they received the Law and the Prophets."[61] Pelikan likewise says that "the most prominent feature of these [apochryphal] books historically, and one that binds them together, is their dubious canonicity and authority."[62]

In contrast to the extrinsic model that the sacramentalist argues for, the intrinsic model affirms that the biblical documents are authoritative because of their divine authorship and that because of this they are *self-attesting and self-authenticating*. This is not a position that is unique to evangelicalism. Orthodox Priest Alexander Schmemann states, "The Church did not 'sanction' the New Testament writings, it recognized them as the Word of God, the source of its existence from the start."[63] Karl Barth, who may

---

60 Bruce M Metzger, *An Introduction to the Apochrypha* (New York, Oxford Univ. Press, 1957), p. 176.

61 Metzger, p. 177.

62 Jaroslav Pelikan, ed., *Sacred Writings, vol. 2, Christianity, the Apochrypha and the New Testament* (New York, Book of the Month Club, 1992), p. xii.

63 Alexander Schmemann, *The Historical Road of Eastern Orthodoxy* (Crestwood, St. Vladimir's Seminary Press, 1977), p. 43.

fairly be described as someone outside the mainstream of evangelical thought, writes, "The Bible itself constitutes the canon. It is the Canon because it imposed itself upon the church."[64] Metzger states similarly, "In the most basic sense neither individuals not councils created the canon; instead they came to perceive and acknowledge the self-authenticating quality of these writings, which imposed themselves as canonical upon the church."[65] Lee McDonald agrees to the early and unique place the Gospels had in the church: "Because the canonical gospels tell the story of Jesus, the most significant authority figure in the early church, they had an implied authority attached to them from their initial circulation. If they were believed to be true, which they were, they could not help but become authoritative in the early churches."[66]

Roman Catholic doctrine claims to affirm the inspiration of Scripture and that the Bible is authored by God, yet in practice it severely undermines both of these positions. "[Catholics] don't reject *sola Scriptura* because they reject the inspiration of the Bible but because there has to be a firmer foundation for the inspiration of the Bible than just the Bible itself."[67] This is an astounding statement! If God himself is the author of Scripture, if he has inspired the writers who penned these books, how could there *possibly* be a firmer foundation for their authority? The Catholic position does not solve any problem, but simply shifts the locus of authority. Kruger summarizes the difficulty well:

---

[64] Karl Barth, *Church Dogmatics*, trans. G. W. Bromiley and T. F. Torrance, 2nd ed (Edinburgh, T&T Clark, 1975), I/1:107.

[65] Bruce M. Metzger, *The New Testament, Its Background, Growth, and Content*, 2nd ed. (Nashville, Abingdon, 1983), p. 276.

[66] Lee Martin McDonald, *Forgotten Scriptures: The Selection and Rejection of Early Religious Writings* (Louisville, Westminster John Knox Press, 2009), p. 155.

[67] Dwight Longenecker, *More Christianity* (Huntington, IN, Our Sunday Visitor, Inc., 2002), p. 51.

The only option left to the Catholic model is to declare that the church's authority is self-authenticating and needs no external authority to validate it. Or, more bluntly put, we ought to believe in the infallibility of the Roman Catholic Church because it says so. The Catholic Church, then, finds itself in the awkward place of having chided the Reformers for having a self-authenticating authority (sola scriptura), when all the while it has engaged in that very same activity by setting itself up as a self-authenticating authority (sola ecclesia). On the Catholic model, the Scripture's own claims should not be received on their own authority, but apparently the church's own claims should be received on their own authority. The Roman Catholic Church, functionally speaking, is committed to sola ecclesia.[68]

Summary

Oral communication quite logically precedes a fixed, written record of God's Word. But in the history of Israel, the transition to a written and authoritative testament superseded the oral. As Jews, thoroughly familiar with the covenantal milieu of the nation, the apostles and the earliest disciples would have expected that documents likewise would accompany the new covenant that Jesus proclaimed. In the apostolic preaching we find the repeated and consistent use of Scripture as the proof of the gospel message. The church fathers displayed an early acceptance of the apostolic documents as possessing the highest authority. It is unnecessary, indeed naïve, to expect the Scriptures to contain a definitive statement as to their own authority. What conveys the inherent authority of the Scriptures most powerfully is how the apostles used them; a pattern that was taken up by the apologists and fathers.

---

[68] Michael J. Kruger, *Canon Revisited: Establishing the Origins and Authority of the New Testament Books* (Wheaton, Crossway Publishers), Kindle Locations 914-921.

The development of the Canon shows that, instead of being the product of conciliar decisions, or a pronouncement of some church hierarchy, the writings that were later collected as the New Testament were recognized quite early as having a unique and self-attesting authority. Authority and Canon are not to be confused. We can speak of the former as being in place long before the latter. Indeed, the Canon is a formal recognition of the authority these writings already possessed. To insist that the church had no Bible until a hierarchy or council acted is simply false. The extrinsic model of Canon undermines the authority of the Bible by making it wholly dependent on the Church. This is precisely what we see worked out in Sacramentalism. At the Council of Trent, the issue of Scripture and tradition was certainly part of the agenda, in answer to the Reformers. Jacopo Nacchianti, the bishop of Chioggio, pronounced at the council that, "To put Scripture and traditions on the same level is impious."[69] Sadly, his view did not carry the day. For when the Tridentine profession of faith was drawn up, before any mention of Scripture is made, we find the statement, "I most firmly accept and embrace the apostolic and ecclesiastical traditions and all the observances of the same [Roman] church. I likewise accept Holy Scripture according to the sense that Holy Mother Church has held and does hold, to whom it belongs to judge the true meaning and interpretation of the Sacred Scriptures."[70] The sacramentalist view of the Scriptures makes them secondary to and dependent upon tradition and to the Church. Evangelicals should recognize that in adopting the sacramentalist paradigm, they are accepting a view of revelation and Scripture that is quite different than what the earliest church understood, and are in fact rejecting the intrinsic authority of God speaking through his Scriptures.

---

[69] John W. O'Malley, *Trent: What Happened at the Council* (Cambridge, The Belknap Press Of Harvard University, 2013), p. 95.
[70] Citied in O'Malley, p. 283.

5
"That you might know": Certainty

Those considering a move away from the evangelical faith into the sacramental traditions must face the question of doctrinal development. Indeed, all believers must address this, but for the evangelical, it is made less troublesome in part because of the sources being circumscribed. The collection of documents is fixed, and it is the biblical record that comprises the authority for the evangelical faith. This is not to say that no difficulties arise, or that there are not disagreements, but delineating the acceptable evidence provides a defense against the excesses and theological Rube Goldberg machines that sacramentalism has often produced. As G.L. Prestige says, "The Gospels afford a collection of material for theological construction; the creed puts forward inferences and conclusions based on that material. The one represents the evidence, the other the verdict. And be that verdict ever so correct, the fact remains that it was the evidence, and not the formal verdict which was once deposited to the saints."[1] In a very real sense, the differences between sacramentalism and evangelicalism spring from the fact that sacramentalism has repeatedly moved the verdict into the evidence column. This is the essence of ecclesiastical tradition becoming normative for the faith.

A creed becomes not a summary or précis of biblical teaching, but assumes an authority all of its own. It moves into the role of a mediating body of truth. Those who then embrace the creed as authoritative for doctrine ask not what do the Scriptures say, but does this accord with the creed? Every tradition likes to think its creed is biblical, but it is not on the same level as Scripture, neither inspired nor inerrant.

Historian Jarsolav Pelikan captures the position of the early church on the question of doctrinal development. "Although the

---

[1] G.L. Prestige, *Fathers and Heretics* (London, SPCK, 1968), p. 3.

speaking of God in the doctrines of the prophets could be said to have taken place 'in many and various ways,' now that He had spoken 'in these last days,' any further change or novelty was precluded by the finality of the revelation given in Christ."[2] There could be explanation and elucidation, but not newly discovered doctrines. Even among those who identify as evangelical but argue for more engagement with tradition and the patristic era, the plea is much the same. Robert Webber, often considered the father of the "Ancient-Future" view of the church says, "The church throughout history is called to be a witness to this truth. It is not to change it, to alter it, to add to it, or take away from it. It is to guard, preserve, transmit, expound, and teach it. That is, in all of its interpretation, it is to remain faithful to it by doing its thinking in such a way that it always points to it as the truth revealed, received, and kept. The church's understanding of this truth may grow and deepen as it is called within a particular geographical place, cultural situation, or historical time to proclaim, explain, and defend it intelligently and perceptively, but the church is to proclaim no new doctrine or deny that which has been given."[3] Doubtless this is an ideal, but in practice theologians have not always found it so easy to explain the difference.

The Vincentian Canon

As the decades and centuries marched on, the glaring fact of doctrinal change could not be ignored. Vincent of Lerins (died circa 445) was one of the earlier theologians to propose a solution to this question. The "Vincentian Canon" was a series of rules he formulated to determine what is, or is not, true doctrine and thus to be held, or rejected. It is often summarized by "Quod semper,

---

[2] Jaroslav Pelikan, *Historical Theology: Continuity and Change in Christian Doctrine* (New York, Corpus, 1971), p. 4.

[3] Robert Webber, *Common Roots: A Call to Evangelical Maturity* (Grand Rapids, Zondervan, 1978), p. 154.

quod ubique, quod ab omnibus" – what has been believed always, everywhere, and by all. The rule is threefold:

> We shall observe this rule if we follow universality, antiquity, consent. We shall follow universality if we confess that one Faith to be true which the whole church throughout the whole world confesses; antiquity if we in no wise depart from those interpretations which it is plain that our holy ancestors and fathers proclaimed; consent if in antiquity itself we eagerly follow the definitions of all, or certainly nearly all, priests and doctors alike.[4]

By the multiple caveats that Vincent attached to his canon, we can see that he recognized the difficulties of a simplistic encapsulation such as this. How are we to deal with customs that are decidedly not universal? The Orthodox Church, for example, to this day holds that the bread used for the Eucharist must be made of leavened bread, while the West uses unleavened (azymes). Most people would consider this a secondary issue, yet it forces us to enter into a parsing of what is truly essential and what is not, something Vincent's rule does not address. The popular aphorism states, "In essentials unity, in non-essentials diversity, in all things charity." One person's non-essential is quite often another's essential, (as the case of the *filioque*[5] clause in the Nicene creed illustrates), so this does nothing to solve the difficulty. The Orthodox forbid married bishops, and celibacy extends to all Catholic clergy. A non-essential? This has been held

---

[4] J. Stevenson, ed., *Creeds, Councils, And Controversies: Documents Illustrating the History of the Church, AD 337-461* (London, SPCK, 1966), p. 322-323.

[5] *Filioque* is Latin for "and the son," a phrase which the Western Church added to the Nicene Creed, to stipulate that the Holy Spirit proceeded from the Father and the Son. The Eastern Church rejected this addition as a corruption and a heresy. This was one of the issues that ultimately led to the Great Schism between the two in 1054.

with a very tight fist for something that is secondary.

Antiquity creates even thornier issues than universality. It is one thing for Vincent, writing in 434, to invoke the ancient traditions of the past, for his past was decidedly shorter than ours. It would be 600 years after him before the rosary would come along. Pope Clement VI did not define the doctrine of the "treasury of merit," wherein the merits of Mary and the saints are applied to other Christians for the decrease of temporal punishment, until 1343. There are, according to Catholic theologian John Thiel, "other beliefs, however, that the Church at some moment affirms as the apostolic deposit but that historical study shows cannot be traced in an unbroken line from the apostolic age to the later moment of affirmation. The Catholic belief in the Immaculate Conception of Mary is a good example."[6] If Vincent's criteria are applied to these particular doctrines, they fail the test. When defined in 1854, the Immaculate Conception was declared a dogma, which it is necessary to believe. In the Catholic definition, therefore, it is decidedly not secondary.

Eschatology is another example where the view of antiquity has been set aside. Men such as Papias, Irenaeus, Ignatius, Tatian, Melito, Justin Martyr, and Tertullian, among others, believed that there would be a literal earthly reign of Christ that would last a thousand years.[7] (Augustine himself was a chiliast earlier in his life.) Though both Catholicism and Orthodoxy currently teach an amillennial view of eschatology, denying any future earthly kingdom, it is true that the earliest fathers held to a literal millennial reign of Christ.[8] (Orthodoxy, however, for the most part

---

[6] John E. Thiel, *Senses of Tradition: Continuity and Development in Catholic Faith* (Oxford, Oxford University Press, 2000), p. 93.

[7] George N.H. Peters, *The Theocratic Kingdom, Vol. 1* (Grand Rapids, Kregel Publications, 1988), p. 451.

[8] Cf. also Brian E. Daley, S.J., *The Hope of the Early Church: A Handbook of Patristic Eschatology* (Cambridge, Cambridge Univ. Press) for other examples of early belief in an earthly, millennial reign of Christ.

ignores the subject of eschatology.) Here, too, the current view of the hierarchical church would fail the Vincentian test. It is curious to find convert David Currie argue against a premillennial position on the ground that it is not a Catholic understanding of eschatology: "One can enter virtually any Evangelical denomination as a premillennialist. But one cannot become a Catholic and remain premillennialist. Premillennialist conclusions directly contradict the teaching Magisterium of the Church."[9] Currie does not hesitate to set aside the fact that the early church's understanding of the kingdom was in fact premillennial, and that many of the first bishops were premillennial in their eschatology.

When we turn to consent, a favorite catchphrase is the "unanimous consent of the Fathers." Yet here too we meet not with unanimity, but with diversity. W.H.C. Frend comments on the ecclesiastical polity that is found among certain early fathers: "No amount of ingenuity can fully reconcile the differing accounts of the ministry to be found in *1 Clement*, the *Letters* of Ignatius and the *Didache* respectively. Ignatius writes as though the norm of Church government was the bishop, priest, and deacon, with absolute power in the hands of the bishop. The *Didache* treats the bishop on a lower level than the prophet and teacher, while *1 Clement*, though asserting the preeminence of bishops gives no clue whether there was to be one bishop or a college of presbyter-bishops in each See."[10]

Another example is the rigorist strain of Christianity practiced in North Africa by men such as Cyprian and Tertullian. Cyprian "held that baptism given outside the sphere of the Spirit-filled community was no baptism."[11] He came into sharp disagreement

---

[9] David Currie, *Born Fundamentalist, Born Again Catholic* (San Francisco, Ignatius Press, 1996), p. 139.

[10] W.H.C. Frend, *The Early Church* (Minneapolis, Fortress Press, 1982), p. 38.

[11] Henry Chadwick, *The Penguin History of the Church, Vol. I: The Early Church*, Rev. Edition (London, Penguin Books, 1993), p. 119.

over the issue with Stephen, the Roman bishop. These varying accounts of church government and discipline would also fail the Vincentian test "to have been held, written, and taught, not by one or two only, but by all equally and with one consent, openly, frequently, and persistently."[12] One can argue that Rome eventually prevailed in the conflict over baptism, but that is just the point: there was conflict rather than unanimity. One of the ironies of the Vincentian Canon is that its immediate purpose "seems to have been to attack the predestinarianism of Augustine and his supporters for being an innovation and a deviation from the tradition of orthodoxy."[13] Pelikan elsewhere terms the Vincentian Canon a "tacit polemic against Augustinianism. St. Augustine, too, was a man of great piety, learning, and genius, an ornament of the Church; but even an ornament such as he could fall into error."[14]

The medieval theologian Peter Abelard played the gadfly when he offered his *Sic Et Non*, or *Yes and No*, which was a florilegium of patristic excerpts, illustrating both sides of a question, and which "suggested that the inconsistencies and downright contradictions in the patristic tradition, together with methods of dealing with these, were to be its theme."[15] Abelard reminds us that bare tradition in and of itself is no sure guide to what we can believe, and that the fathers must be read critically and carefully. "There is little doubt that in its contents fundamental issues are encountered. It is clear that a perception of contradictions has led to these being put on record, probably because at the time

[12] J. Stevenson, p. 323.
[13] Jaroslav Pelikan, *The Christian Tradition: A History of the Development of Doctrine, Vol. 1: The Emergence of the Catholic Tradition (100-600)* (Chicago, University of Chicago Press, 1971), p. 333.
[14] Jaroslav Pelikan, *Historical Theology: Continuity and Change in Christian Doctrine* (New York, Corpus, 1971), p. 7.
[15] Jaroslav Pelikan, *The Christian Tradition: A History of the Development of Doctrine, Vol. 3: The Growth of Medieval Theology (600-1300),* (Chicago, University of Chicago Press, 1978), p. 223.

reconciliation of the opposing views could not be constructed."[16] Patristic consensus is thus a product of later history, useful to reinforce what one already believes, but ultimately ineffectual to settle difficult hermeneutical questions.

There is no doubt that Vincent sought to provide clear guidance for how we might know what is true; however, he "showed the flaw in his all-too-clear definition when he said that universality could deceive if the whole Church fell into heresy. His ultimate canon was universal consensus; his argument was in fact tautological. Interpretations of Scripture vary, he said; consequently tradition must act as a check on the exegesis both of scripture and of patristic texts."[17] An appeal to tradition does not lessen the difficulty if there are just as many traditions as there are interpretations. Evangelical and patristic scholar D.H. Williams, though an advocate of greater engagement with history, says that it is untrue that the early church was uniform, historically or theologically. "Both Athanasius and Arius vehemently declared that their respective views represented the Christian tradition. It may be that Arius was ultimately wrong, but it was nevertheless true that both of them were drawing on selected portions of a body of tradition that existed and yet was not formulated to answer the new questions of their time that were being raised."[18] Quite apart from any dispute Catholicism or Orthodoxy may have with evangelicalism, this is just the situation between Orthodoxy and Catholicism, each claiming a purer, more apostolic form of tradition than the other. This schism between these two branches of sacramentalism appears no closer to being healed.

---

16 J. Ramsay McCallum, *Abelard's Christian Theology* (Merrick, NY, Richwood Publishing Co, 1976), p. 100.

17 Karl F. Morrison, *Tradition and Authority in the Western Church 300-1140* (Princeton, Princeton University Press, 1969), p. 5.

18 D.H. Williams, "Similis Et Dissimilis: Gauging Our Expectations of the Early Fathers," in *Ancient Faith for the Church's Future*, Mark Husbands and Jeffrey P. Greenman, eds. (Downers Grove, IVP Academic, 2007), p. 78.

On What Does Certainty Rest?

In the quest for certainty that converts from evangelicalism seek, it is important to recognize that the solutions offered by sacramentalism are fundamentally different from the evangelical solutions. Indeed, even the questions being asked are different. It is far less "How can I know what the Bible means?", and much more of "How can I know for certain what I am to believe?" Of former Catholics that were converted, "Most report that they never read the Bible themselves while in the RCC. Instead they relied on the priest to interpret the Bible or on the Missal to filter it. [One convert,] Matthew claims, 'I was taught that the Bible was something for the priest to read and tell us what it meant.'"[19] But in the priests' training for the priesthood, the Bible formed no important part of the curriculum. "Adam writes of his time in seminary, and one has to wonder if this remains the norm today: 'Among the studies for the priesthood, we had three textbooks on the Bible, but not the Bible.'"[20]

Ted Pallock, a convert from Orthodoxy, found certainty not from what the Church told him, but when he heard the gospel of grace. Though he was part of the Church from infancy, Ted says that he didn't hear the gospel there. "In junior high school, I had a friend who took me to Mississippi Valley Youth for Christ, and that's where I heard the gospel."[21] He relates that what he heard there was a very different message than what he had been hearing at the Orthodox Church. "I remember the priest speaking from the pulpit saying he didn't know if he was good enough to go to heaven, and I thought to myself, 'What hope do I have?' Years later, I read an 'evangelical tool' used by the Orthodox Church. It relied heavily on the book of James and works and that this is why

---

[19] Scot McKnight and Hauna Ondrey, *Finding Faith, Losing Faith: Stories of Conversion and Apostasy* (Waco, Baylor Univ. Press, 2008), p. 138.
[20] McKnight and Ondrey, p. 139.
[21] Ted Pallock, (Oct 5, 2014) Personal interview.

the Evangelical faith was wrong because it's your works that commend you, and yet it was at the expense of the rest of scripture, and the hope of the gospel."[22]

"The Orthodox were striving to be holy in a way; there was a striving and yet a hopelessness in the Orthodox faith. The message that I heard [in the gospel], is that God knew who I was and in spite of that, while I was yet a sinner, Christ died for me. It was not my righteousness at all, but it was Christ's righteousness – *immeasurable* gift. A stark contrast between no hope to overwhelming hope."[23]

Ted began immediately attending the church where the friend from Youth for Christ attended. "My sister and my mother, and eventually my other sister and my aunt were all converted. They were disenchanted with the hopelessness of the Orthodox Church, and were amazed at the gospel also, and so that was a very sweet thing."

"I never thought of going back to the Orthodox Church. Staying would not at all have been in agreement with the gospel. In their eyes, when I left the Orthodox Church, I was outside of the kingdom of God. There wasn't a hope of changing the Orthodox Church – the 'pure, the original Church', basically has remained the same, and that was their claim to fame. They weren't going to grow in their understanding, they already had the scriptures and the book of tradition – the early Church Fathers, and so they were going to stand fast on that. The Scriptures were important, but I was taught that the writings of the early church fathers were just as important."[24]

Wrestling with the text of Scripture, and discussing its meaning – these are among the most important activities for believers within evangelicalism. Inevitably, there are challenges in arriving at a coherent meaning for some parts of the Bible. As an ancient

---

22 Ted Pallock
23 Ted Pallock
24 Ted Pallock

text, originating in the Levant, it is in some ways worlds away from contemporary society. However, the Bible as God's Word *must* speak to us today if there is to be any basis for faith whatsoever. Frustrated by the multiple interpretations from a plethora of voices, converts to sacramentalism adopt not so much a different interpretation, as a capitulation on the entire question. The church as final authority in what the text of Scripture means is not a hermeneutical principle so much as a hermeneutical surrender. At no time in history have there been more tools available for the believer to read, study, and explore the Bible than there are today. The passage of time, however, has at once made it both easier and more difficult. It is easier in the sense that one does not have to know Hebrew and Greek to read the Scriptures, but more difficult in that 20 centuries of thought and commentary on the Bible mean the voices are not a few, but a vast chorus. In the year 200, one could not go to the local Christian bookstore and select from scores of commentaries on the Gospel of John, as one can today.

Whether it is the Catholic magisterium, or the Orthodox proposal of patristic consensus, what these two approaches share in common is that they very often excise the believer from personal engagement with the Bible itself. As I noted in Chapter 2, a separate class, to whom pronouncements of certainty have been entrusted, is simply not found in the New Testament. The difficulties notwithstanding, engaging with the text of Scripture itself is the way to find not only certainty, but to grow into Christlikeness. Handing off the task of interpreting the Scriptures to a separate entity may provide a kind of contrived certitude, but it is abandoning real interaction with Scripture – and the blessing of that activity. The sacramental posture toward Scripture, that believers cannot know its meaning or discern its sense, is again a denial of the self-authenticating nature of Scripture as God's word, of its ability to speak to us in an unmediated fashion. Because it cannot be known or discerned apart from the authority of the church, certainty for the believer is not attainable from the Bible itself.

Convert Christian Smith offers a critique of what he refers to as Biblicism, the reading of Scripture that he believes to be uniquely evangelical, but which has reduced the Bible to little more than a handbook for living.[25] If a biblicist reading of Scripture reduces the Bible to a self-help guide, a personal improvement manual, what then is the solution? Smith proposes a Christological reading of the text, but he acknowledges this is not a unique or a new approach, nor is it missing from the writings of various evangelical scholars.[26] Smith's criticisms are less valid for evangelicalism as a whole than for a populist slice of evangelical subculture. Smith knows better than anyone how varied evangelicalism is, and to equate Pentecostalism with Anabaptists, for example, is to speak of two vastly different communities – yet both would be termed evangelical. This also strengthens the impression that what Smith is criticizing is a particular segment of evangelical populism. If seminary professors and other theologians of the evangelical movement likewise affirm that the central message of the entire Bible is Jesus Christ, and that it must be read accordingly, the corrective to the narrow biblicism Smith criticizes is less a

---

[25] Christian Smith, *The Bible Made Impossible: Why Biblicism Is Not a Truly Evangelical Reading of Scripture* (Grand Rapids, Brazos Press, 2011), p. 4-5. Smith's parameters of Biblicism are necessarily somewhat elastic. To bolster the view that extra-scriptural support is sometimes needed for doctrinal positions, he notes that the term "Trinity" is nowhere found in Scripture, yet it is utterly central to orthodox Christian belief (p. 83). None would argue with him as to the centrality of the doctrine, because the three persons of the Godhead are clearly taught in Scripture. If the word trinity is not found there, it is but convenient shorthand for speaking of the doctrine. Do we then have a genuine need for extra-scriptural theological concepts, as Smith affirms? This is not a case in point, precisely because the trinity *is* a scriptural concept. Smith well knows his own adopted tradition has run afoul of sound teaching by just such concepts that are truly extra-scriptural. Excesses in Marian devotion are one example that the church hierarchy itself has had to step in to correct. (cf. p. 193 below).
[26] Smith, p. 103-105.

question of jettisoning a view of the Scriptures as our ultimate authority, and more one of paying careful attention to the sound exposition of them.

It is less convincing to argue, as Smith does, that the true word of God is Jesus himself, rather than the Bible.[27] To be sure, he anticipates the argument that the only way anyone actually knows about Jesus is through the Bible. But for Smith and his fellow sacramentalists, the Bible is but one avenue for communion with God. The Eucharist, prayer, fellowship with others – these are also ways in which Jesus makes himself known to the Christian. Yet these aspects of fellowship should not be confused with *revelation* about Jesus. For this, the Scriptures *are* our primary source. It therefore serves to undermine the gospel if we depreciate the scriptures to suggest that "Faith does not rest simply on texts, but – also and more – on persons and events."[28] The persons and events on which we base our faith are made known to us in Scripture. Smith acknowledges this, yet seeks to draw a distinction between the person and the text, warning that a view of Scripture that is overly exalted will lead us to make an idol of a book.

At the start of Luke's Gospel, which it would seem he has written primarily to Theophilus, the evangelist says, "It seemed good to me also, having followed all things closely for some time past, to write an orderly account for you, most excellent Theophilus, that you may have certainty concerning the things you have been taught (Luke 1:3-4)." To divide the Word between Jesus and the written record is therefore to disregard one purpose of the Scripture. The reason Luke has written is so that Theophilus might have certainty. The written text is an aid to and a basis for this certainty. No matter what interpreters have done with the Bible,

---

[27] Smith, p. 119-120.
[28] James Barr, "Bibelkritik als Theologische Aufklärung", in *Glaube und Toleranz: Das Theologische Erbe der Aufklärung*, ed. T. Rendtorff (Gütersloh, Gütersloher Verlagshaus, G. Mohn, 1982), p. 41, quoted in Christian Smith, p. 118.

the statements within the Scriptures indicate they are the foundation of our confidence. John similarly affirms, "But these are written so that you may believe that Jesus is the Christ, the Son of God, and that by believing you may have life in his name." (John 20:31). Faith is predicated on the written word as the foundation of our certainty. In both instances, Luke and John expressly state that faith does indeed rest on texts, especially when the authors of these texts have passed from the scene.

The danger of "bibliolatry" is not one that the apostles apparently feared. Paul tells Timothy to give attention to public reading of Scripture, and to "continue in what you have learned and have firmly believed, knowing from whom you learned it and how from childhood you have been acquainted with the sacred writings, which are able to make you wise for salvation through faith in Christ Jesus. All Scripture is breathed out by God and profitable for teaching, for reproof, for correction, and for training in righteousness, that the man of God may be competent, equipped for every good work" (2 Tim. 3:14-17). The passage points out that because of his Jewish mother, Timothy had been taught the Hebrew Scriptures, and that Paul ascribes to these writings a particular power and authority which he does not ascribe to the church. They bear witness to Jesus and point to his substitutionary atonement. But further, Scripture has another purpose, one that blunts some of Christian Smith's criticism of the evangelical use of Scripture. While the Bible bears primary witness to Jesus and his salvific death, we can say that it also provides guidance in holiness and daily living – reproof, correction, and training in righteousness. It need not be one or the other, but is indeed both. The problems of biblicism that Smith seeks to correct are due less to the misuse of Scripture than to the disuse of it.

The Rule of Faith

It is sometimes argued that the rule of faith, or *regula fidei,* functioned as an authority in the early life of the church, serving as an extra-biblical canon for Christians. If this is the case, the argument states, we have precedent for an extra-scriptural, yet authoritative measure of teaching. We need to bear two things in mind when considering the *regula fidei:* Its content, and how and with whom it was used. Rather than being an exhaustive doctrinal statement, it was instead a synopsis of the fundamental features of orthodox belief. Tertullian's version is as follows:

Now, with regard to this rule of faith – that we may from this point acknowledge what it is which we defend – it is, you must know, that which prescribes the belief that there is one only God, and that He is none other than the Creator of the world, who produced all things out of nothing through His own Word, first of all sent forth; that this Word is called His Son, and, under the name of God, was seen "in diverse manners" by the patriarchs, heard at all times in the prophets, at last brought down by the Spirit and Power of the Father into the Virgin Mary, was made flesh in her womb, and, being born of her, went forth as Jesus Christ; thenceforth He preached the new law and the new promise of the kingdom of heaven, worked miracles; having been crucified, He rose again the third day;(then) having ascended into the heavens, He sat at the right hand of the Father; sent instead of Himself the Power of the Holy Ghost to lead such as believe; will come with glory to take the saints to the enjoyment of everlasting life and of the heavenly promises, and to condemn the wicked to everlasting fire, after the resurrection of both these classes shall have happened, together with the restoration of their flesh. This rule, as it will be proved, was taught by Christ, and raises amongst ourselves no other questions than those which heresies introduce, and which make men heretics.[29]

Tertullian presents the basic elements of the gospel, the facts about the life, suffering, death, and resurrection of Jesus. But his rule includes nothing related to church order, sacraments, church government or anything but the most cursory references to eschatology. The rule of faith would serve to mark off the boundaries of orthodox Christology and contain elements of soteriology, but nothing beyond this. The Gnostics, Docetics, Valentinians, and Marcionites would all take objection to this rule because of what it said about the person of Christ. Irenaeus' rule differs somewhat from Tertullian's, but still serves as a basic outline of faith, rather than a detailed exposition of life and practices in the church:

The Church, though dispersed through our the whole world, even to the ends of the earth, has received from the apostles and their disciples this faith:

[She believes] in one God, the Father Almighty, Maker of heaven, and earth, and the sea, and all things that are in them; and in one Christ Jesus, the Son of God, who became incarnate for our salvation; and in the Holy Spirit, who proclaimed through the prophets the dispensations of God, and the advents, and the birth from a virgin, and the passion, and the resurrection from the dead, and the ascension into heaven in the flesh of the beloved Christ Jesus, our Lord, and His [future] manifestation from heaven in the glory of the Father "to gather all things in one," and to raise up anew all flesh of the whole human race, in order that to Christ Jesus, our Lord, and God, and Saviour, and King, according to the will of the invisible Father, "every knee should bow, of things in heaven, and things in earth, and things

---

[29] Tertullian, *Prescription Against Heretics*, 13, http://www.ccel.org/ccel/schaff/anf03.pdf.

under the earth, and that every tongue should confess" to Him, and that He should execute just judgment towards all; that He may send "spiritual wickednesses," and the angels who transgressed and became apostates, together with the ungodly, and unrighteous, and wicked, and profane among men, into everlasting fire; but may, in the exercise of His grace, confer immortality on the righteous, and holy, and those who have kept His commandments, and have persevered in His love, some from the beginning [of their Christian course], and others from [the date of] their repentance, and may surround them with everlasting glory.[30]

Again in Irenaeus' rule, nothing concerning church order, sacraments, or other matters of ecclesiastical life are found. There is perhaps a bit more here about eschatology than we find in Tertullian, but still nothing in the way of a complete doctrinal exposition such as we would find in the homilies or commentaries on Scripture that came from the Fathers. And as Allert notes, "the Rule of Faith was not a fixed universal formula or creed."[31] The rule was used to silence heretics, not to argue doctrinal or disciplinary points with other Christians. Those who insisted that Jesus was a mere creature, or that he had only seemed to suffer and die, or that there was no connection whatever between the God revealed in the Old Testament and the revelation of himself in the New – this was the audience for the *regula fidei*. Inside the church, however, the rule was not applied, for it would have been superfluous to do so. *All* agreed as to the deity of Christ, his substitutionary death and resurrection. These were the parameters of orthodoxy, and so when disputes arose within the church, the appeal was made to Scripture. T.D. Barnes points out that when speaking to Christians, Tertullian's authority was always the Scriptures. In the *Scorpiace*, or *Scorpian's Sting*, Barnes notes, "His

---

[30] Irenaeus, *Against Heresies*, 1.10.
[31] Craig Allert, *A High View of Scripture?* (Grand Rapids, Baker Academic, 2008), p. 122.

audience was the orthodox Christian community at Carthage, his purpose to strengthen their resolve. As the best form of argument therefore, he selected biblical exegesis."[32] Tertullian argues for "the resurrection of the flesh according to the Old and New Testaments. Again, however, a preliminary task intrudes: Tertullian must repel attempts to interpret the Bible allegorically. Finally, the exposition of the scriptures proceeds: it is Tertullian's favorite mode of argument."[33]

In this preference for Scripture over tradition, it is evident that Tertullian is joined by Irenaeus. Kelly says that, "a careful analysis of his *Adversus Haereses* reveals that while the Gnostics' appeal to their supposed secret tradition forced him to stress the superiority of the Church's public tradition, his real defence of orthodoxy was founded on Scripture. [The] 'canon', so far from being something distinct from Scripture, was simply a condensation of the message contained in it."[34] So dependent was Irenaeus' rule on Scripture that "this rule is not a supplement to the biblical truth derived from the apostles and prophets, nor a tradition of independent material, but a key to interpret the Scriptures which is compatible with the Scriptures as whole."[35]

Bearing in mind this purpose, then, the rule of faith cannot be cast as an extra-biblical tradition, for the Fathers believed it to be nothing other than a summary of what the Scriptures taught. Hanson agrees that "the idea of the rule of faith as supplementing or complementing, or indeed adding anything whatever to the Bible, is wholly absent from their thoughts; indeed, such an idea would be in complete contradiction to their conception of the

---

[32] Timothy David Barnes, *Tertullian: A Historical and Literary Study* (Oxford, Clarendon Press, 1971), p. 172.

[33] Barnes, p. 127.

[34] J.N.D. Kelly, *Early Christian Doctrines*, rev. ed. (San Francisco, HarperSanFrancisco, 1978), p. 38-39.

[35] Stuart G. Hall, *Doctrine and Practice in the Early Church* (Grand Rapids, Eerdmans, 1991) p. 62.

relation of rule to Bible."[36] Nor can it be seen as a tool to bring recalcitrant believers back in line. To deny the deity of Christ or his resurrection was to put oneself outside the faith, outside the body of Christ. These things are what the rule addressed.

Finally, if we are seeking a hermeneutical principle, this also is not part of it. The rule is too brief to expound in any meaningful way how the Scriptures are to be interpreted, thus in any dialogue about the proper way to interpret the Bible, the *regula fidei* does not provide any significant guidance. Bryan Litfin writes that "there is hardly any soteriology or bibliology in the Rule, its eschatology is very basic, and its ecclesiology is meager (though we should note that its very existence presupposes a robust view of the church)."[37] It would be inaccurate therefore to suggest that the rule provides exegetical guidance since it barely touches on these important doctrines. Hanson agrees that the rule "is not even a principle nor a universally received regulation for interpreting Scripture."[38]

Tradition: A Reliable Guide?

Adherents to sacramentalism have noted that tradition should not raise an objection for anyone, because it is found in Scripture itself. Paul tells the Thessalonians to "stand firm and hold to the traditions that you were taught by us, either by our spoken word or by our letter. " (2 Thess. 2:15). The word for tradition is *paradosis*, or handing on. The idea of passing truth from hand to hand finds no objection with evangelicals. This is further strengthened by Paul's counsel to Timothy, "What you have heard from me in the

---

36 R.P.C. Hanson, *Tradition in the Early Church* (Philadelphia, The Westminster Press, 1962), p. 126.
37 Bryan Litfin, "Learning from Patristic Use of the Rule of Faith," in *The Contemporary Church and the Early Church: Case Studies in Ressourcement*, Paul A. Hartog, ed. (Eugene, OR, Pickwick Publications, 2010), p. 79.
38 Hanson, p. 124.

presence of many witnesses entrust to faithful men who will be able to teach others also." (2 Tim. 2:2). Sacramentalism has often focused on this "handing on" as a practice, something that was done very early in the life of the church, and thus the act itself is prescriptive. But this is to miss the point. The importance is not in the *act* of passing on from one generation to another, but in the *content* of what is passed on. The content of tradition becomes problematic when it is no longer the faith that was "once for all delivered to the saints" as Jude urges us to contend for, but includes an ever-increasing catalogue of practices and dogmas. Everett Ferguson affirms this change in understanding.

In the fourth century, therefore, the usage of tradition was narrowed to what is transmitted in the church, and the distinction between written scripture and unwritten tradition became a standard formulation, but tradition was still primarily applied to church practices. Tradition came to prominence in a polemical context, first in response to Gnostic claims, and then in internal church conflicts. Like other successful arguments, the argument from tradition became a part of the doctrines it was designed to defend. But on many controverted issues it was a two-edged sword, with both sides claiming tradition in their favor.[39]

The irony is that tradition, presumed to represent a body of doctrine unchanged and unaltered, has itself become the object of repeated additions and amendments.

Applied to interpretation, does tradition itself provide the guidance any reader of Scripture needs? Father George Tavard expresses a lack of confidence in tradition as any kind of authoritative guide to exegesis. "Today's concern is more for a

---

[39] Everett Ferguson, "*Paradosis* and *Traditio*: A Word Study", in *Tradition and the Rule of Faith in the Early Church*, Ronnie J. Rombs and Alexander Y. Hwang, eds. (Washington, The Catholic University of America Press, 2010), p. 28.

historical knowledge, in depth, of the biblical message. The history of the church and of theology in postapostolic times cannot be the source of such a knowledge. As a result, the historical dimension of religious thought which we call tradition loses some of its former status."[40] Episcopalian Christopher A. Hall paints his own caricature of evangelical exegesis: "Why bother about church traditions? Why do we need any authorities or authority outside of the Bible? Can we not simply affirm *sola Scriptura* and be done with it? Many Christians, including a vast number of evangelicals, would affirm yes. We have our Bible and the inner illumination of the Holy Spirit, and we attend an excellent church where our pastor interprets the Bible thoroughly, faithfully, and insightfully. What need for more?"[41] As I've previously noted, this is not a fair picture of the evangelical treatment of Scripture. Evangelicals interpret every bit as much in the context of the church as anyone. The difference is they do not hold that a college of bishops has ultimate say, nor church councils.

McKnight and Ondrey address just such a misconception as Hall presents. "Even if one can deconstruct Protestantism this way, this radical democratization of interpretation is a principle only. It does not actually work out this way because most learn to read the Bible within an interpretive tradition that exercises considerable heft."[42] Hall surely knows that the Reformers made their appeal to the fathers. Their plea was that the church had strayed from the apostolic witness and the body of biblical truth, as understood by the fathers. Halls spends the next several pages of his essay arguing for an interpretive model that locates itself within tradition,

---

[40] George H. Tavard, "Tradition in Theology: A Problematic Approach" in Robert M. Grant, Robert E. McNally, George H. Tavard, *Perspectives on Scripture and Tradition: Essays* (Notre Dame, Fides Publishers, 1976), p. 85.
[41] Christopher A. Hall, "Tradition, Authority, Magesterium," in *Ancient Faith for the Church's Future*, Mark Husbands and Jeffrey P. Greenman, eds. (Downers Grove, IVP Academic, 2007), p. 28.
[42] McKnight and Ondrey, p. 219.

noting, among other things, that the fathers' use of the *regula fidei* was a safeguard against exegetical excess. (We saw in the last section that it is not accurate to cast the *regula fidei* as an exegetical rule, but as a tool against heretics.) Yet he admits that tradition is not entirely reliable. How may we distinguish between authentic developments and invalid mutations? "The crucial criterion for evaluating the authenticity of a development, it seems to me, is whether the development faithfully, wisely, and coherently expresses the truth found in Scripture."[43] In other words, when there is a determination to be made of what is true, Hall reverts to the same *sola scriptura* principle that he is so suspicious of. When he takes his own logic to its end, Hall must admit that despite his consternation over the diversity of interpretation he finds within evangelicalism, tradition does not provide anything in the way of a definitive guide. We must return to the biblical record itself.

Along with Hall, there has been a group of theologians and historians in the last several decades who identify as evangelicals and who have urged a more intentional engagement with history and the patristic heritage. D. H. Williams has written of his dismay over evangelicals' disregard and, in some cases disdain, for history, and how God has led the church. For Williams and others such as Thomas Oden, the solution is for evangelicals to recover the "Great Tradition," which they believe will provide the guidance that evangelicalism has cast off in reaction against the hierarchical church: "It is time for evangelicals to reach back and affirm a truly 'catholic' Tradition by returning to the ancient sources, to correct the former correction."[44] The former correction was of course the Reformation, and in Williams' estimation, evangelicalism has gone too far in its disregard for history and

---

[43] Hall, p. 41

[44] D.H. Williams, *Retrieving the Tradition and Renewing Evangelicalism: A Primer for Suspicious Protestants* (Grand Rapids, Wm. B. Eerdmans, 1999), p. 15.

tradition. Williams likewise highlights many of the problems I discussed in Chapter 1. "Theology is disappearing in the churches because the drive for truth, and the significance of ideas, has been replaced by an emphasis on technique."[45] Later, he laments the sectarianism he finds to be a persistent problem within evangelicalism. "Evangelicals and Free Church believers need to hear again the great Protestant historian Philip Schaff, who warned us 150 years ago of the 'poisonous plant of sectarianism which has grown so ponderously upon the ground of Protestantism.'"[46] But Williams' theories as to the causes of this doctrinal dereliction rest on assumptions that are incorrect. The first is that the divisions and sects of evangelicalism have arisen due to a lack of regard for tradition. For this to be valid, one would expect to see unanimity and cohesion in sacramentalism, but this is not the case, as I will later demonstrate in Chapter 9.

If those who take their place as part of the Great Tradition themselves manifest division and diversity of views, then the explanation that evangelical schism is due to a lack of regard for tradition is a non sequitur. Asked differently, would a return to tradition, as Williams suggests, provide a solution to the theological variety that he identifies within evangelicalism? Will this both heal the sectarian breaches and provide the theological cohesion that he claims is now lacking? Again, the fact that those who are close adherents to tradition have these same issues argues against this providing unity or theological integrity.

Within the sacramental Church, an alternative justification for didactic tradition is sometimes put forth as *Lex Orandi, Lex Credendi*, or, as the Church prays, it believes. Attributed to Prosper of Aquitaine in the fifth century, the formulation states that *how* the Church worships governs *what* the Church teaches. In other words, liturgy is the wellspring of doctrine. Popular devotion has sometimes run ahead of dogmatic instruction, and when biblical

---

[45] Williams, p. 24.
[46] Williams, p. 202.

support for practices could not be found, the apologists for a practice or tradition fell back on the justification that "the faithful have done so for long ages." Looking to practice as a guide for doctrinal positions opens all manner of ways to worship God, but does not ask whether these things are biblical. Much of contemporary Latin American Catholicism is permeated by syncretism with native religious practices, but just because some worshipers do these things, does this give them reliability as sources of doctrine? The dangers of this are plain. Practices and traditions are fluid and evanescent, but the biblical record is not. We embrace customs that are wholly without evidence in scripture if we look to practice as a guide and support. Hanson and Fuller aptly summarize the fallacy this encompasses: "It is not Scripture, it is not even tradition in the strict sense that is the test of belief, but 'the sense or sentiment of the faithful', 'the instinct', the 'present thought of the Church', 'the intention of the heart', 'the feeling' of the faithful. Within certain very broad limits and under given conditions, in matters doctrinal, whatever is, is right – because it is."[47]

Lex Orandi, Lex Credendi was also to play the decisive role in the iconoclastic controversies that eventually resulted in the victory of the iconodules at the seventh ecumenical council. The practice of the faithful was really the only evidence for icons, for as Mango says, "No matter what the theologians argued, it is clear that icons had acquired a very important place in popular piety."[48] Norwich likewise comments, "For some time the cult of icons had been growing steadily more uncontrolled, to the point where holy images were openly worshipped in their own right and

---

[47] Richard Hanson, Reginald Fuller, *The Church of Rome: A Dissuasive* (London, SCM Press, 1950), p. 69.
[48] Cyril Mango, *Byzantium, The Empire of New Rome* (New York, Charles Scribners & Sons, 1980), p. 98.

occasionally served as godparents at baptisms."[49] The problem
with the growth of the cult of icons in this fashion is that the
scriptural evidence was entirely lacking. As Pelikan notes, "When
they were not simply scoring debating points on behalf of the case
for icons, the orthodox were obliged to admit that, for a practice
that was supposed to be based on the tradition of the apostles and
the church fathers, this one had very little written testimony, either
in Scripture or in ancient Christian writers, to support it."[50] In the
consideration of *Lex Orandi, Lex Credendi*, evangelicals should not
delude themselves into thinking this is anything other than a re-
versal of authority. How we worship should be governed by what
we know of God, which is based on what the Scriptures contain.

The appeal to tradition as a safeguard to faith is not new, and
in the several points where I have examined tradition we have
seen that it is inaccurate to speak of tradition in the singular.
Rather, we have seen that "traditions" is a more precise
description of what church history shows us. East and West may
represent the largest gulf, and since 1054, the two expressions of
sacramental Christianity have been divided. But within the East,
there are Coptic and Jacobite churches under the rubric of
Orthodoxy, but they are not united with the other Orthodox
communions. When we turn to the West, there are likewise a
myriad of different practices and hybrids. Anglicans do not
consider any council past Chalcedon to be ecumenical, and thus
believe that the later ones are not binding in terms of providing
guidance for faith and practice. Anglo-Catholicism is yet another
variety.

Inevitably, advocates of tradition must always issue their own
caveats. Robert Webber warns of any additions to the body of

---

[49] John Julius Norwich, *A Short History of Byzantium* (New York, Vintage
Books, 1999), p. 111.

[50] Jaroslav Pelikan, *The Christian Tradition: A History of the Development of
Doctrine, Vol. 2: The Spirit of Eastern Christendom (600-1700)* (Chicago,
University of Chicago Press, 1974), p. 98-99.

Christian doctrine. Christopher Hall cautions us that interpretations must "faithfully, wisely, and coherently express the truths found in scripture."[51] And D. H. Williams likewise notes that "We should not be blind to the fact that various doctrines have been put forth in the name of 'tradition' that have no warrant in scripture or in the consensual teaching of the church."[52] What is plain with each of these writers is that they all have their borders beyond which orthodoxy cannot stray. It is not a question of admitting tradition, but rather *which* tradition. Thus it is not whether any of us draw lines – we all do – but rather where the lines are drawn. For Williams, "the tradition is the various incarnations of the Christian faith articulated during the first five or six centuries."[53] He therefore apparently rules as inadmissible to the tradition those things that were later developments. No Christian can escape the adjudication of evidence and of history. Every believer enters into this, and does so as an individual. It is easy to claim consensus for a particular view, because adherents to it are often readily available. Nor is this situation recent, or post-Reformational. "In advocacy of any doctrine the words with weight are 'general' or 'standard', *katholikos* or *orthodoxos*. No further explanation or defense may be thought necessary. All sides of a dispute will insist theirs is the really catholic one. Ambrose complains of the fact."[54]

Christian Smith notes, "Presumably the authors of the New Testament would have wholeheartedly endorsed the outcomes of the first four ecumenical councils. But when they were alive and writing, centuries earlier, they simply had not worked out the full implications of the truth that they knew, as later subsequent

---

[51] Hall, p. 41.

[52] D.H. Williams, *Evangelicals and Tradition: The Formative Influence of the Early Church* (Grand Rapids, Baker Academic, 2005), p. 39.

[53] Ibid., p. 50.

[54] Ramsay MacMullen, *Voting About God in Early Church Councils* (New Haven, Yale University Press, 2006), p. 69.

Christians needed to and did."[55] But he must admit this is a presumption, because we do not have the apostles' view on these subsequent councils. Do these four councils provide the certainty believers today need? The Orthodox Church likewise argues for the Great Tradition, but their parameters are different from Williams and Smith in that they affirm the first seven ecumenical councils as definitive. What argument does Williams, as an evangelical, have to tell the Orthodox that icons are not really part of the patristic faith? Williams protests, "One ought not to have to leave the Free Church in order to embrace the norms of the ancient Christian Tradition."[56] At least one Roman Catholic reviewer sees where his logic leads and says, "One might well argue with Williams on this last point, as I certainly would."[57]

Some have pointed out that all expressions of Christianity have traditions, and therefore it is disingenuous for evangelicals to point to adherence to tradition as anything to be eschewed. Indeed, every group has its traditions, and without doubt evangelicals have some of their own. But the question is not whether something is practiced, but whether it is made authoritative. Here is where evangelicals generally draw the line and say no to investing with authority anything not found in Scripture. For example, a local church may have an "anniversary Sunday," where there is a commemoration of the time they first began meeting together as a church. But if this congregation insists that other groups celebrate this in the same way, or that it is a matter of faith and doctrine to do so, then it becomes the imperious tradition we see operating within sacramentalism. Edith Humphrey has identified the "quiet

---

[55] Smith, p. 167.

[56] D.H. Williams, *Retrieving the Tradition and Renewing Evangelicalism: A Primer for Suspicious Protestants* (Grand Rapids, Wm. B. Eerdmans, 1999), p. 31.

[57] Addison Hart, "Evangelical Ressourcement," http://touchstonemag.com/archives/print.php?id=14-03-038-b#ixzz33FftbMz8

time" of daily Bible reading and prayer as an evangelical tradition.[58] It is true that many evangelicals do practice this "tradition," but it carries no authoritative mandate. No one dictates that Christians *must* do this. It is simply a good idea to engage with God through his Word, but this is in no way the equivalent of what sacramentalism imposes as its traditions.

Tradition implies antiquity and absence of change, but as we saw earlier, there has definitely been change in the way the church has understood doctrine and practice, even to the point of inventing new doctrines. We saw in the previous chapter that Basil of Caesarea introduced a "startling innovation" with his doctrine of unwritten tradition. Heiko Oberman observes that, "Whereas Ireneaus (c. 200) and Tertullian (c. 220) had taught the sufficiency of Scripture, in Augustine we encounter an authoritative extrascriptural oral tradition. While on the one hand, the Church 'moves' the faithful to discover the authority of scripture, scripture, on the other hand, refers the faithful back to the authority of the Church on a series of issues with which the Apostles did not deal in writing. In this case Augustine refers to the validity of baptism by heretics, Abelard later to Mariology, Bonaventura to the *filioque*, Aquinas to the form of the sacrament of confirmation and the veneration of images."[59] What is the Christian of today to do with this Augustinian innovation? To the extent that a tradition is not apostolic, can believers be enjoined to obey it and adhere to it, simply because the Church says so? We come once more to ecclesiology as the defining doctrine for sacramentalism.

Catholic Robert Louis Wilken has taken a different stance in his book *The Myth of Christian Beginnings: History's Impact on Belief.* Wilken identifies a particular mindset, which he refers to as the "Eusebian model" of church history, so named for Eusebius of

---

[58] Edith M. Humphrey, *Scripture and Tradition: What the Bible Really Says* (Grand Rapids, Baker Academic, 2013), p. 7.
[59] Heiko A. Oberman, *Forerunners of the Reformation: The Shape of Late Medieval Thought* (New York, Holt, Rinehart and Winston, 1966), p. 54-55.

Caesarea, the first church historian. Eusebius viewed the church as a pure virgin that became tainted by heretical teaching after a time. "In the Eusebian view, the past assumes the role of an *imperative* for present and future. Whatever was a genuine mark of Christianity in the past *should* also mark the church of the present."[60] What I have argued for is in accord with this; the past *is* imperative for the future, but with an important qualification. It is not simply the past that is authoritative, but the Scriptures. In that the New Testament writings belong to the apostolic age, they are by that fact part of the past. But I am not arguing for the Eusebian construct of a virginal state of the Church. As I noted in Chapter 3, drawing a line at Constantine and saying that prior to this the church was pure, is fictitious. From the evidence we have surveyed, we have seen that from the beginning heresy and dissension were present.

Wilken casts doubt on the view of an authoritative past, regarding it as naïve. "Apostolicity is a historical construction of the past arising out of Christian experience. If the picture of the past we have inherited is the result of experiences of Christians in former ages, our age has the right, indeed the mandate, to critically examine our view of the past in light of new experiences. Hopefully, we will be able to give as great a place to change, innovation, and diversity as Christians in the past have given to tradition, permanence, and authority."[61]

Wilken recognizes the fact that when any of us views the past, we are seeing it from the vantage point of our own time and circumstance, and this colors our understanding. And we doubtless do have the responsibility to examine the past – and to judge it for its fidelity to the Scriptures. But he goes further than sacramental traditions would in denying any authoritative role for the past in regulating our present understanding. If equal weight is

---

[60] Robert Louis Wilken, *The Myth of Christian Beginnings: History's Impact on Belief* (Garden City, Doubleday & Co., 1971), p. 190.
[61] Ibid, p. 26.

132

given to change, innovation, and diversity, the parameters of orthodoxy are perpetually open to reinterpretation. By this reasoning, even Islam may be viewed as a legitimate historical development within Christianity. God gave Mohammed a message, and who is to say it was not God speaking to him if there are no criteria against which to judge it? If the past, and in particular, the documents of the New Testament do not have any authority for our *present* understanding of Christianity, then developments of any kind are admissible as genuine.

It is just this sort of continuing development that Cardinal Newman argues for in his *Essay on the Development of Christian Doctrine*: "It is a first strong point that, in an idea such as Christianity, developments cannot but be, and those surely divine, because it is divine; a second that, if so, they are those very ones which exist, because there are no others; and a third point is the fact that they are found just there, where true developments ought to be found – namely, in the historic seats of Apostolical teaching and in the authoritative homes of immemorial tradition."[62]

The logic Newman follows cannot support his claims. If we see developments in doctrine, this is to be expected. But Newman offers no explanation as to why we should expect developments. When Jeroboam introduced the "development" of sacrificing on the high places in Israel, it was not regarded as "surely divine" because it occurred in the congregation of God's chosen people. When the people were at last taken captive to Assyria, the writer of 2 Kings points back to what by that time was a "tradition" of some 200 years: "Judah also did not keep the commandments of the Lord their God, but walked in the customs that Israel had introduced....The people of Israel walked in all the sins that Jeroboam did. They did not depart from them." (2 Kings 17:19,22). Paul affirmed that he had delivered over to the Ephesians the whole counsel of God, and Tertullian vociferously objected to the

62 John Henry Newman, *An Essay on the Development of Christian Doctrine* (Kindle Edition, 2011), p. 61-62.

suggestion that the apostles had held anything back in their teaching. Contrary to what Newman suggests, there is every indication that development in doctrine is decidedly not to be expected.

Moreover, to suggest that "they are those very ones which exist, because there are no others," is absurd and nonsensical. There surely have been other developments. Church councils were repeatedly called to deal with doctrinal developments that were regarded as heterodox. These developments occurred within the Church and in many cases, it was legitimately consecrated bishops that were the originators of such heresy. Paul of Samosata, Photinus of Sirmium, Eunomius of Cyzicus, Acacius of Caeseara, Nestorius of Constantinople - all of these men were condemned for heresy, yet were part of the Church hierarchy, and in some cases, bishops of "the historic seats of Apostolical teaching and in the authoritative homes of immemorial tradition."

Newman presents a sanitized view of church history that is popular among adherents to the hierarchical view of ecclesiology, but is simply not a true picture. Newman's *a priori* assumption is that because developments occur in the church, they are legitimate. But Scripture and history both argue forcefully against this stance. His criteria of whether a development is a true one is whether it originates in the Church, the institution that he believes to be infallible, and not whether it accords with the biblical revelation.[63] The Church for him is a self-authenticating institution, but it is a circular argument to contend that any doctrinal developments found in the church are therefore legitimate.

For those seeking certainty, as McKnight has said many evangelicals are, nothing in the history of doctrinal development provides the certitude that putatively comes with sacramental

---

[63] It is noteworthy that Newman held to a view of infallibility that embraced the whole people of God, and not the hierarchy or the Pope. Though he was invited to Vatican I, he declined the invitation, due to his reservations about the declaration of papal infallibility.

ecclesiology. The Vincentian Canon came about because of alarm over change – and change within the Church. No believer is able to outsource his faith decisions to others. Each of us must do the hard work of examining the Scriptures. This does not mean having a disregard for what believers of another age have concluded, but we likewise must acknowledge that antiquity is not equal to orthodoxy.

6

"Do you understand what you're reading?"
The Role of Hermeneutics

Many things condition our understanding of the Bible. The theological traditions we grow up with, our fellow believers, our institutional associations – all of these things influence our understanding of Scripture. Most people will acknowledge that it is impossible to be completely unbiased in our view of the Scriptures. The idea of interpreting the Bible according to the tradition of the church, however, implies that there has been a fixed and stable manner of dealing with the text through the centuries. This has not been the case. If we do insist on a single method such the Rule of Faith, as we noted in Chapter 5, we are again speaking in generalities, rather than specifics, and the rule provides no assistance in the true difficulties of hermeneutics.

According to the sacramental position, if the multitude of interpretations has been a cause of division, then locating the interpretation of the Bible within the context of the church is a way to resolve this difficulty. As I noted earlier, evangelicals do not shun the communal understanding and interpretation of the Bible, but the difference in their position rests on what one means by the context of the church. The Roman Catholic position is that the right to interpret the scriptures belongs to the magisterium alone. The *Catechism* states, "The task of giving an authentic interpretation of the Word of God, whether in its written form or in the form of Tradition, has been entrusted to the living, teaching office of the Church alone. Its authority in this matter is exercised in the name of Jesus Christ. This means that the task of interpretation has been entrusted to the bishops in communion with the successor of Peter, the Bishop of Rome."[1]

---

[1] *Catechism of the Catholic Church* (New York, Image Books, 1995), p. 32.

The Orthodox Church likewise claims that the proper locus of hermeneutics is the Church, but there is no magisterium. Instead, the writings of the Fathers and their interpretations form the basis of how the Orthodox read Scripture. It is evident that in both of these cases, the church is that which is composed of the bishops, which these traditions believe to be in direct succession from the apostles. Again we encounter the true issue in sacramental authority – ecclesiology.

In making these statements about where true interpretation is found, sacramentalism is at the same time making statements about the Bible. The authority of the Bible as the Word of God is undermined if knowing its true meaning requires the Church. Are we dealing with a book whose ultimate author is God, a book that is God-breathed? Is the word of God living and active, as Hebrews 4:12 states? Or, when Paul tells Timothy that the Scriptures are "able to make you wise unto salvation through faith which is in Christ Jesus," has he simply assumed Timothy will understand the necessity of the hierarchical church? Stated differently, does the inherent authority that we saw at work in Canon formation abruptly stop there, so that, once collected into a canon, their authority depends entirely on the Church? Perhaps it is attributable to the polarization of Reformation and Counter-Reformation polemics, but this was indeed the attitude expressed by Stanislaus Hosius, papal legate to the Council of Trent. "The Scriptures have only as much force as the fables of Aesop, if destitute of the authority of the Church."[2]

If sacramentalists insist that the proper interpretation of the Scriptures can only be based on the church's understanding and

---

[2] *Confutatio Prolegomenon Brentii, Opera, 1.530.* English translation from Francis Turretin, Institutes of Elenctic Theology, trans. George Musgrave Giger, ed. James T. Dennison Jr., 3 vols. (Phillipsburg, NJ: P & R, 1992–1997), 1:86 (2.6.2). Cited in Michael J. Kruger, *Canon Revisited: Establishing the Origins and Authority of the New Testament Books*, Kindle Locations, 1395-1397, (Wheaton, Crossway Books, 2012).

its tradition, it prompts the question, which tradition? Throughout the centuries, the way in which the church has handled and understood the Scriptures has changed and evolved, at times in dramatic fashion. It is not a problem for the evangelical to declare that someone in the past (or present) erred in his or her view of the Scriptures – men are fallible and are liable to error. The church fathers could, and did, err. For one who adheres to the idea that the church is infallible and the teaching authority of the church is where true interpretation alone is found, it becomes a game of theological hair-splitting to explain how it is that a certain church father who taught something that the church no longer teaches was not erroneous in his views.

For the Orthodox, who form a collection of autocephalous churches, the historic witness of the fathers is the key to interpretive coherence. But as we saw with the Vincentian Canon, it can prove difficult, if not embarrassing, to hold to the "unanimous consent" when men of different provenance and different centuries begin to contradict one another. As Pelikan notes,

> Such an exhortation as "let us reverently hold fast to the confession of the fathers" seemed to assume, by its use of "confession" in the singular and of "fathers" in the plural, that there was readily available a patristic consensus on the doctrines with which the fathers had dealt in previous controversy and on the doctrines over which debate had not yet arisen – but was about to arise. When it did arise, the existence of such a patristic consensus became problematic. When an orthodox church father such as Gregory of Nyssa appeared to be in agreement with a heretic such as Origen on the eventual salvation of all men, it was necessary to explain away this agreement. When it appeared that there was a contradiction between two passages in Gregory of Nazianzus, closer study would show "their true harmony."[3]

---

[3] Jaroslav Pelikan, *The Christian Tradition: A History of the Development of Doctrine, Vol. 2: The Spirit of Eastern Christendom (600-1700)* (Chicago, University of Chicago Press, 1974), p. 21.

Thus by a kind of theological sleight of hand, clashes in the fathers were made to appear harmonious, and the "patristic consensus" could be maintained, even if it required a good bit of creativity to do so. But Orthodoxy had manufactured this difficulty by bestowing upon the writings of the fathers a kind of canonical status, which would admit no conflict. Recognizing that the fathers were fallible men, whose writings about scripture could be wrong solves this problem for the evangelical. Space will not permit a full review of all the important commentators on scripture throughout the ages, but focusing on a few key individuals and thinkers will allow us to draw conclusions on the lasting influence of their ideas.

The early adversaries of biblical interpretation were perceived to be two. In one camp were the heretics and Gnostics. These were men such as Marcion, Valentinian, and others, who taught a Christology that was unsustainable from Scripture, yet harmonious with the Greek systems of the day. To combat this faction, Irenaeus of Lyon wrote his treatise *Adverus Haereses*, which presents a rebuttal of the Gnostic system. One of the things he articulates is an early example of what has been called the perspicuity of Scripture, though he also acknowledges that the apostolic writings require careful study. "All Scripture, which has been given to us by God, shall be found by us perfectly consistent; and the parables shall harmonize with those passages which are perfectly plain; and those statements the meaning of which is clear, shall serve to explain the parables; and through the many diversified utterances [of Scripture] there shall be heard one harmonious melody in us."[4] Coming to the end of his critique of the Gnostic claims of the origins of creation and the divine ordering, he says, "Such, then, is their system, which neither the prophets announced, nor the Lord taught, nor the apostles delivered, but of which they boast that beyond all others they have

---

[4] *Ante-Nicene Fathers, Vol. 1*, ed. Philip Schaff (Grand Rapids, Christian Classics Ethereal Library, n.d.), p. 1027.

a perfect knowledge. They gather their views from other sources than the Scriptures."[5] Two principles are evident. Obscure passages are to be interpreted by the plain passages, and the doctrines of Christianity are contained in Scripture alone. Other sources are ruled out by Irenaeus. These principles are embraced by evangelicals of today, but not by the sacramental church.

Tertullian's approach to the Scriptures was to take the text at its plain meaning. His training as a lawyer and in rhetoric prepared him to hew to the ordinary significance of words. "In law courts, the principle most frequently invoked was one of a simple, literal reading. Cicero's prime rule was the use of the ordinary sense of words. This was Tertullian's most basic rule also."[6] This does not mean that Tertullian did not recognize figurative language in the text; this too is in fact recognizing the plain significance of words. The other important feature of Tertullian's exegesis is that in recognizing typology he insisted on types being firmly grounded to their historical events.

The second camp of adversaries was the Jews. Early apologists such as Justin Martyr sought to appropriate the Old Testament as a wholly Christian book; one that the Jews at best were interpreting incorrectly, and at worst had no right to at all. In his *Dialogue with Trypho*, Justin reproves Trypho for not being able to discern the prophetic witness to Christ. "They are contained in your Scriptures, or rather not yours, but ours. For we believe them; but you, though you read them, do not catch the spirit that is in them."[7] The Jews were seen as competitors in the arena of faith, and, because it could not be denied that they were instrumental actors in the Old Testament drama, the tactic was to discredit their interpretation of the oracles of God.

---

[5] Ante-Nicene Fathers, Vol. 2, p. 868.

[6] Maureen A. Tilley, *The Bible in Christian North Africa: the Donatist World* (Minneapolis, Fortress Press, 1997), p. 21-22.

[7] Ante-Nicene Fathers, Vol. 1, p. 600.

The School of Alexandria

Early interpreters were more influenced by a strain of Jewish exegesis than they were prepared to admit. The straightforward manner in which men such as Irenaeus and Tertullian read Scripture represents one the earliest approaches to the Bible, but it did not endure. Dual exegetical traditions developed in the ancient world, located in two established centers of Christianity – Alexandria and Antioch. Alexandrian interpretation of the Scriptures focused on the allegorical meaning of the text, drawing out from it the putatively hidden and deeper meaning. The Alexandrian Jew, Philo, had a significant influence on later Christian exegetes, but Greek thought had influenced Philo himself. "From the Stoics Philo had learned to divide allegorization into two classes, the 'physical', and the 'ethical.' In the first classification he could place interpretations of scripture that referred to God and the nature of the world; in the second, interpretations which referred to the duties of man. For example, he and his predecessors agree that the seven-branched candelabrum really means the seven planets (physical allegory), and that Abraham and Sarah stand for Mind and Virtue (ethical)."[8]

Allegorization represents a view of Scripture that divorces the plain meaning of words from their context, where events narrated in scripture are quite often emptied of their significance, or even their historicity. "This method insisted that the literal sense, particularly of historical passages, did not exhaust the divinely purposed meaning of such passages, but that they also included a deeper, higher, spiritual, and mystical sense. The literal sense indicated what was said or done, while the allegorical showed what should be believed. The allegorical approach, then, was

---

[8] Robert M. Grant, David Tracy, *A Short History of the Interpretation of the Bible* (Philadelphia, Fortress Press, 1984), p. 52-53.

adopted for apologetic and theological purposes."[9] Clement of Alexandria provides a few examples of the odd hermeneutical results that are characteristic of the Alexandrian School. His exposition of the mystical meaning of the tabernacle furniture and the high priestly garments is strange, and one that no modern exegete would agree with. "Now the high priest's robe is the symbol of the world of sense. The seven planets are represented by the five stones and the two carbuncles, for Saturn and the Moon. The former is southern, and moist, and earthy, and heavy; the latter aerial, whence she is called by some Artemis, as if Ærotomos (cutting the air); and the air is cloudy."[10] Commenting on the twelve stones that are part of Aaron's breastplate, Clement says, "The twelve stones, set in four rows on the breast, describe for us the circle of the zodiac, in the four changes of the year."[11]

Origen, a pupil of Clement, was to prove even more influential than his teacher. Origen's scholarship and erudition are unquestionable, and though he was eventually to be censured by a later council, his personal piety and zeal were never doubted. G.L. Prestige has sarcastically noted, "Origen is the greatest of that happily small company of saints who, having lived and died in grace, suffered sentence of expulsion from the Church on earth after they had already entered into the joy of their Lord."[12]

This encomium needs to be tempered by looking at the approach Origen used in his interpretation of the biblical text. For Origen, Scripture held at least three levels of meaning: the literal, the moral, and the spiritual. These he conceived of in ascending sequence; thus, the spiritual was the highest application. Origen

---

[9] David S. Dockery, *Biblical Interpretation Then and Now: Contemporary Hermeneutics in Light of the Early Church* (Grand Rapids, Baker, 1992), p. 83.

[10] *Ante-Nicene Fathers, Vol. 2*, ed. Philip Schaff (Grand Rapids, Christian Classics Ethereal Library, n.d.), p. 957.

[11] Ante-Nicene Fathers, Vol. 2, p. 958.

[12] G.L. Prestige, *Fathers and Heretics* (London, SPCK, 1968), p. 43.

was deeply influenced by the philosophical environment of Alexandria. Frances Young observes, "Origen, it has been said, really worked from Clement's position that, as all religious language was in the form of oracles, enigmas, mysteries, and symbols – this was true of Plato's myths as well as the mystery religions – that the truth of scripture also came through a veil, and the key to unlock the hidden mysteries was Christ."[13] But Origen did not approach the Scriptures to see what they said of Christ so much as impose his own beliefs about Jesus on passages that did not in fact speak directly about him. Kelly notes that Origen was prone "to ascribe too readily to the inspiration of the Spirit the fanciful spiritual symbolism which his fertile imagination discovered in almost every word of image of the Bible. Every proper name, every number, all the animals, plants and metals mentioned there seemed to him to be allegories of theological or spiritual truths."[14]

Bertrand de Margerie, S.J., highlights the dangers of the Alexandrian system as exemplified in Origen. "The principle according to which every passage of Scripture has a symbolic sense is foreign to the primitive Christian conception. It is the principle of universal allegory. Origen is so penetrated with this principle that he does not hesitate to write: 'Everything in Scripture is mystery.' Two negative consequences follow from this. On the one hand, the typological interpretation of Scripture is frequently reduced in Origen to hardly convincing subtleties (especially in the case of Leviticus); on the other hand, his perception of a historical development in the Old Testament is sometimes imperiled. The general

---

13 Frances Young, "Alexandrian and Antiochene Exegesis," in *A History of Biblical Interpretation, Vol. 1, The Ancient Period*, Alan J. Hauser, Duane F. Watson, eds. (Grand Rapids, Eerdmans, 2003), p. 336.
14 J.N.D. Kelly, *Early Christian Doctrines*, rev. ed. (San Francisco, HarperSanFrancisco, 1978), p. 74.

tendency of allegorism is toward the negation of history."[15]

This negation of history is illustrated by the difference between type and allegory. A type does not negate the historical significance of an Old Testament narrative, as allegory may. Indeed, for the validity of a type, the historical *must* be affirmed. Isaac is a type of Christ not only because he foreshadows the sacrifice of the father offering up his only son, but because the event with Abraham and Isaac on Mount Moriah truly occurred. Similarly, Jesus himself identifies Jonah as a type of his own death and burial. Some exegetes explicitly limit the identification of types to only those that are named in the New Testament, as these two examples are. An allegory, especially as pursued by Alexandrian exegesis, need not have occurred in history. Origen readily dismissed the historicity of certain events in the Old Testament that he found morally offensive, (Lot and his daughters, for example).

The School of Antioch

Alongside Alexandria, the other major center of scriptural exegesis is found in Antioch. The Syrian capital was an important metropolis in the early centuries of the church, being one of the five major sees (Jerusalem, Rome, Constantinople, and Alexandria were the others). In the fourth century, Basil of Caesarea considered Antioch "the Mother-Church of the East, and perhaps of Christendom."[16] In contrast to Alexandria, Antiochene exegesis shunned allegory in favor of a more literal reading of the text. Diodorus of Tarsus and his student Theodore of Mopsuestia (born in 352) were important practitioners of this school, as was John

---

[15] Bertrand de Margerie, Leonard Maluf, trans., *An Introduction to the History of Exegesis, Vol. 1: The Greek Fathers* (Petersham , Saint Bede's Publications, 1994), p. 110-111.

[16] W.H.C. Frend, *The Early Church* (Minneapolis, Fortress Press, 1982), p. 174.

Chrysostom, the patriarch of Constantinople. Diodorus "set out to combat allegorical interpretation, which he regarded as an imposition upon the text of a meaning unseen and unintended by its inspired author."[17] His student, Theodore, is often held forth as the foremost exponent of the Antiochene School. He joins Origen in being the object of posthumous condemnation, but Reventlow avers that, "in its condemnation of his teachings, the fifth ecumenical Council of Constantinople of 553 presumably did him an injustice, because during his lifetime he was considered a true defender of the Nicene confession against Arians and other heretics."[18]

Theodore anticipates features of the historical-grammatical principle that most contemporary theologians employ. He is "an absolute exception among early church biblical interpreters [in] that he engages in textual criticism."[19] He recognizes literary form and stylistic devices in the text, such as two verbs for a single action (dieresis), figurative use of terms such as the part for the whole (synechdoche: e.g., the use of "soul", "flesh", "heart", "tongue" for the whole person), and the concrete for the abstract (metonymy: the "right hand" of God for help).[20] He shares the view of his contemporaries that the Old Testament speaks of Christ, but his approach is markedly different than the Alexandrians. "His search for a historical occasion for each psalm – this too is a characteristic trait of Antiochene exegesis – leads him to suppose this in David's life itself (as already had been done in some of the psalm headings)."[21] Theodore's approach to the Old

---

17 Joseph W. Trigg, *Biblical Interpretation* (Wilmington, Del., Michael Glazier, 1988), p. 32.

18 Henning Graf Reventlow, James O. Duke, trans., *History of Biblical Interpretation, Vol. 2: From Late Antiquity to the End of the Middle Ages* (Atlanta, Society of Biblical Literature, 2009), p. 6.

19 Reventlow, p. 7.

20 Reventlow, Loc. Cit.

21 Reventlow, p. 8.

Testament differs greatly from the Alexandrians. "He tries to identify for each prophecy the historical setting to which it refers. That Scripture is a 'true history of events' is important to him."[22] Trigg agrees, saying, "Theodore concentrated on the meaning of texts in their surrounding verses, on their historical references and chronological significance, and on principles of translation. Theodore's respect for history led him not only to reject allegory, but, as is the case with Tertullian, to restrict the typological or prophetic interpretation of the Old Testament."[23] Contemporary interpreters take many of these principles as sound exegetical methods, but they were not universally applied in the ancient world.

As noted above, the other famous Antiochene exegete is John Chrysostom, whose surname means the "Golden-mouthed," given for his oratorical skills. John was Patriarch of Constantinople beginning in 397, and though he was later exiled, this is attributed to the political machinations of the day, rather than to anything heterodox in his teaching. In John's exposition, Frances Young says, "like others in the Antiochene tradition of exegesis, Chrysostom repudiates allegorical flights of fancy and treats the text as straightforwardly as possible. He does not shrink from accepting that much of the Old Testament refers to mundane and even immoral matters and is to be taken as history, not symbol, as literal (though interim) commandments, not spiritual directives in veiled form; indeed he regards it as a universal law of scripture that it supplies the interpretation if an allegory is intended, so as to prevent the uncontrolled passion of those bent on allegorizing from penetrating everywhere without system or principle."[24]

This survey of the highlights of these two schools of thought is not necessarily to prove that one is superior to the other (though

---

[22] Reventlow, p. 10.

[23] Trigg, p. 33.

[24] Frances M. Young, *From Nicaea to Chalcedon: A Guide to the Literature and Its Background* (Philadelphia, Fortress Press, 1983), p. 156.

much of the Alexandrian school has now been set aside as irresponsible exegesis), but to demonstrate the difficulty of formulating a consistent hermeneutic "within the Church." Both of these traditions functioned within the Church, and yet their results were sometimes very different. Moreover, as the centuries passed, different viewpoints were brought forth as representing interpretation within the Church. To the extent that these later interpretations set aside the earlier ones, they represent a *de facto* repudiation of what had been previously held by the Church.

The Allegorical Legacy in Sacramentalism

Though Origen's theology was later rejected and condemned (and a large amount of his extant writings were destroyed), his hermeneutical method was preserved and proved influential for later church fathers, even those who shared none of his heterodox positions. Chief among these hermeneutical heirs was Augustine, whose influence in the theology of the Western church is difficult to overstate. Robert Norris observes that because of thinkers such as Jerome and Ambrose, Augustine stands, "broadly speaking, in the Alexandrian tradition of biblical interpretation."[25] His need to find some meaning in each detail of the text, no matter how minor, is demonstrated by his well-known exposition of the parable of the Good Samaritan:

A certain man went down from Jerusalem to Jericho: Adam himself is meant; Jerusalem is the holy city of peace from whose blessedness Adam fell; Jericho means the moon, and signifies our mortality, because it is born, waxes, wanes, and dies. Thieves are the devil and his angels. Who strip him, namely, of his immortality; and beat him, by

---

[25] Richard A. Norris, Jr., "Augustine and the Close of the Ancient Period", in Alan J. Hauser, Duane F. Watson, eds., *A History of Biblical Interpretation, Vol. 1* (Grand Rapids, Eerdmans, 2003), p. 386.

persuading him to sin; and left him half-dead, because in so far as man can understand and know God, he lives, but in so far as he is wasted and oppressed by sin, he is dead; he is therefore called half-dead. The priest and Levite who saw him and passed by, signify the priesthood and ministry of the Old Testament, which could profit nothing for salvation. Samaritan means Guardian, and therefore the Lord Himself is signified by this name. The binding of the wounds is the restraint of sin. Oil is the comfort of good hope; wine the exhortation to work with fervent spirit. The beast is the flesh in which He deigned to come to us. The being set upon the beast is belief in the incarnation of Christ. The inn is the Church, where travelers are refreshed on their return from pilgrimage to their heavenly country. The morrow is after the resurrection of the Lord. The two pence are either the two precepts of love, or the promise of this life and of that which is to come. The innkeeper is the Apostle (Paul). The supererogatory payment is either his counsel of celibacy, or the fact that he worked with his own hands lest he should be a burden to any of the weaker brethren when the Gospel was new, though it was lawful for him "to live by the Gospel."[26]

It is evident through this exposition that Augustine is operating very much in the Alexandrian tradition. No actor or object is beyond signifying something. Augustine even manages to find the apostle Paul in the parable. Richard N. Soulen comments that "the interpretation follows the rule of faith. It is not of his devising. It is the authoritative teaching of the church: Adam is assisted in his movement toward God by the healing love (charity) of Christ, in the figure of the Good Samaritan, while the cupidity of both priest and Levite leave them even less close to God than before."[27]

---

26 Cited in Richard N. Soulen, *Sacred Scripture: A Short History of Interpretation* (Louisville, Westminster John Knox Press, 2009), p. 91.
27 Soulen, Loc. Cit.

But whether Augustine's exegesis accords with the understanding of the rule of faith of his day, is the interpretation true to the text, and indeed to the wider context of the Gospels and the entirety of Scripture? Does it convincingly explain the truth that Jesus sought to convey in telling this parable? It is evident that Augustine's *a priori* assumptions influence his interpretation. Bernard McGinn comments that, for Augustine, "all progress toward God can only take place within the church."[28] Thus the bishop must locate the church as the inn within the parable, and Paul as the innkeeper.

When we look at other commentators, we see a very different interpretation of the Good Samaritan. David Gooding focuses our attention on the one actor that Augustine misses in his analysis – the lawyer who posed the question to Jesus: "Who is my neighbor?" "From the practical point of view that was all the guidance the lawyer, or anyone else, needed; whenever we come across in our pathway someone in great need, we are to have compassion on them and help them as we would like them to help us if were in need."[29] R.C.H. Lenksi points us to a Christological center, rather than approaching the parable as a kind of literary riddle. "Jesus is touching this lawyer's conscience. His command, which is so brief and simple, if it is acted on by this lawyer will soon show him all his selfish lack of love, and thus make him ready to see what prophets and kings long to see, what the disciples did see (v. 24), the blessedness of grace which the Messiah Jesus brings to all who accept him by faith."[30]

Comparing these views of the parable with Augustine's, the

---

28 Bernard McGinn, *The Presence of God: A History of Western Christian Mysticism, Vol. 1: Foundations of Mysticism: Origins to the Fifth Century* (New York, Crossroad Publishing Co., 1994), p. 238.

29 David Gooding, *According to Luke: A New Exposition of the Third Gospel* (Grand Rapids, Wm. B. Eerdmans, 1987), p. 203.

30 R.C.H. Lenski, *The Interpretation of St. Luke's Gospel* (Minneapolis, Augsburg Publishing House, 1946), p. 609.

pitfalls of allegory are plain. Augustine misses what is clearly the main point of Jesus' answer to the lawyer. Perhaps this is why, though located within the church, allegorical interpretation has been rejected by modern scholarship. Even the Pontifical Bible Institute noted, "the allegorical interpretation of scripture so characteristic of patristic exegesis runs the risk of being something of an embarrassment to people today."[31] As I noted also in Chapter 4, (see pages 89-90), other scholars within the sacramental tradition have grown highly suspicious of allegory as any sort of sure foundation for interpretation. But the damage has already been done. Sacramentalism and all its accouterments are based squarely on mystery, which is supported by centuries of allegorical interpretation. The practices of sacramentalism has become so entrenched in both Catholicism and Orthodoxy that even if the hermeneutical principle that birthed them has been invalidated, sacramental authority lives on, because it is sanctioned by long tradition.

Augustine and the other fathers who indulged in allegory were men of their time, influenced by their contemporaries and their culture. It is in one sense, therefore, not surprising to find them interpreting the Scripture in this manner. What is surprising is to find those today who still insist on "interpretation within the Church" (meaning the hierarchical church) as the only sure way of arriving at the true meaning of a text of Scripture. The objective of this is not to simply point out that Augustine was wrong in his interpretation, but to recognize that being a bishop, being part of the hierarchy (though no one conceived of a magisterium in Augustine's day), is in no way a guarantee to arrive at a coherent reading of Scripture.

Augustine himself did not confine interpretation only to the hierarchical church. The *Book of Rules* by the Donatist Bishop of North Africa, Tyconius, was the first attempt in the West at a

---

[31] Pontifical Bible Institute, *The Interpretation of the Bible in the Church, J.L. Houlden, ed.* (London, SCM Press, Ltd., 1995), p. 68.

hermeneutical manual, was warmly recommended by Augustine. What is significant about this is that Tyconius was decidedly outside of the hierarchy, and, as a Donatist, was considered in schism with the church Augustine represented.[32] Yet we find Augustine not only commenting on his *Rules*, but also recommending them as a helpful aid to understanding the Scripture. Augustine had a quibble about the labeling of a few of Tyconius' principles, and he remarks that Tyconius was part of the Donatist church, "however, Augustine's endorsement was complete and enthusiastic."[33] The bishop of Hippo finds guidance and help for interpreting the Scriptures outside of the hierarchy and, indeed, outside of the official church.

Kannengieser assesses the implication of what Augustine does in his recommendation of Tyconius. "A vigilant supervisor of a strict form of ecclesiastical orthodoxy undertakes to introduce a hermeneutical system of a man excluded from the Catholic communion and well-known as a life-long schismatic, in order to give 'to such an elaborate and useful work' a paradigmatic value in the Catholic exegesis of scripture! If Roman Church authorities, two centuries earlier, had publicly recommended Marcion's understanding of the Christian canon, they would have fairly anticipated the initiative of Augustine quoting Tyconius."[34] With such an example, can it be credibly argued that biblical interpretation "has been entrusted to the living, teaching office of

---

[32] Like others "outside the mainstream" that were briefly profiled in Chapter 3, the Donatists were not heretical in their view of Christ, but insisted on holiness in their priests. The group was born during a time of persecution when some within the church, under pressure, handed over the Scriptures to persecutors.

[33] Karlfried Froehlich, *Biblical Interpretation in the Early Church* (Philadelphia, Fortress Press, 1984), p. 26.

[34] Charles Kannengieser, "Augustine and Tyconius: A Conflict of Christian Hermeneutics in Roman Africa," in Pamela Bright, (ed. and trans.), *Augustine and the Bible* (Notre Dame, University of Notre Dame Press, 1999), p. 153.

the Church alone"? This very model of ecclesiastical authority was set aside by Augustine to cull the truth from an unlikely source. The hierarchical church itself contains examples of looking outside the church for guidance on interpretation.

Summary

This survey of hermeneutics through the centuries has demonstrated several things. Firstly, we cannot speak of a hermeneutical rule that the Church always applied which has resulted in a consistent and coherent interpretation of the Scriptures. Whether we begin with the sub-apostolic church or look later at the esteemed theologians of late antiquity, or the exegetes of Scholasticism, in each age we find not consistency, but diversity. Moreover, one of the chief goals of exegesis was to support the received interpretation, to bolster the authority of the Church in the way it defined a Christian's relationship to God.

While the sacramental church may have disavowed the allegorical approach to Scripture of the Alexandrian School, the fact that it reigned so long and so pervasively has meant that its influence has remained firmly in place, even if allegorical principles have now been supplanted by the historical-critical method. This is chiefly seen in the mystery that infuses everything about sacramentalism. Alexandrian exegesis provided the tools to view the Scriptures as mystery, with the sacraments the vessels and the Church the steward of those mysteries. In this way the Church takes her place between the believer and Christ, supported by a dubious exegetical method that has redefined how the grace of God is received and experienced in the life of the Christian.

It is important to remember that the clarion of justification by faith alone that re-emerged during the Reformation was a *conclusion* of exegesis, not an *a priori* assumption. Luther, says Peter Stuhlmacher, "more and more abandoned allegory and established research into the literal meaning of scripture as the decisive exegetical task."[35] One of the chief differences from earlier exegesis is that the Reformers were willing to cede authority to the Scriptures, to place the Church under their authority. "Proceeding from the original meaning of the texts, they aim at a reflective theological dialogue with the historical and dogmatic tradition of the church, a tradition in part instructive and in part full of error and miscalculation."[36] This latter realization that the Church could and did err in its handling of the Bible is what separated the Reformers from the hierarchical Church of their day. It is still a defining difference between evangelicalism and sacramentalism.

Evangelical converts must reckon with this diversity of interpretation as well. In choosing to move to a sacramental tradition, one is not casting in one's lot with the "historical church," or the apostolic church for that matter. Rather, it is a decision to join oneself to *one* particular tradition, but by no means the only one, nor the oldest. Affirming that interpretation must be located in the Church, or, more particularly, in the hierarchy of the bishops, is to deny what has taken place historically. Sacramental churches of today have their own interpretation of what history shows, but even among their own ranks, there is disagreement. It is sometimes difficult to come to a right interpretation of a passage of Scripture, but outsourcing these decisions to a hierarchy is no sure or responsible course to follow. The apostolic admonition still stands: "Do your best to present yourself to God as one approved, a worker who does not need to be ashamed and who correctly handles the word of truth" (2 Tim. 2:15 NIV).

---

35 Peter Stuhlmacher, Roy A. Harrisville, trans., *Historical Criticism and Theological Interpretation of Scripture* (Philadelphia, Fortress Press, 1977), p. 34.
36 Stuhlmacher, p. 35.

7

Sacraments as Vehicles of Grace

In the hierarchical traditions, the term sacrament is used freely and sometimes indiscriminately. *Sacramentum* is the Latin translation of the Greek *mysterion*, or mystery. The word sacrament does not precisely mean mystery, but this is how Jerome translated it in his Latin Vulgate. Many things are described as sacraments, from the commonly known seven sacraments of today in Roman Catholic teaching, to the church, the world itself, and other acts and practices called sacramentals. When a rite or practice is involved in a sacrament it is thought to impart grace to the one who performs it.

The Sacramental Paradigm

The full-orbed doctrine of sacramentalism took centuries to completely develop, and in the West, as with many aspects of theology, Augustine proves to be an important source. With Augustine, Alexandre Ganoczy says, "there occurred a truly epochal turning point in the Christian sacramental understanding. Using a neo-Platonist epistemology and ontology, he was able to construct a consistent and systematic theology of sacraments."[1] Acts and rituals were for Augustine symbols that conveyed the sacred. Professor Ganoczy goes on to ask, concerning the two sacraments of baptism and the Eucharist, "Are both of these sacraments simply interpretive symbols? It would be possible to assume this from Augustine's philosophical approach. And yet the answer turns out differently: The sacrament of Christian ritual effects what it symbolizes. It communicates that to the recipient

---

[1] Alexandre Ganoczy, William Thomas, and Anthony Sherman, trans., *An Introduction to Catholic Sacramental Theology* (New York, Paulist Press, 1984), p. 20.

154

which the analogy points up: baptism communicates cleansing, justifying faith; the Eucharist communicates the unifying power of the true body and true blood of Christ."[2]

Some theologians, extending the Augustinian paradigm of sacraments effecting what they symbolize, include words themselves. Scott Hahn writes, "There are times when words do more than describe, there are times when words are deeds. This is the contention of 'speech-act' theory, which was first proposed by philosopher J.L. Austin in the 1960s and has since become an influential school of thought. Austin pointed out that, while most words are merely descriptive, there are certain phrases that really accomplish what they describe. Once they are uttered, they change things."[3] Oddly, Hahn seems not to have made the connection between this view and Pentecostal word-faith teaching, in which speaking something can make it come to pass. These doctrines of word-faith teachers, reaching their full flowering in prosperity gospel preaching, have been quite destructive. Where these two converge is that in both Pentecostalism and sacramental doctrine there are creative forces at work. "The sacraments are seen as sacred signs, but signs which actually bring about what is being signified."[4]

Viewed in this way, sacraments perform a mediating function on behalf of the believer. We experience God through the Church and through the sacraments. According to sacramentalism and the allegorical approach to Scripture I examined in Chapter 6, divine knowledge is cloaked in mystery. The rites of the Church therefore assume for believers a critical importance as the conduits of experiencing and knowing God. Father Geoffrey Preston describes the mystery associated with the sacramental view:

[2] Ibid, p. 24.

[3] Scott Hahn, *Swear to God: The Promise and Power of the Sacraments* (New York, Doubleday, 2004), p. 92.

[4] David K. O'Rourke, *A Process Called Conversion* (Garden City, Doubleday, 1985), p. 140.

The sacramental encounter is the whole of the sacramental celebration in which the word is the soul and sense of the sacramental gestures. If we are to raise the question of truth or falsity in relation to the sacraments, it is the whole celebration at which we must look. In such a celebration there is a nebula of meaning of a pre-theological kind, and sacramental theology exists as a "second-order" elucidation of this nebula. What is true or, conceivably, false about a sacramental occasion is not any one of its meanings or possible frames of reference, nor any one theology of the sacraments to the exclusion of all the others. The reality of Christ shows itself – if it *does* show itself – in ways which cannot be exhaustively expressed in concepts and so need such imaginative representation. The ritual gestures of the sacraments, many of which are rooted in the human will of the historical Jesus, are bearers of a meaning which cannot be adequately stated in words. By their very nature the images are multivalent and enable the whole man to grasp the ultimate reality of the things of God. This is another reason why one must have confidence in the validity of external behaviour and not demand "sincerity" as a non-negotiable minimum.[5]

For the worshiper, Preston implies that faith in the acts themselves will suffice for grace to be imparted. Although the Catechism stresses that the reception of grace is dependent on the proper disposition of the worshipper, it does not elaborate on the nature of that disposition. It may be based on the fact that the worshiper has no unconfessed sin. Yet even if the worshiper were in a right state, what scriptural foundation is there that the sacramental gesture brings about what it signifies? The other component is the condition of the priest. When Father Preston dismisses the need for sincerity, it is assumed that he refers to the spiritual condition of a priest. Whatever state of sin the priest may

---

[5] Geoffrey Preston, Aidan Nichols, eds., *Faces of the Church: Meditations on a Mystery and Its Images* (Grand Rapids, Eerdmans, 1997), p. 110.

be in, the sacrament is unaffected. The "validity of external behaviour" does not demand sincerity. In the vernacular, a priest can quite literally go through the motions, and the efficacy of the sacrament remains in force. Evangelicals have rightly viewed such attitudes with deep suspicion.

In the early church, many condemned this division of sacramental act from Christian life. Cyprian had no doubt that a priest who was unholy in his conduct was unworthy to preside at the Eucharist: "Nor let the people flatter themselves that they can be free from the contagion of sin, while communicating with a priest who is a sinner, and yielding their consent to the unjust and unlawful episcopacy of their overseer, when the divine reproof by Hosea the prophet threatens, and says, "Their sacrifices shall be as the bread of mourning; all that eat thereof shall be polluted" (Hos. 9:4) teaching manifestly and showing that all are absolutely bound to the sin who have been contaminated by the sacrifice of a profane and unrighteous priest."[6] Later theologians may have discarded Cyprian's view, but it is nonetheless the record that fathers such as he who are so valued by today's Catholics and Orthodox do not support the unconditional powers of sacramental acts advocated by Father Preston.

Orthodoxy has often been even more mystical than Catholicism in this view of how God is known, and how we grow in our knowledge of him. Vladimir Lossky, describing the distinctly Eastern phenomenon of apophatic theology, says, "It is by *unknowing* (ἀγνωσία) that one may know Him who is above every possible object of knowledge. Proceeding by negations, one ascends from the inferior degrees of being to the highest, by progressively setting aside all that can be known, in order to draw near to the Unknown in the darkness of absolute ignorance."[7]

---

6 Cyprian, Epistle 67:3, in *Ante-Nicene Fathers, Vol. 5*, Phillip Schaff, ed. (Grand Rapids, Christian Classics Ethereal Library, n.d), p. 893.

7 Vladimir Lossky, *The Mystical Theology of the Eastern Church* (Crestwood, NY, St. Vladimir's Seminary Press, 1976), p. 25.

Lossky could just as easily be describing the Buddhist concept of Nirvana.

In his book, *The Gagging of God*, D.A. Carson tells the story of a trip to Europe for a missionary conference where a husband and wife approached him. The husband had been greatly helped by a "rebirthing" seminar he had attended. Due to an abusive childhood, he had never been able to truly experience the love of God, and the concept of "father" was distorted for him. After the rebirthing training, he was marvelously enabled to give and receive love, and for the first time could really enter into the love of Jesus. Carson relates that he did not call into question that the man had indeed been helped in this way, but goes on to say that he told the man, "At best you have experienced second best, and at worst you have been seduced into idolatry. My dear brother, all the emotional catharsis, all the tears, all the integration, might well have been yours *along biblical lines*" (emphasis his).[8]

Carson points out to this man all the places in Scripture where he might find the love of God emphatically displayed, chief among them the cross. "For the fact of the matter is that you now associate your emotional release not with the cross, but with rebirthing techniques. You will be less inclined to think of the gospel as that which is the power of God unto salvation. You will think of the gospel as providing some sort of pardon, and rebirthing techniques as providing healing, power, restoration. All the associational links are wrong. They are diverting. They bring you some measure of relief, while distracting you from the cross."[9] The problem that Carson emphasizes is exactly that which we see in the many liturgical forms and sacraments. Sacramentalism diverts from the gospel as the power of God unto salvation, and substitutes other things as providing restoration, power, and forgiveness. Whether it is praying to a particular saint, repeating a

---

[8] D.A. Carson, *The Gagging of God* (Grand Rapids, Zondervan Publishing House, 1996), p. 468.

[9] Ibid, p. 468-469.

certain number of novenas, or fulfilling the requirements a priest has dictated as part of penance, these things assume the role conveying the grace of God to the believer.

For the hierarchical church, baptism and the Eucharist are the two sacraments of primary importance and I will examine them, along with confession, for their significance in sacramental doctrine.

Baptism: A Life-Giving Sacrament?

I am aware of the large amount of literature on the topic of baptism, and that within Protestantism itself there is disagreement as to the mode and meaning of the ordinance. In examining baptism here, my task is to focus on the claims made in the sacramental traditions for what it accomplishes. These claims differ from those made by Protestants who practice infant baptism. In sacramentalist understanding, one enters the Church and is granted forgiveness of sins through the sacrament of baptism. Without doubt, baptism is a New Testament practice, but the questions that divide Christians are its mode, who a candidate for baptism is, and what exactly transpires in baptism. The evangelical usually holds to believer's baptism, or credo-baptism. One must profess faith in Christ to be a candidate for baptism. Baptism presents a physical picture of the spiritual reality of death, burial, and resurrection with Jesus. "Do you not know that all of us who have been baptized into Christ Jesus were baptized into his death? We were buried therefore with him by baptism into death, in order that, just as Christ was raised from the dead by the glory of the Father, we too might walk in newness of life" (Rom 6:3-4). The picture of one going under the water accurately depicts death and the grave – our dying with Christ,[10] as Paul says.

---

[10] It is universally acknowledged that the mode of baptism in the apostolic and sub-apostolic era was by immersion. This is demonstrated by the

Within evangelicalism, the importance of baptism is sometimes overlooked, and it is decidedly not the teaching of the New Testament that baptism is optional. Thomas Schreiner notes, "It is striking that there is no sustained discussion of baptism in any of the epistles, presumably because the NT authors were writing to those who were already believers to whom the significance of baptism was explained upon their conversion. When Paul does refer to baptism, he assumes that all believers are baptized. Hence, we cannot deduce from the infrequent references to baptism that baptism was unimportant."[11] The concept of an unbaptized Christian is simply foreign to the New Testament. The extent to which evangelicals have failed to call attention to the importance of baptism as something obedient Christians should do demonstrates their failure.

Within sacramentalism, the importance of baptism is stressed, albeit at times to an outsized proportion. Sacramentalism practices infant baptism as both an entrance rite into the new covenant with God and as that which cleanses from sin. Indeed, in this view one cannot be saved apart from baptism: "Through baptism we are freed from sin and reborn as sons of God; we become members of Christ, are incorporated into the Church and made sharers in her mission."[12] The sacramental view ascribes profound accomplishments to baptism: regeneration itself, and cleansing the baptized one from the stain of sin.

How did the sacramental church move away from believers' baptism in favor of infant baptism? In the New Testament, we meet with no certain evidence of infant baptism. In the book of Acts, where we find various instances of baptism, it is always upon

---

examples we have in Scripture, as well as by archaeological evidence of baptisteries, which were akin to small pools.

[11] Thomas Schreiner, "Baptism in the Epistles: An Initiation Rite for Believers," in *Believer's Baptism*, Shawn D. Wright and Thomas Schreiner, eds. (B&H Publishing, Kindle Edition, 2007), p. 58.

[12] *Catechism of the Catholic Church* (New York, Image Books, 1995), p. 342.

belief. After Peter's Pentecost sermon, "So those who received his word were baptized, and there were added that day about three thousand souls" (Acts 2:41). The Ethiopian eunuch, hearing Philip expound the gospel says, "'See, here is water! What prevents me from being baptized?" And Philip said, 'If you believe with all your heart, you may.' And he replied, 'I believe that Jesus Christ is the Son of God'" (Acts 8:36-37).

In Acts 10, Peter had been called to the house of Cornelius, a Roman centurion, who was a God-fearer, or a Gentile who attached himself to the Mosaic Law. After his gospel preaching, all who heard believed, causing Peter to ask, "Can anyone withhold water for baptizing these people, who have received the Holy Spirit just as we have?" And he commanded them to be baptized in the name of Jesus Christ (See Acts 10:47-48). Baptism obviously followed belief in both of these cases.

The Philippian jailer's conversion is sometimes cited as evidence of infant baptism, or of household baptism, but this can only be by inference: "And he took them the same hour of the night and washed their wounds; and he was baptized at once, he and all his family" (Acts 16:33). Were there small children or infants in the family? It is conjecture to assume this, as nothing is stated in the text. In short, nothing in the New Testament demonstrates any evidence of infant baptism. Rather, baptism upon profession of faith is instead seen again and again. New Testament textual critic Kurt Aland comments, "It is true that we hear frequently of the baptism of whole households, e.g., Acts 16.15,32f., 18.8, I Cor. 1.16. But the last passage taken in conjunction with I Cor. 7.14 does not tell in favour of the view that infant baptism was usual at that time. For in that case Paul could not have written: 'else would your children be unholy.'"[13] In other words, if it were the practice of the apostles to baptize whole households, including infants and children, there would be no

---

[13] Kurt Aland, G.R. Beasley-Murray, trans., *Did the Early Church Baptize Infants?* (London, SCM Press, Ltd., 1963), p. 1.

logic in speaking of these children as "unholy." Had they undergone baptism, would not Paul have spoken of them as being part of the Church and as among the saints? New Testament scholar James D.G. Dunn comments, "It is one of the standing ironies of the diversity of Christian theology and practice that the chief means of accomplishing regeneration for so many centuries has had so little foothold in the NT, and has not clearly been encompassed even within the wide-ranging diversity of first-century Christian practice. For it has to be recognized that *infant baptism can find no real support in the theology of baptism which any NT writer can be shown to espouse*"[14] (emphasis his).

What of the patristic evidence? Tertullian favors a delay in baptism: "The delay of baptism is preferable; principally, however, in the case of little children."[15] He goes on to indicate that it is better if those who come for baptism can themselves understand what they are entering into: "Let them 'come,' then, while they are growing up; let them 'come' while they are learning, while they are learning whither to come; let them become Christians when they have become able to know Christ."[16] Tertullian indicates an age of accountability, implying that it is better if people attain an age when they are themselves able to understand the faith. Even when we come to a time when the practice of infant baptism became more widespread, it is the case that "of known named individuals in those centuries who were both of Christian parentage and baptized at known dates, the great majority were baptized on profession of faith."[17] Wright notes the evidence:

---

[14] James D. G. Dunn, *Unity and Diversity in the New Testament: An Enquiry into the Character of Earliest Christianity*, 2nd Ed. (London, SCM Press, 1990), p. 160.

[15] Tertullian, "On Baptism", in *Ante-Nicene Fathers, Vol. 3*, Philip Schaff, ed., (Grand Rapids, Christian Classics Ethereal Library, n.d.), p. 1512.

[16] Tertullian, p. 1513.

[17] David F. Wright, *What Has Infant Baptism Done to Baptism? An Enquiry at the End of Christendom* (London, Paternoster, 2005), p. 6.

We encounter that widespread group of later fourth-century churchmen and churchwomen nurtured in Christian families but not baptized until they were of independent years. It is extensive: Ambrose (and his brother Satyrus and probably also their sister Marcellina), Augustine, Basil the Great, Ephraem Syrus, Gregory Nazianzen (and his brother Caesarius and sister Gorgonia), Gregory of Nyssa (and his sister Macrina, in all likelihood), Jerome (and his friend Heliodorus), John Chrysostom, Paulinus of Nola (and his brother), Rufinus of Aquileia, and quite possibly others, like Ulfilas and Cassian." Some of these instances come very close to death-bed baptism (in which otherwise the Christian emperors were specialists). But although several of these persons later became vocal among the ranks of preachers condemning baptismal delay, only in the case of Augustine is criticism voiced of his own parent's default.[18]

The questions this raises are twofold. If infant baptism were the norm, and widespread, why is there such a list of esteemed individuals in the early church who were not baptized as infants? Secondly, if baptism were really thought to impart the life of Christ to the person receiving it, would it be right to imperil the soul of an individual by delay? The second question is answered by a differing view in antiquity of the innocence that children were thought to possess. Aland says that, "In the Apostolic Fathers we repeatedly find the presumption of the 'innocence' (in the original meaning of the term) of children unambiguously intimated."[19] Athenagoras, in his treatise, "On the Resurrection of the Dead," says that the purpose of the resurrection is not solely for judgment;

---

[18]David F. Wright, *Infant Baptism in Historical Perspective* (Eugene, Wipf & Stock, 2007), p. 65.
[19] Aland, p. 105.

else very young children would not be included, for they are those that "had done neither evil nor good."[20]

To Augustine belongs the fully developed doctrine of original sin, which became one of the reasons for his insistence on infant baptism. A full exposition of Augustinian doctrine on original sin is beyond my scope here, but it is without doubt that his view has had a profound impact on all the various Christian traditions, including Catholic and Protestant. Wright observes, "For him, newborn babies had to be baptized in order to escape from the guilt of original sin and its entail, eternal damnation. Since Augustine earlier in his career had been uncertain why babies should be baptized, he may be said to have eventually applied to baby baptism what he knew to be true of older candidates, who were baptized for the remission of sin." [21]

The Augustinian concept of original sin dovetails with that of baptismal regeneration. If the stain of original sin is removed through baptism, as the Catechism notes, then it is evident why sacramentalism assigns such prominence to baptism. Stated differently, if baptism is absolutely necessary for salvation, then its importance becomes clear. A catena of scriptural references can be cited to show that salvation is conditioned upon faith in Jesus, rather than on an external act done on their behalf without their knowledge or consent, but evangelicals should know these. Again, for an evangelical, moving to sacramentalism requires the paradigm shift in the basis of authority to accept the hierarchical church's redefinition of what baptism is, and what it imparts.

Does the New Testament teach that baptism is a requirement of salvation? Peter's plea to his hearers at Pentecost ends with the appeal, "Repent and be baptized every one of you in the name of

[20] Athenagoras, "On the Resurrection of the Dead", in *Ante-Nicene Fathers*, *Vol. 2*, Philip Schaff, ed. (Grand Rapids, Christian Classics Ethereal Library, n.d.), p. 352-353.
[21] David F. Wright, *What Has Infant Baptism Done to Baptism? An Enquiry at the End of Christendom* (London, Paternoster, 2005), p. 7.

Jesus Christ for the forgiveness of your sins" (Acts 2:38). This passage is often cited as proof of the necessity of baptism. But Peter's insistence on repentance carries the implication of faith with it. To repent is to change one's mind, and the change of mind Peter pleads for is to believe that Jesus is the Messiah. Here baptism is in no way separated from faith, but accompanies it.

The other passage often brought forth is in 1 Peter 3:21, where we read "Baptism, which corresponds to this, now saves you, not as a removal of dirt from the body but as an appeal to God for a good conscience, through the resurrection of Jesus Christ." Concerning this, Schreiner observes:

> Peter repudiates an ex opere operato view of baptism, for he immediately qualifies the statement that baptism saves. It does not save mechanically or externally as if there are magical properties in the water. Peter comments that the mere removal of dirt from the body does not bring salvation, demonstrating that the water itself does not save. Baptism is only saving if there is an appeal to God for a good conscience through the resurrection of Jesus Christ. The waters themselves do not cleanse as is the case when a bath removes dirt from the body. Indeed, the objective work of Jesus Christ in his death and resurrection does not save unless there is a subjective element as well. The one receiving baptism also appeals to God for a good conscience, which means that he asks God to cleanse him of his sins on the basis of Christ's death and resurrection.[22]

In this passage, as well as in Acts 2, faith is present and indeed precedes baptism. What might be termed corollary passages inform us on this question as well. If baptism has the effect of removing sin, and imparting life, of bringing one into God's family, it is strange indeed to find Paul thanking God that "I baptized none of you, except Crispus and Gaius"(1 Cor. 1:14).

---

[22] Schreiner, p. 60.

Lest it be thought that he is simply decrying the divisions in the Corinthian congregation, in verse 17 he explicitly sets baptism in contrast to the preaching of the gospel, and affirms the latter to be his purpose. "For Christ did not send me to baptize but to preach the gospel, and not with words of eloquent wisdom, lest the cross of Christ be emptied of its power." If baptism were an act that imparted new life, why would Paul not seek to baptize infants and children at every opportunity? As he writes later, "that by all means I might save some" (1 Cor. 9:22).

It is one thing to consider what baptism meant in the apostolic and sub-apostolic era and another to ask, as David F. Wright does, what it means "at the end of Christendom." Wright speaks of a "massive baptismal reductionism which the long reign of infant baptism has inflicted on baptism."[23] Two extremes prevail which have contributed to this. On the one side are those who insist, as sacramentalism does, that baptism is efficacious to save, to wash away sin, and to put one into the body of Christ. The fact that an infant cannot himself believe or exercise faith is entirely unimportant in this view. The parents are acting as proxies; their answers render as the infant's answer, their faith as the infant's faith. Wright notes that, "Universal infant baptism was one of the constitutive elements of the unitary world of church-state Christianity which is what Christendom commonly denotes."[24] In short, the practice that came to prevail of baptizing all infants led to a situation where faith is entirely unimportant; on the part of parents, or children, baptism was simply something one did as a member of a society dominated by the hierarchical church.

The deleterious effects of this are evident. It has emptied baptism of any of the meaning assigned to it in the New Testament. The identification with Christ in his death, burial, and resurrection is changed to a rite of initiation into the professing family of God. The looming question which sacramentalism must

---

23 Wright, p. 87.
24 Ibid, p. 9.

answer is this: If baptism is indeed effective in imparting new life, in washing away sin, in putting one into the church, how is it that so many people who have undergone infant baptism manifest no signs of divine life whatsoever? There are huge numbers of people who are considered part of the Roman Catholic Church or part of the Orthodox Church because they have undergone infant baptism, yet do not participate in the church or cannot be considered members of the church in any realistic way. The only conclusion is that the effectiveness of the sacrament has failed. The incongruity of what we see in the professing church with what is claimed for infant baptism argues that the practice has been emptied of value for what it claims to do.

Infant baptism is of course not limited to sacramentalism. High church Protestantism kept the practice, though its ministers changed the underlying meaning somewhat. Adherents to this draw parallels with circumcision as a rite of initiation into the covenant. Yet this is a misunderstanding of the New Testament teaching on baptism. Calvin and other magisterial reformers were sometimes in agreement with Catholics on the church as a visible society of the faithful. Verduin notes, "In one view the Church is *Corpus Christi*, the body of Christ, which consists of believing folk and them solely; in the other view the Church is *Corpus Christianum*, the body of a 'christened' society."[25] Infant baptism was the initiation into this christened society. Luther and his colleagues often treated Anabaptists, the so-called radical reformers, as they would treat heretics. When pressed to explain exactly what the significance of infant baptism is, Protestants who hold to infant baptism equate it with infant dedication. None of these Protestants would insist that it removes sin, or imparts the life of Christ, and so it has a very different meaning from what the sacramental church affirms.

---

[25] Leonard Verduin, *The Reformers and Their Stepchildren* (Grand Rapids, Eerdmans, 1964), p. 17.

The Eucharist

When Jesus ate the Passover meal with his disciples just before going to Calvary, he instituted something new. In Luke 22, we read, "And he took bread, and when he had given thanks, he broke it and gave it to them, saying, 'This is my body, which is given for you. Do this in remembrance of me.' And likewise the cup after they had eaten, saying, 'This cup that is poured out for you is the new covenant in my blood'" (Luke 22:19-20). This was the Last Supper, which came to be known as the Lord's Supper because Jesus had instituted a new ordinance. The commandment to do this as a part of worship is not expounded in the Gospels. John's Gospel does not even record the introduction of the Lord's Supper. When we turn to the book of Acts, we see the first disciples engaged in a fourfold practice: "And they devoted themselves to the apostles' teaching and the fellowship, to the breaking of bread and the prayers" (Acts 2:42). It is quite likely that the "breaking of bread" here was a communal meal that ended with the Lord's Supper, very much as the Passover meal had been taken together when Jesus first introduced the aspect of remembering his death. This is further evidenced a few verses later in Acts 2:46: "And day by day, attending the temple together and breaking bread in their homes, they received their food with glad and generous hearts."

There have been numerous examinations of the Lord's Supper or the Eucharist.[26] In the sacramental Church, the belief that the bread and wine become the actual body and blood of Jesus forms a very important part of the doctrine of the Eucharist. Rather than present a full-scale examination of this view, I wish to show how and why the Lord's Supper moved from being regarded as a

---

[26] See, for example, *The Lord's Supper: Five Views*, Gordon T. Smith, ed. (Downer's Grove, IVP Academic, 2008); and *The Lord's Supper: Remembering and Proclaiming Christ Until He Comes*, Thomas R. Schreiner, Matthew R. Crawford, eds. (Nashville, B&H Academic, 2010).

memorial to becoming a sacrifice. Paul outlines the doctrine of the Lord's Supper in 1 Corinthians 11:23-26:

> For I received from the Lord what I also delivered to you, that the Lord Jesus on the night when he was betrayed took bread, and when he had given thanks, he broke it, and said, "This is my body which is for you. Do this in remembrance of me." In the same way also he took the cup, after supper, saying, "This cup is the new covenant in my blood. Do this, as often as you drink it, in remembrance of me." For as often as you eat this bread and drink the cup, you proclaim the Lord's death until he comes.

The elements of the Supper, the bread and wine, are taken in remembrance of Jesus. That is, the focus of these is to bring to mind his death. Partaking in the Supper is a proclamation of the gospel. It reminds believers that by giving his life Jesus purchased their redemption. The emphasis, then, is that partaking of the Lord's Supper is both a *remembrance* and a *proclamation*. A growth in grace, or strengthening of believers through the actual substance of bread and wine, is not part of Paul's doctrine. Dunn affirms a third meaning to the Lord's Supper, that of *participation*. "The emphasis is not so much on what was eaten and drunk as on the sharing (*koinonia*) of the same bread and same cup (v. 16); believers were one because they shared the same loaf. (v.17) not because of some efficacy in the bread itself."[27]

Earlier, in 1 Cor. 10, the apostle had presented the contrast between pagan and Christian worship: "What do I imply then? That food offered to idols is anything, or that an idol is anything? No, I imply that what pagans sacrifice they offer to demons and not to God. I do not want you to be participants with demons" (1 Cor. 11:19-20). Paul disavows any inherent change to the food offered to an idol. It is nothing, he says. Rather, the real

---

27 Dunn, p. 165.

significance is what is behind the food, and what is behind the idol, the demonic power. Similarly, he indicates that the power in the Supper is not in the bread and wine, but rather in the Lord to whom these point. J.W. Hunkin writes, "It is worth noting that S. Paul never actually speaks of eating the Lord's *body*, but always of eating the *bread*; never of drinking the Lord's *blood*, but always of drinking the *wine*."[28] It is a *spiritual* significance, just as Paul explains the typology of the rock from which the Israelites drank to be a spiritual rock, pointing ultimately to Christ.[29]

Our participation in the Supper is an acknowledgement that we have been formed into one body by Christ's death on our behalf: "Because there is one bread, we who are many are one body, for we all partake of the one bread" (1 Cor. 10:17). John 6, where Jesus speaks of eating his flesh and drinking his blood, has also been used as a justification for the real presence. But Jesus ends the discourse by saying, "It is the Spirit who gives life; the flesh is no help at all. The words that I have spoken to you are spirit and life" (v. 63). In other words, Jesus explains to the disciples that he is speaking figuratively. Later in John's Gospel, Jesus calls himself both a vine and a door, but there is no suggestion that these figures should be taken literally. It is odd that John 6 is one of the only passages in Scripture which sacramentalists insist must be taken literally, abandoning their customary allegorical interpretation.

The centrality of the death of Christ in the message of the gospel is self-evident. Without his death, there is no resurrection, and without both, there is no gospel, no triumph over sin, indeed no Christianity. The Lord's Supper, as a proclamation of Jesus' death, is a vital component in our preaching of the gospel to one another in gathered worship. Too often evangelicals have minimized its importance in the worship of the church. One way

---

[28] J.W. Hunkin, "The Origin of Eucharist Doctrine" in *The Evangelical Doctrine of Holy Communion*, A.J. MacDonald, ed. (Cambridge, W. Heffer & Sons, Ltd., 1930), p. 26. (italics his).
[29] Dunn, Loc. cit.

this has occurred is by celebrating it infrequently. Relegating the celebration of the Lord's Supper to once a month, or in some cases, quarterly, is to diminish a very important part of congregational life. Paul affirms that when believers do this, they proclaim the Lord's death. The implication here, as well as in Acts 20, is that each Lord's Day the gathered church celebrated the Supper.

Why this movement away from the weekly celebration of the Lord's Supper has developed in evangelicalism is likely due to two factors. Firstly, since the expository preaching of the Bible was virtually excised from sacramental tradition, evangelicalism sought to restore the primacy of the Word of God in the church. This can be seen even in the fact that the pulpit, rather than the altar, is at the front and center of evangelical churches. Restoring the supremacy of Scripture meant that expository preaching took the central place in evangelical churches. Secondly, one wonders whether a reaction against the unbiblical ascriptions given to the Lord's Supper by sacramentalism is in part responsible for the diminution of the ordinance in evangelicalism. Yet reacting against the wrong way that one tradition practices something rooted in Scripture is not a good reason to diminish it.

Alexander Schmemann describes how, in the East, the meaning of the Lord's Supper began to move away from its original significance. It is no longer a remembrance of Jesus in his death, of him giving himself for us, but "this offering to God of bread and wine, of the food we must eat in order to live, is our offering to Him of ourselves, of our life and of the whole world. We offer the world and ourselves to God. We come again and again with our lives to offer; we bring and 'sacrifice' – that is, give to God – what He has given to us."[30] The Lord's Supper and the simplicity of remembering Jesus in his death have been transformed into something quite different. It is now a rite with the emphasis not on what he has done, but on what we are offering to him.

---

[30] Alexander Schmemann, *For the Life of the World: Sacraments and Orthodoxy* (Crestwood, NY, St. Vladimir's Seminary Press, 1973), p. 35.

Ben Witherington III ascribes the transformation of the Lord's Supper to the Eucharist to a hermeneutical failing, an incorrect allegorical interpretation:

One of the things that happened when the church moved from meetings in homes to having purpose-built buildings beginning before, but accelerated during, the Constantinian era, is that while the church itself was becoming less Jewish in character, it began to apply a more and more Old Testament hermeneutic to its discussions about church, ministry, and sacraments. The church began to be seen as a temple, or basilica, the Lord's Supper began to be seen as a sacrifice, just as in Leviticus, were seen to be priests. There was the further move in this direction when Sunday began to be seen as the Sabbath, another example of this same sort of hermeneutic. There were considerable problems with this whole hermeneutic from the start, since nowhere in the New Testament is there set up a class of priests or clerics to administer any sacraments.[31]

Witherington points to the Judaizing of Christianity that took hold in the sub-apostolic era as largely responsible for this changed view of the Lord's Supper from a memorial of Jesus' death to a sacrifice offered to God. Again we see that the sacramental church's embrace of allegory has led her down a path that is inconsistent with New Testament truth.

It is easy to marshal the putative evidence for a realist view of the Eucharist from patristic sources. It is similarly easy to assemble evidence of a symbolic view of the Lord's Supper from the patristic sources. To cite one example, A.J. MacDonald notes, "The idea of a real flesh of Jesus in the Eucharist is entirely foreign to Christian thought at the beginning of the second century. It is foreign even to the thought of Ignatius, who used it in the letters to the Smyrnaeans and the Philadelphians. The Ignatian phraseology is

---

31 Ben Witherington III, *Making a Meal Of It: Rethinking the Theology of the Lord's Supper* (Waco, Baylor University Press, 2007), p. 110-111.

symbolical."[32] What is clear is that Ignatius uses figurative language to convey doctrinal concepts: "In Ignatian thought the bread is faith and the cup is love, symbolised by the food received at the fellowship meal, which provide protection against heresy. 'Take ye only Christian food and abstain from strange herbage which is heresy, for these men (the heretics) do mingle poison with Jesus Christ... like persons administering a deadly drug with honied wine... Do ye therefore arm yourselves with gentleness in faith, which is the flesh (σάρξ) of the Lord, and love which is the blood (αἷμα) of the Jesus Christ.'"[33]

Other passages from Ignatius can be cited which seem to support a real presence view, but even an apologist for that view must admit that "the language of St. Ignatius is so difficult, that it is in some passages possible to assign diametrically opposite meanings to him."[34] This same exercise can be undertaken from the writings of Justin Martyr, Tertullian, and other fathers, to show support for both a view of the real presence and that of the symbolic. It therefore becomes very much the same situation as what Francis Sullivan described with conciliar and papal infallibility: "The texts are convincing, it would seem, only to those who are disposed to accept the doctrine."[35]

The aspect of the Eucharist as sacrifice was further expanded at the council of Trent, as a reaction against the Reformers. (It was also at Trent that transubstantiation was formally defined.) The argument was that, just as in the Old Testament priests offered sacrifice, so in the New do the priests of the Church. Claudius Zauis, one of the Trent fathers, said, "And if priests should be in

---

[32] A.J. MacDonald, "The Formulation of Sacramental Doctrine" in *The Evangelical Doctrine of Holy Communion*, A.J. MacDonald, ed. (Cambridge, W. Heffer & Sons, Ltd., 1930), p. 46-47.
[33] Ibid, Loc. Cit.
[34] Felix L. Cirlot, *The Early Eucharist* (London, Society for Promoting Christian Knowledge, 1939), p. 78.
[35] See p. 69 above.

the law of the gospel, it is necessary that there also be sacrifices, as Paul said, for it is proper for them to offer. But there is no other sacrifice in the law of the gospel unless it is the oblation of the eucharist; there this oblation is a sacrifice."[36] Zauis predicates the necessity of sacrifices on the existence of priests, but in fact there are not priests in the "law of the gospel," except for the priesthood of Jesus himself, and that of all Christians. A separate order of priests upon whom powers are conferred by ordination is an invention of later history, consistent with the Judaizing of the Church. Secondly, the shift in viewing the Lord's Supper as a sacrifice could not but change the claims made for what was happening in the Eucharist. The Trent fathers went on to claim that, "because the sacrifice of the cross is propitiatory, as Hebrews 9:13 says, the Mass also is propitiatory because it is a memorial of the cross."[37] But this is contradictory. The Mass cannot be both a re-presentation of Christ's sacrifice[38] and be at the same time propitiatory. If the sacrifice of Jesus on the cross is propitiatory, then it must be in some fashion be insufficient if the Mass is also viewed as propitiatory.

A group of evangelicals who converted *en masse* to Orthodoxy, and whose story is chronicled in Peter Gillquist's *Becoming Orthodox,* display a similar embrace of the Old Testament as normative for New Testament worship. Undertaking a study of the sub-apostolic church, they conclude that the liturgical and sacramental view of the Eucharist is the correct one. "The second part of the early Christian liturgy was the *Eucharist,* that is, the thanksgiving. It's part of the worship that leads up to

---

[36] *Concilium Tridentinum: Diarorum, Actorum, Epsitularum, Tractatum Nova Collectio*, Societas Goerresiana, ed. (Freiburg im Breisgau, Herder and Co., 1901). Cited in Ralph N. McMichael, *Eucharist: A Guide for the Perplexed* (London, T&T Clark, 2010), p. 72.

[37] Ralph N. McMichael, *Eucharist: A Guide for the Perplexed* (London, T&T Clark, 2010), p. 71.

[38] *Catechism of the Catholic Church*, p. 380.

and includes the taking of Communion. The form of this service is based upon the liturgy followed by the Old Testament priest in the temple, with the offering no longer that of bulls and goats, but now the body and blood of Christ."[39] This accords with what Witherington finds, yet again it is an understanding of the Lord's Supper not found in the New Testament, but only in the sub-apostolic shift of looking toward Israel and its worship as didactic for what the church should do. Looking to Old Testament models has facilitated the changed view of the Lord's Supper from memorial meal to a sacrifice we present to God.

Clearly, we are still on the Judaizing ground that Witherington speaks of. If we view the church as not a distinctly New Testament phenomenon that began at Pentecost, but rather as the collection of the people of God throughout the whole of biblical history, then we will look toward Israel for cues as to how we should worship. Such a view fails to note the profound distinction between Israel and her worship, and the church and hers. Jesus indicates the same when he speaks of putting new wine into old wineskins. In sacramental doctrine, the old wine of the Levitical system has been put into the new wineskin of the church. In short, it is a failure to acknowledge that the fulfillment of these things in Jesus means that we cannot go back to the Old Testament types and shadows as instructive for New Testament worship. In the Old Testament, the sons of Aaron alone were priests. In the New Testament, every believer is a priest. In the Old Testament, sacrifices were continually offered which covered over sin, but did not remove it. In the New Testament, Jesus dies once on the cross, saying, "It is finished." The writer of Hebrews also takes up the finality of this: "Nor was it to offer himself repeatedly, as the high priest enters the holy places every year with blood not his own, for then he would have had to suffer repeatedly since the foundation of the world. But as it is, he has appeared once for all at the end of

[39] Peter E. Gillquist, *Becoming Orthodox: A Journey to the Ancient Christian Faith* (Ben Lomond: CA, Conciliar Press, 1992), p. 32.

the ages to put away sin by the sacrifice of himself. And just as it is appointed for man to die once, and after that comes judgment, so Christ, having been offered once to bear the sins of many, will appear a second time, not to deal with sin but to save those who are eagerly waiting for him" (Heb. 9:25-28). "He entered once for all into the holy places, not by means of the blood of goats and calves but by means of his own blood, thus securing an eternal redemption" (Heb. 9:12). In the Old Testament we see an altar where sacrifice is made. In the New Testament, we see the Lord's Table where friends sit down, because peace with God is *already* accomplished. The argument that the Eucharist is itself a sacrifice compromises these truths of the death of Christ as fully sufficient, unique, and not to be repeated. This is not more Christianity, but decidedly less.

In no other epistle is the word "better" used as much as in Hebrews. Here we are presented with a better hope, better promises, a better sacrifice, and the mediator of a better covenant. To suggest that the Eucharist is a sacrifice is to demote all of these things from "better" to "not good enough." It is a *de facto* rejection of the completeness and finality of what Jesus accomplished on the cross. It is to confuse the covenants. It is not surprising that sacramental worship looks so Jewish when this confusion of covenants is endemic to it. The blessing of the Lord's Supper is, just as Jesus commanded, when we take it in remembrance of him. In doing so, we also proclaim our sure hope that he is returning. This evangelical emphasis in the Lord's Supper on the blessed hope of his return has all but been eclipsed in the sacramental doctrine of the Eucharist.

Confession

No one would claim that confessing one's sins is unbiblical, or is not in accordance with the New Testament. Yet the sacramental position that confession of sin must be done in a particular way and be accompanied by penance and the absolution of a priest, is a different matter altogether. It is spurious to claim that a clergyman must be the one to grant forgiveness if the office of priest is part of tradition only. Hahn describes the edifice that has been built up over the years in sacramental theology: "Jesus has delegated His power to forgive to his Church, personified by His priests. He breathed the Holy Spirit upon those first clergymen, the apostles, and He said, 'Receive the Holy Spirit. If you forgive the sins of any, they are forgiven.' And, in doing so, the Gospel here uses the same Greek verb used elsewhere to describe Jesus' unique power to forgive (see Luke 7:48; Mt. 9:2). In a sense nothing has changed. The power of forgiveness still rested with God alone. Only now, God was empowering others to forgive *in His Name*, as a sure and sacramental sign."[40]

Hahn apparently puts much stock in the incident recorded in John's Gospel of Jesus breathing on the disciples in this fashion. The exact meaning of what Jesus did here is far from clear. He had earlier avowed to the disciples, "These things I have spoken to you while I am still with you. But the Helper, the Holy Spirit, whom the Father will send in my name, he will teach you all things, and bring to your remembrance all that I have said to you" (John 14: 25-26). And later, "It is to your advantage that I go away, for if I do not go away, the Helper will not come to you. But if I go, I will send him to you" (John 16:7). In short, whatever occurred in John 20, it was not the sending of the Spirit that Jesus here promises. That occurred at Pentecost, after Jesus' ascension. As these passages indicate, the sending of the Holy Spirit is predicated on

---

[40] Scott Hahn, *Lord Have Mercy: The Healing Power of Confession* (New York, Doubleday, 2003), p. 51.

the return of Jesus to glory. The John 20 incident is admittedly obscure, but it is best viewed as a kind of earnest, or down payment of the Spirit. Others have seen it as finding fulfillment in the proclamation of the gospel itself. The apostles were being prepared for their ministry of building the church through preaching Jesus. In this proclamation is forgiveness of sins. To take another example of an obscure passage, Mormon doctrine teaches that because of the reference by Paul to baptism for the dead (1 Cor. 15:29), this practice has merit. Sacramentalism would disagree, as this is not practiced, but Hahn's claim, too, is built on the exposition of a single, obscure passage. By considering the context of the entire New Testament, we see that baptism for the dead is not an endorsed practice. Similarly, by considering the entire New Testament, we see no examples of what Hahn claims.

Hahn's view that Jesus was here instituting the sacrament of confession and absolution by a priest faces several high hurdles. There is no indication whatever that such a power, even if it were granted to the Twelve, is transferrable to any subsequent generation. As noted in Chapter 2, the apostolic office was a once-for-all position, the privileges of which cannot be duplicated. Secondly, no such thing as a priest exists in the New Testament, aside from all believers collectively being the "called."

The problems with confession and absolution as uniquely residing with a priest become even clearer when Hahn moves on to penance: "Through the priest, Christ forgives sinners and finds some way the sinner can make it up to God. The priest assigns the penance."[41] To speak of making it up to God is to misunderstand the atonement, the offense of sin, and the basis of our forgiveness. David F. Wells terms this a "shallow moralism that defined sins as simply an infraction of the rules. Sin could be eliminated by the compensating weight of good works. And underlying this moralism was a semi-Pelagianism that compromised the biblical understanding of how sin cripples our ability to seek, love, and

---

41 Ibid.

serve God outside of his sovereign redeeming work in our lives. The combination of this semi-Pelagianism and this shallow moralism, coupled with the confusion over how God's grace is received, resulted in justification being misconstrued as a righteousness produced during life rather than a righteousness conferred by Christ."[42] This understanding of forgiveness was a betrayal of the Augustinian understanding of grace, and a legacy of Scholasticism, the shape of which was so profoundly Thomist.[43] It is this that Luther found so antithetical to what he read in the New Testament. Pelikan comments that the first of the 95 theses Luther nailed to the Wittenberg door concerned penance and its abuse: "At its core this thesis addressed that abuse by appealing to a higher court, pitting the authority of the Bible, the message of Jesus as recorded in the gospel, against the long-standing sacramental teaching and penitential practice of the church. Jesus did not say, 'Do penance', *Poenitentiam agite*' (as the Vulgate translated it), that is, go through the prescribed steps of contrition for sin, confession to a priest, and satisfaction and reparation by good works, but 'Repent' (as the original Greek had it), that is, literally, turn your mind around and change your heart through the purifying power of the word of the gospel and through faith in it."[44]

Father John M. T. Barton calls it a false view of penance that insists, as Luther did, that we cannot contribute to our forgiveness: "The Council [of Trent] further defines, as against the Lutheran heresy that no satisfaction is required for the temporal punishment due to sin, that it *is* needed, in order that Christ's satisfaction may be applied to us, and that we may share in the work of our

---

[42] David F. Wells, *Turning to God: Reclaiming Christian Conversion as Unique, Necessary, and Supernatural* (Grand Rapids, Baker Books, 1989-2012), p. 97.

[43] Ibid, p. 96-97.

[44] Jaroslav Pelikan, *Whose Bible Is it? A History of the Scriptures Through the Ages* (New York, Viking Penguin, 2005), p. 164.

salvation, in accordance with St. John the Baptist's command: 'Come, then, yield the acceptable fruit of repentance' (Matt. 3.8)."[45] The evangelical who adopts sacramentalism must therefore reverse course on believing the forgiveness we have is based on Christ's work alone and nothing of ourselves. In its place is the tradition of the Church that, as God has done his part, we must do ours. This is no longer the gospel of God's grace.

Peter Kreeft writes, "Penance forgives all actual sins if they are confessed and sincerely repented of. This sacrament gives us liberation, pardon, and peace."[46] In fact, converts from Catholicism report exactly the opposite. "Trying to work within this system causes great angst for many RCEs [Roman Catholic Converts to Evangelicalism]. Says 'Nicholas', of his experience in Catholicism, 'I lived in constant fear that when I committed a sin on Monday or Tuesday, after receiving penance on a Saturday, I would be cast into the fires of hell for all eternity if I died before the following Saturday when I went again to confession.'"[47] Concerning exactly what was needed to fulfill the penitential mandate, another convert says, "The problem was I could never figure out just how many of these things would be sufficient to save me from eternal damnation."[48] The question this raises is, if Christ has done all that is needed for our forgiveness and pardon, why would those who trust him be liable to eternal damnation?

If a system is set up which finds no basis in Scripture, it is not surprising that it brings no peace or assurance. This too is one of the things that former Catholics report. In their sacramental days, they were told that assurance of salvation was not possible, yet

---

[45] John M. T. Barton, *Penance and Absolution* (New York, Hawthorne Books, 1961), p. 15.
[46] Peter Kreeft, *Catholic Christianity* (San Francisco, Ignatius Press, 2001), p. 123.
[47] Scot McKnight and Hauna Ondrey, *Finding Faith, Losing Faith: Stories of Conversion and Apostasy* (Waco, Baylor Univ. Press, 2008), p. 136
[48] Ibid.

when they begin to read the Scriptures, they find it to be a promise of the gospel that one *can* know and be assured of forgiveness, and that freedom and liberty come precisely because it no longer depends on anything they do, but upon what Jesus has done. Scott Hahn and Peter Kreeft have the advantage of being first exposed to evangelical doctrine, and thus they are equipped to reinterpret these rites, and attempt to shoehorn them into a biblical framework. It is telling that cradle Catholics who have had no other teaching than official Church dogma take a very different meaning from confession and penance.

In the mid 1940s, Father Manuel Perez Vila was ordained to the order of St. Jerome in Segovia, Spain. His desire to serve God was sincere and real. The monastic order was strict, and Perez Vila describes the lengths he and his brothers went to in order to purify themselves spiritually. "We gave ourselves up there to the practice of severe penitences with all the ardor of youth, whipping ourselves until our backs were turned into one great sore. One of our satisfactions was to be able to show the visitors to the restored monastery the marks of our own blood on the cell walls. We also tortured ourselves with sackcloth that we wore around our waists and legs for whole days and nights. Still, no matter how much we sacrificed our bodies, we did not feel the peace that one could logically expect as a result of such penitences. I know that my experience was also that of several companions. My soul felt thirsty for something I was not finding in the Roman Church."[49]

"One day, through what seems to me curiosity but which I now see was an impulse from the Lord, I went to Madrid intending to find out about the teachings of Evangelical Christianity."[50] Vila did find an evangelical pastor, who "talked to me in terms that I had not dreamed of, dealing with me about regeneration through faith in Christ. He did not refer at all to changing from one church to

---

[49] Manuel Perez Vila, *I Found the Ancient Way* (Chicago, Moody Press, 1958), p. 10-11.
[50] Perez Vila, p. 11.

another, but to the necessity of having a sincere personal relationship with God and the assurance of salvation. The more I studied the Holy Scriptures and the Evangelical books I had, the better I began to understand my inner dissatisfaction with the Catholic Church, while the desire grew in my spirit to be free to follow the truth."[51] Father Vila did abandon the priesthood, and he explains this was because though a priest, he was not truly a child of God, nor did confession bring any relief to him at all.

When I heard the gospel preached I realized I had need for pardon from all my sins, through a confession made directly to God with real repentance. I, who had so often given absolution to others, felt the uselessness of that act and the peace that the soul experiences when it goes directly to the only One who has power to forgive sins – Jesus. My life as a priest was neither better nor worse than that of my fellow priests, but when God in mercy turned His eyes on me, He made me a new creature in Christ Jesus. All of my feelings were so changed that I had the strength even to leave off the vice of smoking, which until then had controlled me. I had never understood before what it meant to be born again. Like Nicodemus, I was "a master of Israel" and I did not know the most important secret of the Gospel, spiritual regeneration. But today by the grace of God I can bear witness to this miracle wrought by Jesus toward the end of 1953: I who had been spiritually dead was resurrected by the Holy Spirit of God and given a new life, to walk in the paths that God prepared from eternity for us to walk in. [52]

As defined by the hierarchical Church, the sacrament of confession and penance undermines the gospel in a startling way. The basis of forgiveness is changed in such a manner that the death of Christ is, despite protests to the contrary, rendered insufficient for our forgiveness and pardon. The church moves into

51 Perez Vila, p. 12.
52 Perez Vila, p. 13-14.

the role of arbiter of forgiveness, of granting or denying forgiveness based on what sinners do, rather than their trust in Jesus. Why would an evangelical who clearly apprehends the sufficiency of the death of Christ step back from that truth to embrace something else?

Summary

By looking to the old covenant for guidance in worship, the sacramental Church fails to adhere to the distinctions of the new covenant. Even the furniture – a table, and not an altar – makes a statement about the truth of Jesus' death and the peace that it has brought us. Opening the New Testament, the reader will find nothing of the sacramental system that developed in later centuries. For sacramentalism, the Bible is not so much a blueprint as a launch pad, a starting point. When sacramentalism does look to the Bible, its failure to distinguish between old and new covenant yields a Judaized worship and theology. Rituals, rites – the characteristics of the sacraments themselves – are the channels through which the commodity of grace flows to the believer. It is impossible for the sacraments not to become ends in themselves, rather than simply the means. In this process, the centrality of Christ, his sufficiency and primacy, are eclipsed.

There is an evangelical or, rather, a biblical answer to this. We follow a path to maturity in Christ and growth into his likeness in which the mind and heart are continually brought back to what Jesus accomplished in his death and resurrection. We have been blessed with every spiritual blessing in the heavenly places in Christ, (Eph. 1:3); we have received redemption and forgiveness through his blood (Eph. 1:7). We have obtained an inheritance (Eph. 1:11), and have been sealed with the Holy Spirit when we believed (Eph. 1:13). These are but a few of the glorious truths conveyed to us not by the sacraments, but in the pages of Scripture. The Holy Spirit, who dwells in every believer, applies these truths to our hearts and minds. Paul prays for the Ephesian believers, and thus for all of us, that according to the riches of his glory [God] may grant you to be strengthened with power through his Spirit in your inner being, so that Christ may dwell in your hearts through faith (Eph. 3:16-17). The Church and the sacraments are not requirements for the Spirit to do his work.

The striking difference between the evangelical view of baptism and the Lord's Supper and the view of sacramentalism is that for evangelicals, these ordinances look back on accomplished spiritual facts. Baptism portrays our death, burial, and resurrection with Christ, which happened spiritually at the new birth, upon belief. The Lord's Supper memorializes Jesus' death on our behalf, the giving of himself to provide the ground of our forgiveness. Our pardon is assured (and thus requires no clerical absolution) because the events the ordinances mark are already settled spiritual realities. These ordinances do not create these things, as sacramentalism claims. For in such a claim there is detraction from the original events as insufficient, and a requiring of what the sacraments newly create.

We worship God according to New Testament truth when our practices affirm what is revealed there. We proclaim salvation is all of grace and Christ's one sacrifice is our peace when we gather around the Lord's Table, not an altar. To return to the types and shadows of the old covenant is to fall short of appreciating their fulfillment in Christ. The writer of Hebrews, after explaining the pictures of the Old Testament sacrifices pointing to Jesus says, "Through him then let us continually offer up a sacrifice of praise to God, that is, the fruit of lips that acknowledge his name" (Heb. 13:15). Here is no sacrifice of the altar, but one of our praise for what he has accomplished. Peter likewise affirms, "you yourselves like living stones are being built up as a spiritual house, to be a holy priesthood, to offer spiritual sacrifices acceptable to God through Jesus Christ" (1 Peter 2:5). New Testament truth must be accompanied by New Testament worship, rather than a return to

Old Testament forms. We proclaim the sufficiency of Christ not by practices that belonged to a time before the full revelation of salvation, but by those that reflect our distinct position in Christ.

8
Mary and the Saints

Peggy O'Neill spent fifty years as a Roman Catholic nun. "The second of ten children, I had the example of good parents who were faithful members of their Church. Were my family to be judged by the teachings and traditions of the Catholic Church, we could all reasonably hope for a place in heaven."[1] Yet O'Neill says that during all those years as a nun, she had never heard the true gospel. "I would have said that I had always believed in Jesus, yet now I realize that I had not known the real Jesus, the Jesus revealed in the Scriptures. I had known nothing of the gift of righteousness He had to offer or of the complete forgiveness of sin brought about by His death and resurrection."[2]… "I was carrying out religious practices that showed I did not know Him. I thought it was essential for my salvation to attend Mass because I had not fully accepted his propitiatory sacrifice on the cross. I sought forgiveness for sin in the Sacrament of Reconciliation, not knowing that Jesus had already reconciled me to God. As well as depending on Jesus, I also depended on Mary, the saints, my penances and good works, my hours of adoration before the Blessed Sacrament, rosaries, scapulars, indulgences, purgatory."[3]

O'Neill came to see that the position given to Mary couldn't be reconciled with Scripture. "There was no biblical evidence of anyone praying to Mary or giving her the *hyperdulia* type of veneration recommended by the Catholic Church… John Paul II, speaking of Mary's suffering said, 'It was on Calvary that Mary's suffering beside the suffering of Jesus reached an intensity which

---

[1] Peggy O'Neill, "I Had Never Heard the True Gospel", in *The Truth Set Us Free: Twenty Former Nuns Tell Their Stories*, Richard Bennett, Mary Hertel, eds. (Multkeo, WA: Winepress Publishing, 1997), p. 161.

[2] Peggy O'Neill, p. 164.

[3] Ibid.

can hardly be imagined from a human point of view, but which was mysteriously and supernaturally fruitful for the redemption of the world.' Notwithstanding her exalted position in Catholicism, Mary was a human being, and like any believer, she performed works of righteousness during her lifetime. However, the words of Isaiah 64:6 apply to her, the same as to all mankind, *'All our righteousnesses are as filthy rags.'* Mary's sufferings could make no contribution to the redemption of the world."[4]

The former Sister Aidan does not denigrate Mary, but focuses rather on the faith she displayed, as any other believer should. "We thank God for Mary, a wonderful woman of faith and obedience to God. Elizabeth in her greeting said, 'Blessed is she that believed.'"[5] O'Neill instead came to look to the merits of Christ alone for the assurance of salvation. "I had never really believed, as I had never accepted salvation as a gift. By God's mercy, I was convicted of the sin of not totally trusting in Jesus and His finished work. I repented of the dead works and from trusting in my own righteousness and I accepted the finished work of Jesus on the cross. I experienced salvation. I was born again in the way that Jesus said to Nicodemus, 'You must be born again.'"[6]

As I demonstrated previously, the experience of the sacraments opens the believer to mysticism and an external mediation between the Christian and God. Father Richard McBrien recognizes the "inherent risk in Catholicism's constant stress on the principle of mediation."[7] Acknowledging Protestant concerns, McBrien notes, "Just as the principle of sacramentality edges close to the brink of idolatry, so the principle of mediation moves one along the path toward magic. Just as there has been evidence of idolatry in some Catholic piety, so there has been evidence of a

---

[4] Peggy O'Neill, p. 171.

[5] Ibid.

[6] Peggy O'Neill, p. 165.

[7] Richard P. McBrien, *Catholicism* (San Francisco, HarperSanFrancisco, 1994), p. 12.

magical view of the divine-human encounter in certain forms of Catholic devotional life."[8] It is no coincidence that Mariology has developed only in sacramentalism. Where Scripture is held as final authority, this has simply never been a factor, because of the exceedingly meager scriptural evidence for what later grew to be an elaborate Mariology. Even within liturgical traditions there is variation. The Orthodox and Anglican communions reject the view of the immaculate conception of Mary because there is no biblical support for this. Yet this is an issue only for those who regard it as necessary that doctrines be grounded in Scripture. Perhaps no other area of dogma rests so directly on tradition and on the fiat of the Church hierarchy, rather than upon the biblical record, as Marian doctrine. But because the cult of Mary has grown so vast through the centuries, it justifies a detailed examination of this aspect of sacramentalism, as well as the ancillary teaching of the intercession of the saints.

The Biblical Record on Mary

There are obviously areas of agreement among all traditions – the virgin birth of Jesus, for example. Evangelicals share this belief with sacramental traditions because there is clear biblical reference to it. It is explicitly stated in that the conception of Jesus is miraculous. When the angel appears to Mary, she questions the manner of this, saying, "How can this be, since I am a virgin?" The Holy Spirit's power would accomplish this. The virgin birth is therefore part of Jesus' identity as the Son of God. It makes no sense to speak of incarnation if his birth were not of God. Incarnation refers specifically to the putting on of flesh by the second person of the Trinity: the Son.

This is where the agreement between evangelicals and sacramentalism tends to end. The references to Mary in the New Testament are few. The wedding at Cana is non-determinative in

---

8 McBrien, p. 11.

any doctrinal sense, yet even here, exegetes in the sacramental tradition have not agreed as to what the exchange between Jesus and Mary means. Some have seen Jesus' reply to her comment that they have no wine as a gentle rebuke: "Woman, what is that to you and me? My hour is not yet come" (John 2:4). Some have seen it to mean that Mary was requesting a miracle in providing wine. The passage in Matthew 12 argues in fact against any special status for Mary. Jesus is told his mother, and brothers are outside, but he answers, "'Who is my mother and who are my brothers?' And stretching out his hand toward his disciples he said, 'Here are my mother and my brothers! For whoever does the will of my Father in heaven is my brother and sister and mother'" (Matt 12:48-50). The natural relationships of blood, which under the Jewish economy were important, were being replaced with a spiritual bond. Mark's Gospel records a single reference to Mary, referring to Jesus as "the son of Mary" (Mark 6:3).

The Luke passages are the most extensive, and have been cited as the basis for much of the later developments of Marian dogma. If these passages teach a special place for Mary in the Christian faith, have evangelicals overlooked or downplayed this aspect of her? The angel Gabriel greets Mary with the words, "Greetings, O favored one, the Lord is with you!" (Luke 1:28). The word "greetings" is a salutation; it is used derisively of Jesus when the Jews say "Hail, King of the Jews!" on the way to the crucifixion. But it also means to rejoice or be glad. "When Herod saw Jesus, he was very *glad* (Luke 23:8)." "Then they left the presence of the council, *rejoicing* that they were counted worthy to suffer dishonor for the name" (Acts 5:41). The angelic greeting is both a salutation and an invitation to rejoice at the news that Gabriel is about to deliver, but there is nothing soteriological or Christological about the greeting in itself. The appellation of "O favored one" is invested with special significance by sacramental traditions, which view

Mary as "enriched by God with the gifts that befit such a role."[9]

The Catechism presents a depiction of Mary that exalts and praises her, and ascribes unique qualities to her. "Through the centuries the Church has become ever more aware that Mary, 'full of grace' through God was redeemed from the moment of her conception."[10] "The Father blessed Mary more than any other created person 'in Christ, with every spiritual blessing in the heavenly places' and chose her 'in Christ before the foundation of the world to be holy and blameless before him in love."[11] This interpretation is emblematic of what is often done in Roman Catholic dogma: taking what is spoken of all Christians, and applying it to a select few. The quotations from Ephesians referenced in the Catechism come in the middle of a declaration by Paul of all the blessings that are the common heritage of every single believer in Christ. To apply what was clearly intended for all Christians as unique to Mary, or truer of her than any other created being, is simply unsupportable by the text.

Two other phrases in the Lucan record receive particular focus in Marian dogma. When Mary visits, Elizabeth exclaims, "Blessed are you among women, and blessed is the fruit of your womb." (Luke 1:42). The word translated here as "blessed" is often used in speaking of God (and in the second part of the verse, no one would question that the blessing pronounced on the fruit of Mary's womb is applicable to Jesus). The word is Εὐλογημένη, from which we get the English word eulogy. "*Blessed* is he who comes in the name of the Lord!" (Matt. 21:9). It is spoken to give thanks to God: "Then he ordered the crowds to sit down on the grass, and taking the five loaves and the two fish, he looked up to heaven and said a *blessing*." (Matt 14:19). It is also used of Christians in general: "So then, those who are of faith are *blessed* along with Abraham, the man of faith"(Gal. 3:9). We are commanded to "*Bless* those who

---

9 *Lumen Gentium*, 56.
10 *Cathechism of the Catholic Church*, 491.
11 Ibid, 492.

persecute you; *bless* and do not curse them" (Rom. 12:14). Is Elizabeth singling out Mary in order to elevate her or exalt her above others? Or is she rather commenting that Mary is magnificently privileged to receive this gift from God, to bear his Son? While it is clear that Mary is set *apart* from others to be the one to give birth to Jesus, it does not follow that she is therefore set *above* all others. To cite this text as investing Mary with a title or claim to blessedness in the sense of intrinsic holiness or exaltation is to misapply it. We would need to accord the same status to Jael, the wife of Heber the Kenite. The fourth chapter of the book of Judges records that she drove a tent peg through the skull of Sisera, who commanded the Canaanite army. Deborah and Barak praise her, saying, "Most blessed of women be Jael, the wife of Heber the Kenite" (Judges 5:24). In the Septuagint version, this adjective is the same Greek word, *eulogeo*, which is spoken by Elizabeth to Mary. No one would suggest that this honor elevates Jael to a level that places her above every other woman; yet if we build a doctrine on a single word, this would be the result.

Elizabeth ends by saying, "And blessed is she that believed; for there shall be a fulfillment of the things which have been spoken to her from the Lord" (Luke 1:45, ASV). Here the word is μακάριος, sometimes translated *happy*, or *fortunate*, as well as *blessed*. It is the word that begins each of the beatitudes, but also the word used when Paul stands before King Agrippa to make his defense and says "I consider myself *fortunate*" (Acts 26:2). Is this second blessing from Elizabeth conferring something extraordinary on Mary, or saying something about her cooperation with the divine plan? Vatican II posits this understanding of her: "Rightly therefore the holy Fathers see her as used by God not merely in a passive way, but as freely cooperating in the work of human salvation through faith and obedience. For, as St. 148 says, she 'being obedient, became the cause of salvation for herself and for the whole human race.'"[12] We should note other situations where divine intervention brought about a miraculous birth, and yet there was a decided lack of faith. Zacharias, the father of John the Baptist, expressed doubt about the promise the angel announced to him. Though Zacharias was disciplined by being mute until after the birth of John, this in no way jeopardized the fulfillment of it. Sarah laughed at the suggestion that she would bear a son, yet this in no way impeded God's promise. God did not need Sarah's cooperation or faith to effect his plan. Similarly, Anglican priest Tim Perry says, "Mary's trust is not the basis of the divine favor; rather, the fulfillment of the promise is the divine favor."[13]

Mary was indeed happy and fortunate to be chosen to bear the Savior, but God's accomplishment of the incarnation was not conditional upon Mary's faith, or her obedience. She provides an example of submission to God, just as many do whose faith is recorded in the Scriptures. Hebrews 11 is a catalog of similar exemplars who trusted in God and were favored and blessed because of it. Evangelicals have reacted against the excesses of Marian devotion, sometimes by denigrating her, or by not appreciating her role in God's plan. This should not be the case. Christians should recognize Mary's faith in trusting in God's plan as announced by the angel. Our esteem for her should be no less, but certainly no more, than what the Scriptures portray.

The second portion of Luke's Gospel record that has received much attention is the Magnificat, where Mary's response to the annunciation is to speak a song of praise to God for his goodness to the nation of Israel and to her. In Luke 1:48, Mary says, "For behold, from now on all generations will call me blessed." Sacramentalists look upon this verse as justification for the particular honor paid to Mary: "Hence after the Synod of Ephesus the cult of the people of God toward Mary wonderfully increased

---

[12] *Lumen Gentium*, 56.

[13] Tim Perry, *Mary for Evangelicals: Toward an Understanding of the Mother of Our Lord* (Downers Grove, Intervarsity Press, 2006), p. 75-76.

in veneration and love, in invocation and imitation, according to her own prophetic words: 'All generations shall call me blessed, because He that is mighty hath done great things to me.'"[14] But is this to be understood as ascribing to her an honor that is unique to her, because she is more worthy or holy than others? David Gustafson points out that the fact that "they would call her blessed wasn't a paying of honor to *her* but an acknowledgement that grace had been shown to her by *God*."[15] Indeed, the hierarchy has at various points of history been forced to reckon with excesses of devotion toward Mary, and to correct these extravagances. *Lumen Gentium* cautions: "But [the Church] exhorts theologians and preachers of the divine word to abstain zealously both from all gross exaggerations as well as from petty narrow-mindedness in considering the singular dignity of the Mother of God. Let them assiduously keep away from whatever, either by word or deed, could lead separated brethren or any other into error regarding the true doctrine of the Church."[16] If the correct place of Mary in Church teaching is so clear, what need is there for such a warning?

When we leave the gospel records, further mention of Mary in the New Testament is sparse indeed. The last reference to her by name is in Acts 1:14: "All these with one accord were devoting themselves to prayer, together with the women and Mary the mother of Jesus, and his brothers." There is no further commentary in the text as to what role she played; it simply notes her presence with the disciples. However, the other fact the verse delineates concerns the brothers of Jesus, which we will investigate further.

The epistles do not reference Mary at all, which raises the question of her importance in the first decades of the church. In Romans 1:3, Paul refers to Jesus as "descended from David,

---

14 *Lumen Gentium*, 66.
15 Dwight Longenecker, David Gustafson, *Mary: A Catholic-Evangelical Debate* (Eastborne, Brazos Press, 2003), p. 170.
16 *Lumen Gentium*, 67.

according to the flesh," but most scholars consider this a commentary on Jesus' humanity, rather than any reference to Mary: "Whether a human birth or an incarnation is meant, the context stresses Jesus' humanity."[17] The reference in Galatians 4:4-5 is the only reference Paul makes to Mary, and even here it is somewhat indirect. "But when the fullness of time had come, God sent forth his Son, born of woman, born under the law, to redeem those who were under the law, so that we might receive adoption as sons." Paul does not refer to Mary by name, simply stating that Jesus was "born of woman." Jaroslav Pelikan notes that "Most New Testament scholars would agree that 'made of a woman' did not mean or even imply 'but not of a man' (although it also did not exclude the idea of the virgin birth), but rather that it was a Semitic expression for 'human being', as in the statement 'Man that is born of woman is of few days and full of trouble.'"[18] Just as in Romans, Paul is making a statement about the full humanity of Jesus, but is not making any claim about Mary. Finally, it is interesting that Paul, who traveled with Luke in his missionary journeys, would have next to nothing to say about Mary. That is, if Luke's Gospel forms such an important part of Marian dogma, the apostle apparently gleaned nothing from the evangelist on this point, for Paul's references to Mary are nearly non-existent.

The other passage which has been interpreted as Marian is Revelation 12:1-6:

And a great sign appeared in heaven: a woman clothed with the sun, with the moon under her feet, and on her head a crown of twelve stars. She was pregnant and was crying out in birth pains and the agony of giving birth. And another sign appeared in heaven: behold, a great red dragon, with seven heads and ten horns, and on his heads seven diadems. His tail swept down a third of the stars of heaven and

---

17 Perry, p. 25.

18 Jaroslav Pelikan, *Mary Through the Centuries: Her Place in the History of Culture* (New York, History Book Club, 2005), p. 14-15.

cast them to the earth. And the dragon stood before the woman who was about to give birth, so that when she bore her child he might devour it. She gave birth to a male child, one who is to rule all the nations with a rod of iron, but her child was caught up to God and to his throne, and the woman fled into the wilderness, where she has a place prepared by God, in which she is to be nourished for 1,260 days.

Does the woman refer to Mary? It is obvious that the male child is Jesus, for he is to rule all the nations with a rod of iron. Mary gave birth to Jesus, so on the face of it this passage seems to refer to her. However, we must recall that the entire Apocalypse is given in signs, and therefore a symbolic meaning for many of the actors in the book is not unusual. Personification is used elsewhere in the book. In Chapter 17, a woman is seen to represent Babylon, and all the evil that opposes God. Robert Mounce comments, "The woman is not Mary the mother of Jesus but the messianic community, the ideal Israel. Zion as the mother of the people of God is a common theme in Jewish writings (Is 54:1; II Esdr. 10:7; cf. Gal 4:26)."[19] Other commentators likewise view this passage as not referring to Mary, but to Israel from whose stock the Christ was born: "We are on more secure ground if we take proper account of the Old Testament representation of the ideal Zion as the mother of God's people."[20]

A collection of Roman Catholic and Lutheran scholars comes to the same conclusion: The primary reference to the woman in Chapter 12 is "to the people of God, Israel and the Church."[21] They hold out the possibility of a secondary reference to Mary, but

---

[19] Robert H. Mounce, *The Book of Revelation* (Grand Rapids, Wm. B. Eerdmans, 1977), p. 236.

[20] Stephen S. Smalley, *The Revelation of John: A Commentary on the Greek Text of the Apocalypse* (Downers Grove, InterVarsity Press, 2005), p. 314.

[21] *Mary in the New Testament*, Raymond E. Brown, Karl P. Donfried, Joseph A Fitzmyer, John Reumann, eds. (Philadelphia, Fortress Press, 1978), p. 235.

list a number of difficulties with this interpretation. Among these are that no such interpretation is known until the fourth century.[22] "The fact that the mariological emphasis on Revelation 12 is relatively recent raises the question of whether it represents an exegesis of the text itself or simply an imaginative theological application as part of a search for biblical support for Marian doctrine."[23]

The Later Witness to Mary

When we search the patristic writers for their views on Mary, the literature is of course extensive, and we will only be able to examine a sampling. Not surprisingly, none of the patristic writers questions the virginal conception of Jesus. To doubt the ante-partem virginity of Mary is to question the witness of Scripture, and the doctrine of the incarnation. Moreover, because the testimony of Scripture is unequivocal on this point, none of the fathers believes other than what the Bible affirms: Mary was a virgin who bore the Son of God because of the activity of the Holy Spirit. However, it is only later that we begin to find suggestions that she remained a virgin in the act of giving birth (*in partu*).

The source of the view that Mary remained a virgin *in partu* comes from the apocryphal *Ascension of Isaiah*. Because of this, Tertullian rejects *in partu* virginity: "He had a good reason for denying this, which, after all, rested only on apochryphal evidence; for it might lend substance to the heretical Gnostic view that Christ had not really taken flesh from the Virgin Mary, but had only 'passed through her.'"[24] Athanasius likewise did not teach the virginity *in partu*, but affirmed, "he who was born opened the

---

[22] Loc. cit.

[23] Ibid, p. 236.

[24] Hilda Graef, *Mary: A History of Doctrine and Devotion* (Notre Dame, Ave Maria Press, 2009), p. 33.

womb."[25] The important point with both Tertullian and Athanasius is that they view *in partu* virginity as allowing for the belief that the humanity of Jesus was not genuine.

While the early evidence for devotion to Mary is scant, it grew intense as the centuries passed. A decisive factor seems to be the growth of monasticism and the view that virginity was a higher spiritual state than married life. Helvedius, a fourth-century theologian, "undertook to defend the equal value of marriage and virginity against the prevailing teaching of the superiority of the latter. For this purpose he wrote a treatise (which has not survived) in which he declared Mary an example of both, of perfect virginity before the birth of Christ and of married love and motherhood afterwards; for according to him the 'brethren of the Lord' were the sons and daughters of Mary and Joseph."[26] Jerome vociferously opposed Helvedius, which demonstrates that views about Mary that were later elevated to dogmatic status were not universally held in the early centuries.

Orthodox theologian Sergius Bulgakov believes that, despite the biblical record, the view that Mary and Joseph had other children is a failure to honor her and her virginity properly. He ascribes this putatively novel view of her to the Reformation. The patristic evidence shows this to be false, but in an example of devotion gone awry, Bulgakov writes, "This failure to be mindful of the Virgin Mary is often found in Protestantism to such extreme beliefs as that the Virgin might have had other children by Joseph."[27] It is bewildering that Bulgakov considers the possibility of a normal marital relationship between Mary and Joseph "extreme." In fact, the New Testament refers to Jesus' brothers and sisters, and early patristic witness confirms this belief as well. Is it

---

[25] Ibid, p. 40.

[26] Ibid, p. 69.

[27] Segius Bulgakov, "The Virgin and the Saints in Orthodoxy," in *Eastern Orthodoxy Theology: A Reader*, Daniel Clendenin, ed. (Grand Rapids, Baker Books, 1995), p. 66.

not rather the extreme position to deny what the New Testament plainly depicts?

Even in earlier centuries, not everyone was comfortable with the growing devotion to Mary. Epiphanius, the bishop of Salamis in the fourth century, writes, "But we must not honor the saints to excess; we must honor their Master. It is time for the error of those who have gone astray to cease. Mary is not God and does not have her body from heaven but by human conception, though, like Isaac, she was provided by promise. And no one should make offerings in her name, for he is destroying his own soul."[28] The same dangers that Epiphanius highlighted are still with us today.

Former evangelical Jon M. Sweeney says, "Her roles and her names are similar to that and those of the Holy Spirit. In fact, in many ways, Mary is for devout Catholics what the Holy Spirit is for the devout Protestant."[29] Indeed she is, and Sweeney has perhaps unwittingly demonstrated a prime danger of sacramentalism: that of putting something or someone in the place that belongs solely to God. Without question, within sacramentalism Mary is elevated to a place that the Bible knows nothing of. To compare her with the Holy Spirit is dangerous indeed. The sacramental system has given her a position that is entirely unsupportable by Scripture; including a unique role in mediating grace in the life of the faithful. But though they refer to her as "mediatrix of all graces," this rests on no biblical evidence whatsoever. The accretions of the centuries and the excessive devotion of various mystics form the core of Marian dogma, rather than any explicit (or even implicit) teaching of scripture.

Just as when experience and mystery are unduly elevated (and scripture is thereby denigrated), by ascribing the qualities they do to Mary, sacramentalists at the same time say things about Jesus

---

[28] Epiphanius of Salamis, *The Panarion, Books II and III, De Fide*, trans. Frank Williams, 2nd edition (Leiden; Boston, Brill, 2013), p. 635-636.
[29] Jon M. Sweeney, *Strange Heaven: The Virgin Mary as Woman, Mother, Disciple, and Advocate* (Brewster, MA, Paraclete Press, 2006), p. 99.

and his work that are untrue, and ultimately denigrating to him. Aelred of Rievaulx, writing in the twelfth century, says, "as his queen she averts his wrath 'so that she herself has often placed back into its sheath his naked sword, which was at that very moment raging against mankind.'"[30] It is a common theme in medieval theology that Jesus is wrathful and full of vengeance toward mankind, and that only by the agency of Mary may he be appeased. Later theologians and mystics seem almost to try to outdo one another in this aspect of their devotion to Mary. Louie-Marie Grignion de Montfort (d. 1716) in his treatise *True Devotion to the Blessed Virgin* goes to great lengths in urging consecration to Mary: "Our good works are more capable of converting sinners and of comforting souls in purgatory if they pass through Mary's hands than if they do not. For if we offer Jesus anything by ourselves he will examine the offering and frequently reject it because it is stained by self-love, whereas, if we present our works through Mary 'we take him by his weak side' and so he does not consider the gift so much as the Mother who presents it."[31] Montfort goes on to say, "Moreover, we should never dare to approach Christ on our own, however sweet and merciful he may be, but always avail ourselves of the intercession of our blessed Lady."[32]

It is not only in medieval theologians where such devotion to Mary is found. In contemporary sacramentalism, the cult of Mary has only grown. John Paul II promulgated the papal encyclical *Redemptoris Mater* in 1987, in which he puts Mary in the place of intercessor. "Mary places herself between her Son and mankind in the reality of their wants, needs and sufferings. She puts herself 'in the middle,' that is to say she acts as a mediatrix not as an outsider, but in her position as mother. She knows that as such she can point out to her Son the needs of mankind, and in fact, she

---

[30] Graef, p. 195-196.

[31] Ibid, Loc. Cit.

[32] Ibid, p. 323.

'has the right' to do so."[33] One wonders at the suggestion that Jesus, who is God, needs anyone to point out the needs of mankind to him. Any believer should recognize this as aberrant theology.

Anyone familiar with Scripture at once notices the picture of Jesus these citations paint is a caricature of the Son of God. The Bible presents him as our faithful and merciful high priest, and urges us to draw near. Paul affirms that Jesus "loved me and gave himself for me" (Gal. 2:20). We draw near to Jesus because his death and resurrection have already provided everything for our salvation. Paul states it emphatically at the start of Romans 5: "Therefore, since we *have been justified* by faith, *we have peace* with God through our Lord Jesus Christ. *Through him* we have also obtained access by faith into this grace in which we stand, and we rejoice in hope of the glory of God." These are present realities, not aspirations. Peace with God is not something we strive for, but something we now enjoy as the birthright of being in God's family. 1 John states that our advocate before the father is Jesus (1 John 2:1), and Paul writes to Timothy that there is one mediator between God and man, the man Christ Jesus (1 Tim. 2:5). Mary is never contemplated in the New Testament in any role of mediation whatsoever. An evangelical who embraces sacramentalism embraces these views of Mary as another mediator at the same time. Putting her in this position is wholly without foundation in Scripture, and redirects one's attention away from Christ and his work. Is this where God would lead believers?

The Communion of the Saints

In some Protestant churches, the Apostles' Creed is still recited, and one phrase within it states, "I believe in the communion of the saints." If one were to ask Protestants what this signifies, a likely

---

[33] *Redemptoris Mater*, 21.

answer would be that all Christians are one and that we enjoy a common fellowship with Jesus and with one another. Yet for the sacramental traditions, particularly the Roman Catholic Church, the communion of the saints has a very different meaning. It is not simply the idea of fellowship, but of *transfer*. The Catechism states, "Therefore, the riches of Christ are communicated to all the members, through the sacraments. As this Church is governed by one and the same Spirit, all the goods she has received necessarily become a common fund."[34] McBrien comments on those who have died, saying, "Such persons intercede for those of us on earth and place their merits at our disposal."[35]

Ott expands upon this, saying, "The Faithful on earth, can, by their good works performed in the state of grace, render atonement for one another. The effect of the atonement is the remission of temporal punishment for sin. The possibility of vicarious atonement is founded in the unity of the Mystical Body. As Christ, the Head, in His expiatory sufferings, took the place of the members, so also one member can take the place of another."[36] What Ott says is staggering. A host of theological questions come with this assertion; chief among them is why, if Jesus has died for our sins, is any punishment at all left for the believer? Evangelicals who embrace Catholicism should consider the implications this has to the doctrine of the atonement. The death of Christ cannot but be insufficient if there is something more to be paid, some further punishment for sins. Moreover, if the merits of one Christian can be applied to another, is salvation any more by grace? Ott's matter-of-fact suggestion that, just as Jesus was our substitute, so can one person take the place of another is profoundly misguided, to say the least. He apparently puts no

---

[34] *Catechism of the Catholic Church*, p. 269.

[35] Richard P. McBrien, *Catholicism* (San Francisco, HarperSanFrancisco, 1994), p. 1127.

[36] Ludwig Ott, Patrick Lynch, trans., James Bastible, ed., *Fundamentals of Catholic Dogma* (Rockford, IL, Tan Books and Publishers, 1955), p 317.

importance on Jesus being sinless and having no sin of his own to atone for. This is what makes him the perfect Lamb of God. Other sinners are just that – imperfect and sinful humans who cannot effect their own pardon, much less that of another person. Such an exchange of one sinner for another as Ott suggests is simply not possible according to the gospel. The guilt and sin of each one of us demands a perfect Savior to atone for us, and no one but Jesus is fit for this. It is clear that Ott both misunderstands the nature of sin, as well as the person of the Savior, if he believes the Scriptures teach vicarious atonement by anyone other than Christ alone.

Colossians 1:24 is sometimes cited as proof of the vicarious atonement of one individual by another. Paul writes there, "Now I rejoice in my sufferings for your sake, and in my flesh I am filling up what is lacking in Christ's afflictions for the sake of his body, that is, the church." A full exposition of this passage would require many pages, but a few things can be said. First, we must ask whether Paul is implying that there is something inadequate in the death of Christ, or that his atonement is somehow deficient? To suggest this is to impugn his purpose in coming to earth, and in becoming incarnate, for the Scriptures clearly portray the death of Christ as the central reason for the incarnation. The writer of Hebrews, contrasting the sacrifices of the old covenant with the one sacrifice of Jesus, says, "We have been sanctified through the offering of the body of Jesus Christ once for all" (Heb. 10:10). The finality and sufficiency of Jesus' death for our sins is clear.

Peter T. O'Brien dismisses the idea of any lack in Jesus' death as inconsistent with the rest of the New Testament. "Paul, like other NT writers, regarded the death of Jesus as the means by which reconciliation was truly and uniquely accomplished. To go no further than Colossians itself Paul states that because of Christ's death on the cross all our trespasses have been forgiven (2:13, 14; 1:12-14, 19-22).[37] In addition to this, it has been pointed out by

---

[37] Col 2:13: "And you, who were dead in your trespasses and the uncircumcision of your flesh, God made alive together with him, having

Staab, Schweizer and others that nowhere else in the NT is the phrase 'Christ's afflictions' used of his redemptive act or general experience of suffering. Instead, Paul uses the concepts 'blood', 'cross', and 'death' to refer to that act of redemption."[38]

Secondly, the sufferings Paul describes in Colossians 1 are said to be "for the sake of his body, that is, the church." To the Corinthians, he writes "Now you are the body of Christ and individually members of it" (1 Cor. 12:27). In other words, what Paul has in view in Colossians is corporate, rather than individual. In his apostolic position, Paul suffered for the furtherance of the gospel. As a chosen vessel, he was appointed to suffer many things for the building up of the church. These became part of his apostolic resume. "For as we share abundantly in Christ's sufferings, so through Christ we share abundantly in comfort too. If we are afflicted, it is for your comfort and salvation; and if we are comforted, it is for your comfort, which you experience when you patiently endure the same sufferings that we suffer. Our hope for you is unshaken, for we know that as you share in our sufferings, you will also share in our comfort" (2 Cor. 1:5-8). Similarly, he tells the Corinthians that they too will suffer in the name of Jesus. These sufferings refine and mature believers, but they are not

---

forgiven us all our trespasses, by canceling the record of debt that stood against us with its legal demands. This he set aside, nailing it to the cross." Col. 1:12-14: "Giving thanks to the Father, who has qualified you to share in the inheritance of the saints in light. He has delivered us from the domain of darkness and transferred us to the kingdom of his beloved Son, in whom we have redemption, the forgiveness of sins." Col. 1:19-22: "For in him all the fullness of God was pleased to dwell, and through him to reconcile to himself all things, whether on earth or in heaven, making peace by the blood of his cross. And you, who once were alienated and hostile in mind, doing evil deeds, he has now reconciled in his body of flesh by his death, in order to present you holy and blameless and above reproach before him."
[38] Peter T. O'Brien, *Word Biblical Commentary: Colossians and Philemon* (Waco, Word Books, 1982), p. 77.

atoning. Nothing in what Paul says to the Corinthians or the Colossians implies these sufferings are for the forgiveness of sin, or the lessening of any punishment, either for himself or other Christians. Indeed, for the Christian, the essence of the gospel is that there remains no punishment for sin because this is what Jesus took upon himself when he died.

Peter also takes up this idea of suffering: "Beloved, do not be surprised at the fiery trial when it comes upon you to test you, as though something strange were happening to you. But rejoice insofar as you share Christ's sufferings, that you may also rejoice and be glad when his glory is revealed. If you are insulted for the name of Christ, you are blessed, because the Spirit of glory" (1 Peter 4:12-14). Hendriksen develops the theme of the Christian now suffering because of being identified with Jesus, saying, "It is in that sense that all true believers are in his stead supplying what, as the enemies see it, is lacking in the afflictions which Jesus endured. Christ's afflictions overflow toward us. Here, too, there is no thought of forgiveness of sins in this suffering. This interpretation is supported by passages such as the following: 'If they called the master of the house Beelzebub, how much more them of his household (Matt. 10:25).' 'You shall be hated of all men for my name's sake (Mark 13:13).'"[39]

Finally, Paul speaks of his desire to be more conformed to Jesus' sufferings. "That I may know Him and the power of His resurrection, and the fellowship of His sufferings, being conformed to His death" (Phil. 3:10 NKJV). The apostle does not think he has arrived. He knows that there is always more room for growth in Christ.

Nothing in Colossians 1:24 hints at anything like the vicarious atonement that sacramentalism claims is here. Jesus, the unique mediator, the one Savior, took our place because he was the spotless and sinless Lamb of God. For a sinful individual to

---

[39] William Hendriksen, *New Testament Commentary: Exposition of Colossians and Philemon* (Grand Rapids, Baker Book House, 1964), p. 87.

provide atonement for another human is utterly foreign, not only to the biblical record, but to the entire ground of the gospel.

The idea of a great spiritual bank account of grace, upon which a believer may draw, is a concept that damages the gospel. It puts the entire basis of salvation on something other than Jesus and his death. It shifts the focus to works, and claims that what we do or will do will provide atonement. It affords one of the clearest examples of the sacramental principle: turning the grace of God into a commodity to be traded, something apart from the person of Christ. In between the believer and this grace stands the Church, to mete out the merits that will reduce one's debt. To embrace this view is to redefine the gospel itself. This doctrine rests solely on the later developments of history and the fiat of the church, but where there is no foundation in scripture, and where the core tenets of the gospel are compromised, evangelicals must clearly recognize that this, too, is part of crossing the Tiber.

Summary

Converts abandon the biblical definition of Jesus as the one mediator, along with the confidence we now have through the new birth, and exchange this for another definition of how a believer approaches God. The New Testament presents a consistent exhortation that a Christian's focus should be on Christ alone, on his death and resurrection as completed, and that this is the entire basis for our peace and justification.

When Mary, the saints, or anything else is brought in, they become, as D.A. Carson says, diverting and distracting. Converts give up all of these truths, and substitute for them something else, something that cannot but be inferior, because it is not found in the New Testament. When these distinctly biblical truths are set aside for sacramentalism, it is a statement that what God has provided in Christ is not enough, that the way of approach to him is lesser to what the church in subsequent ages has defined, and that the Bible itself is insufficient. Without question many evangelical churches do not preach these settled truths of justification in Christ and sanctification in him forcefully enough. Many have lapsed into moralistic guidance only, or topical preaching about steps to a fuller life. But the biblical prescription for growth in Christ is to meditate on the person and work of Christ; what he has done, what he is now doing as our great high priest, and the hope of his return. To avail oneself of the mediation of Mary and the saints as if this will somehow get one more of Christ removes the believer from gospel ground. As with every aspect of the Christian life, the guidance for the way forward, the correction for our mistakes, and conformity to Jesus, are all found through the application of the Scriptures, which always direct us back to Christ.

9

Schism and Unity

Converts from evangelicalism to sacramentalism have very often noted that they no longer want to be associated with the perceived sectarianism of the evangelical movement. They say that the repeated schisms, splits, and new denominations are a mockery of the one body of Christ. In this view, Protestant opposition to the hierarchical Church, the church that was putatively the only one in the beginning, defines the movement. Convert Stephen K. Ray ascribes to Luther the innovation of *sola scriptura* and *sola fide*, saying these two "were developed as a result of his scrupulosity and out of his reaction to the Catholic Church, thus the name Protestant ('protest-ant', or 'one who protests')."[1] Without doubt Luther found much in the Catholic Church of his day to decry, but Ray is repeating an incorrect etymology of the word Protestant. As Fred Sanders has written, the word is derived from "pro + testari, to testify forth, or to hold forth a position on something. Its primary historical meaning has been to assert, to maintain, to proclaim solemnly or state formally."[2] And indeed the positions Luther and the Reformers proclaimed were that the church is subject to Scripture, and that the believer is justified by faith. These are positive positions, not negative ones. That they were novelties of Luther's time is a construction of history. To the degree that sacramentalism says no to these, its proponents are themselves protesting.

While division in the body of Christ is an evil, the sacramental assumption that no real schisms came about until the Reformation

---

[1] Stephen K. Ray, *Crossing the Tiber* (San Francisco, Ignatius Press, 1997), p. 23.

[2] Fred Sanders, "Protestants, not Protesters", http://www.patheos.com/blogs/scriptorium/2011/04/ protestants-not-protesters/, April 19, 2011.

is false. If we leave aside heresies such as Arianism, Gnosticism, Marcionism, and all the other heterodox teachings that by their very nature meant adherents to these things were outside the sphere of true doctrine, we are still left with the reality of other disagreements, sometimes sharp, that divided the church. These controversies often resulted in the severing of fellowship and the censure of one bishop by another. Examples include the Quartodeciman controversy (concerning the proper date of the Easter celebration), the Acacian schism, the Meletian schism, the Donatist schism, and the one that endures to this day, the Great Schism between Orthodoxy and Roman Catholicism. All of these fissures occurred well before the Protestant Reformation. It is spurious to claim that there were no serious schisms prior to this. The second false assumption is that the Roman Catholic Church of today is in fact uniform and does not display the rifts and divisions that are seen in other traditions.

The history we have examined thus far shows that divisions and schisms divided Christians from the beginning. Historian Robert Louis Wilken has written, "It is tempting to romanticize the early Church and imagine a golden age of peace and harmony. In truth there never was a time, even in the first decades, that Christians had no differences. Because Christian faith holds that certain things are true (there is one God, creator of all that exists), controversy over what is to be believed as well as how the faith was to be practiced was present from the beginning."[3] The importance of this is that if we view division and separation as belonging to the relatively recent past, we are apt to believe in the golden age that Wilken says is a fiction. It was as often diversity of practice as it was diversity of doctrine that led to separation between Christians, but schism has a history much longer than the Reformation. So, too, does the labeling of one's opponents as schismatics or heretics with a view towards tarnishing their name.

---

[3] Robert Louis Wilken, *The First Thousand Years: A Global History of Christianity* (New Haven, Yale University Press, 2012), p. 37.

Veiled Schism, Veiled Unity

Sacramental ecclesiology insists on the nature of the church as a visible community, but whether those who are part of this church are in fact Christians is another matter. A key to understanding this view of unity is that sacramentalism has equated Christendom with the church. All who are baptized are part of the Church, whether they have any faith or not. Yet this, as we have seen, was a later understanding of the Church, and therefore an innovation of history. In contrast to this, evangelicalism and Protestantism have held to a view of the church where unity is not based on baptism into the visible communion, let alone outward fealty to the pope or to the magisterium. Unity is due to the fact that we all belong to Christ; we are all members of his body. Membership in the body, the church, is through personal faith in Christ, not through any rite or sacrament. The testimony of Scripture is unequivocal on this: "Whoever believes in him is not condemned, but whoever does not believe is condemned already, because he has not believed in the name of the only Son of God" (John 3:18). Paul calls the gospel "the power of God for salvation to everyone who believes" (Rom. 1:16). To the Ephesians, he writes "in him [Christ] you also, when you heard the word of the truth, the gospel of your salvation, and believed in him, were sealed with the promised Holy Spirit" (Eph. 1:13).

It is, of course, never contemplated that a believer can be in Christ, and yet not in the Church, or that one can be in Christ, and yet not have the Holy Spirit. These are spiritual impossibilities. "Anyone who does not have the Spirit of Christ does not belong to him" (Rom. 8:9). That is to say, he is not a Christian. The Spirit himself puts us into the body – this is the unity of the Spirit we are called upon to keep. Does the maintenance of that unity take the external visible form that sacramentalism insists it must? If we say that it does, then everyone must also confess that it is decidedly not there. The accommodations made by Vatican II toward non-Catholics create more difficulties for the necessity of visible unity. It acknowledges that there are those of other "ecclesial communions" in whom the life of Christ is manifest. They are in Christ, and yet not part of the Roman Catholic Church, a thing that earlier was said to be impossible. Indeed, earlier popes considered this idea unthinkable.[4] *Unitatis Redintigratio* tries to walk a fine line in presenting a Catholic justification for the undeniable fact of Christians outside the Catholic Church.

For men who believe in Christ and have been truly baptized are in communion with the Catholic Church even though this communion is imperfect. The differences that exist in varying degrees between them and the Catholic Church — whether in doctrine and sometimes in discipline, or concerning the structure of the Church — do indeed create many obstacles, sometimes serious ones, to full ecclesiastical communion. The ecumenical movement is striving to overcome these obstacles. But even in spite of them it remains true that all who have been justified by faith in Baptism are members of Christ's body, and have a right to be called Christian, and so are correctly accepted as brothers by the children of the Catholic Church.[5]

In other words, it is no longer tenable to hold that only those inside the Catholic Church are Christians. Those formerly known as heretics were now given the moniker of "separated brethren." The solution was to consider these believers in some imperfect fashion in communion with the Catholic Church. Some evangelicals would disagree on just how much communion there may be, as they cannot affirm much of what is taught by the sacramental Church. Evangelicals, and indeed all Christians, are in

---

[4] Boniface VIII, for example, in his 1302 bull *Unam Sanctum*, declared that "it is altogether necessary to salvation of every human creature to be subject to the Roman pontiff."
[5] *Unitatis Redintegratio*, 3.

communion with those who are in Christ though faith. This includes Catholics and Orthodox, not because of their denominational association, but because if they have been born again, they share a common life in Christ. It is not what we know that unites us, but whom we know. It is notable that the *Unitatis Redintigratio* seems to adopt Protestant language of "justification by faith" – but faith only as it is joined to baptism, rather than faith in Christ's death on their behalf. The Orthodox have not felt the need to be as ecumenically sensitive to those outside their communion. Daniel Clendenin writes, "Whether a non-Orthodox person can even be saved is an open question in Orthodox ecclesiology. Over coffee one day I asked an Orthodox priest whether I, as a protestant theologian, might be considered a true Christian. His response: 'I don't know.'"[6]

Between Catholics and Protestants, there has certainly been a re-examination of the positions that separate these traditions, to an extent that contradicts previous Catholic positions. The warnings of *Mortalium Animos*, the 1928 papal encyclical of Pius XI against the dangers of ecumenism, sound sectarian in the post-Vatican II era. The encyclical notes that ecumenical efforts rest falsely on "a hope that the nations, although they differ among themselves in certain religious matters, will without much difficulty come to agree as brethren in professing certain doctrines, which form as it were a common basis of the spiritual life."[7] But the Vatican was in no way encouraging of any form of ecumenism that did not mean a full return to the Roman Catholic Church: "It is clear that the Apostolic See cannot on any terms take part in their assemblies, nor is it anyway lawful for Catholics either to support or to work for such enterprises; for if they do so they will be giving countenance to a false Christianity, quite alien to the one Church of Christ. Shall We suffer, what would indeed be iniquitous, the

---

[6] Daniel Clendenin, "Why I'm Not Orthodox", *Christianity Today*, January 6, 1997.

[7] *Mortalium Animos*, p. 2.

truth, and a truth divinely revealed, to be made a subject for compromise?"[8]

The call to joint action against a secularized culture was also a cause of bringing evangelicals and Catholics together. The 1994 manifesto *Evangelicals and Catholics Together: The Christian Mission in the Third Millennium* was a highly publicized product of this call. Evangelical Charles Colson, the founder of Prison Fellowship, and Roman Catholic priest (and former Lutheran) Richard John Neuhaus, spearheaded this effort. "It became evident that Christian engagement in the great cultural, social, and political tasks of our time would be largely futile, even counter-productive, unless that engagement was grounded in shared spiritual commitment and gospel truth."[9] The signatories of the document, aside from Colson and Neuhaus, included several luminaries within evangelicalism, such as Bill Bright, founder of Campus Crusade for Christ, J.I. Packer, historian Mark Noll, and Pentecostal Pat Robertson. Among those on the Catholic side, Avery Dulles, Jr., John Cardinal O'Connor, and George Weigel signed on. The document was not uniformly praised. Several prominent evangelical theologians, including John MacArthur and R.C. Sproul, preached or published rebuttals that critiqued ECT as a compromise of the gospel.[10] In view of the fundamental problems with the sacraments that I have discussed in previous chapters, I believe this assessment is correct. Evangelicals who may agree with Catholics on the battles of the culture war should not confuse this unity with doctrinal unity.

Converts to the view of the hierarchical church, whether that headquartered in Rome, or that of the Orthodox, who have a more loosely defined hierarchy but insist that theirs is the only true

---

[8] *Mortalium Animos*, p. 10.

[9] Charles Colson, Richard John Neuhaus, eds., *Evangelicals and Catholics Together: Toward a Common Mission* (Dallas, Word, 1995), p. x.

[10] See, for example, R.C. Sproul, *Faith Alone: The Evangelical Doctrine of Justification* (Grand Rapids, Baker Book House, 1999).

church, are adopting a very different view of unity than one based on life in Christ, a view that is fanciful. Those who draw a circle around themselves state that anyone who is interested in the unity of the Church *must* come over to their side. In this way alone can unity be achieved. Ironically, this is the most sectarian of stances to assume. It is denominationalism, and it is a bit ridiculous to plead that, "We are not a denomination. All other communions are, but we are not. We are the true Church." Any communion that claims the mantle of the "one true Church" makes itself into one large denomination. As I noted earlier, it is very frequently converts from evangelicalism who assume this sectarianism. Scott Hahn reports that when he was investigating Catholicism he encountered priests who in fact discouraged him from converting. Rather, they told him he could be of more help by just staying put as a Presbyterian.[11]

In contrast to the various communions of Protestantism and evangelicalism, the hierarchical church pleads that it is unified. The single voice of the Church in Catholicism is often cited as this unifying factor, or that all Catholics are in communion with the bishop of Rome. This is the stance Brad Gregory takes when he writes, "In sharp contrast to the Catholic magisterium, there are no shared criteria, authorities, institutions, or mechanisms that can resolve Protestant exegetical, doctrinal, or moral disagreements."[12] The claim is in fact a hollow one. The Catholic Church may have a magisterium that teaches, and which provides official dogmatic positions, but does it effect unity? Polls of Catholics done over the last ten years indicate that there is a high degree of private interpretation among Catholic faithful, and the official church teaching often does not carry much weight. A 2005 Gallup poll of

---

11 Scott and Kimberly Hahn, *Rome Sweet Home: Our Journey to Catholicism* (San Francisco, Ignatius Press, 1993), p. 66.
12 Brad S. Gregory, "A Response to Evangelicalism" in *Journeys of Faith, Evangelicalism, Eastern Orthodoxy, Catholicism, and Anglicanism*, Robert L. Plummer, ed. (Grand Rapids, Zondervan, 2012), p. 177.

Catholics found only 41.9% of respondents agreed that the teachings of the Vatican are very important. Some 42% disagreed that Catholicism contains a greater share of truth than other religions. When asked who should have the final say as to a divorced Catholic remarrying without getting an annulment, 41.8% replied that this should be up to the individual, rather than church leaders. And 22.5% said that a person can be a good Catholic without believing that Jesus rose from the dead.[13]

In February 2008, the Center for Applied Research in the Apostolate at Georgetown University conducted a survey of US Catholics to ask them about all aspects of their faith.[14] About six in ten Catholics (57%) agree that Jesus Christ is really present in the bread and wine of the Eucharist. The remaining 43% said the bread and wine are symbols of Jesus, but that he is not truly present. For something so important to the doctrine of the Eucharist, the fact that just over 4 in 10 do not believe what the Church teaches is rather surprising. A more recent poll of over 12,000 Catholics on five continents found similar disagreement with the official positions of the Church.[15] 45% said women should be allowed to become priests. A vast majority, 78%, supports the use of contraception. Given these numbers, it is rather absurd to claim, as Peter Kreeft does, "There is no such thing as a 'cafeteria Catholic.' Catholics do not pick and choose among the church's doctrines and laws; we receive them gratefully from God, we 'eat all the food Mother puts on our plate.'"[16] If Kreeft means to suggest that Catholics *should* accept everything the Church

---

[13] Gallup Poll of Catholics,

http://www.thearda.com/Archive/Files/Codebooks/GALLUP05_CB.asp.

[14] Sacraments Today: Belief and Practice Among US Catholics,

http://cara.georgetown.edu/sacraments.html.

[15] La Voz Del Pueblo,

http://www.univision.com/interactivos/openpage/2014-02-06/la-voz-del-pueblo-matriz-1.

[16] Peter Kreeft, *Catholic Christianity* (San Francisco, Ignatius Press, 2001), p. 105.

teaches, no doubt that is an ideal that the hierarchy strives for. If his position is that only those who do so are in fact Catholics at all, then he summarily cuts the number of true Catholics by a massive amount, and likely holds a view that many priests and bishops do not.

These poll results show that Catholics *do* pick and choose what they want to believe. They are every bit as private in their interpretation as Protestants. Thomas Bergler summarizes, "It seems that most Catholics still believe some important church teachings, but they consider themselves empowered to determine which teachings are central and which can be ignored."[17] Thus there is not much common agreement among those who identify as Roman Catholics of what is important to their faith, or even who should decide what is important. There may be *de jure* unity in the Church, but there is *de facto* schism. In this regard, the Roman Catholic Church shows no difference whatsoever from theologically diverse positions of some evangelicals and Protestants. The difference comes from being perfectly comfortable – and able – to remain within the Catholic Church while believing things the hierarchy says one cannot believe and remain a good Catholic. The situation is one where the Catholic Church has plenty of schism, but it is not immediately visible unless the veneer is peeled back. Similarly, within evangelicalism, it appears there is faction and division, but there is a unity around the gospel that may not be immediately visible.

It is not just within Western Christianity that we see a struggle over unity, but in the Catholic relationship with Orthodoxy. Part of this is because, as Frederica Mathews-Greene writes, there is simply no agreement on what unity means. "From a Roman Catholic perspective, unity is created by the institution of the Church. Within that unity there can be diversity; not everyone agrees with official teaching, some very loudly. But from an

---

17 Thomas Bergler, *The Juvenalization of American Christianity* (Grand Rapids, Eerdmans, 2012), p. 221.

Orthodox perspective, unity is created by believing the same things. It's like the unity among vegetarians or Red Sox fans. You don't need a big bureaucracy to keep them faithful."[18] Mathews-Greene goes on to cite a few examples of the theological and doctrinal development that occurred in the West that the Orthodox Church cannot assent to. In short, the West changed the faith of the early church, and that is why there isn't unity. "Catholic diversity makes it easy for Catholics to embrace us: When they look at us, they see the early church. We fit right in. But when the Orthodox look at Catholics, we see an extra thousand years of theological development, plus rebellion in the pews."[19]

Mathews-Greene is correct in that within contemporary Orthodoxy, there may be more unity of doctrine than Catholicism displays within its ranks. (And while Orthodoxy was completely bypassed by the Reformation, it is interesting to note that in recent years, there is a nascent Reform movement within Orthodoxy).[20] Yet the connection with history is where Orthodoxy manifests schism. Some of the traditions of Orthodoxy may be old, but they are not the oldest. The veneration of icons, the form of their liturgy, these things date from late antiquity. If these things were unknown to the apostolic church, and cannot be found in Scripture, how is it that the Orthodox are unified with the church the apostles left us? Ironically, it is this same principle that prevents evangelicals from uniting with Orthodoxy. When evangelicals look at Orthodoxy, they see the Church of late

---

[18] Frederica Mathews-Greene, "Orthodox-Catholic Unity?", *The Wall Street Journal*, July 15, 2005.

[19] Ibid.

[20] The Ukranian Reformed Orthodox Church is one such case. It allows marriage among bishops and archbishops, something "unreformed" Orthodoxy does not allow. This is not to suggest that these churches are becoming wholly evangelical, but the break with certain traditions is indeed a fact in these communions.

antiquity, with all manner of theological barnacles adhering to it, rather than the early church. Unity is indeed found in believing the same things, but the things that belong to the biblical record, not to the developments of later ages. The theological detritus of Orthodoxy: icons, liturgical innovation, Marian devotion, and in many cases, the ethnic and national influences which have shaped it, make it impossible to find in Orthodoxy the Christianity of the New Testament.

How is Unity Defined?

It is plain from the history we've examined that what is meant by unity among Christians varies between sacramentalism and evangelicalism. With these definitions come questions of what is realistic, and whether we will see unity among Christians. The answer in large part is predicated on how unity is defined. If it is cast in the narrower sense of submission to the Roman Pontiff, as the Catholic Church has insisted for a very long time, then it is doubtful unity can be achieved. That kind of unity certainly does not now exist. If we insist on a definition of unity that includes a hierarchical structure, an episcopal organizational chart in which all who name the name of Jesus must take their place, this presents great difficulties. If we maintain that this form of the church is what Jesus founded, and what he meant when he prayed in his high priestly prayer "that they may all be one," then we are we are forced to ask in what way this has at all succeeded? All who name the name of Christ are *not* now united in this way, and the prospect of this happening is exceedingly dim. To insist that this alone is the unity that Jesus meant is to likewise say that his prayer has not been answered, and that unity has failed. Perhaps it was partially these facts of history at work when Vatican II sought to move more toward a position of invisible unity, adopting the Protestant view that all who know Christ are spiritually united.

The Orthodox Church has been far more binary in its views on the basis of unity. To adopt the Orthodox faith, and subscribe to the dogmas defined by the seven ecumenical councils, this is the ground of unity among believers. Here, too, the prospect of this happening for all who now profess the name of Christ is quite remote. The difference between Catholicism and Orthodoxy here is that the Orthodox have never been too bothered about ecumenism or that other believers are in practice divided from them. Oddly enough, Orthodoxy and evangelicalism may find an agreement in principle, if not in facts. Alexander Schmemann wrote of the Orthodox position with regard to efforts around ecumenical dialogue, saying, "the only adequate ecumenical method from the Orthodox point of view was that of a total and direct doctrinal confrontation, with, as its inescapable and logical conclusion, the acceptance of truth and the rejection of error. Throughout its history Orthodoxy knew only those two categories: the right belief (orthodoxy) and the heresy, without any possibility of compromise between them."[21]

What Father Schmemann articulates is that the starting point for unity is doctrinal. Ecumenism is the *result* of agreement on what is true. Quite often, efforts at unity have focused on a least common denominator, as those who argue for adherence to the "Great Tradition," as well as signatories of *Evangelicals and Catholics Together*, have posited. It is usually an argument from the perspective of practicality – how we can accomplish something, socially or politically – that is behind this. This is the same animating principle behind the Emergent church that I briefly looked at in Chapter 1. In other words, ecumenism is important because one of the problems our division causes is to make us less relevant to the culture around us. Evangelicals would agree with Father Schmemann that truth is of paramount importance, even as

---

[21] Alexander Schmemann, "Moment of Truth for Orthodoxy," in *Eastern Orthodox Theology: A Contemporary Reader*, Daniel Clendenin, ed. (Grand Rapids, Baker, 1995), p. 206-207.

they disagree on what that truth is and where it is found. Moreover, it is fair to ask whether these efforts at aligning everyone to the Great Tradition result in robust doctrinal integrity. Do those of the sacramental traditions have a greater commitment to the gospel of grace?

The other point Father Schmemann highlights is the tangible division in the value of unity itself. For people such as those who signed *Evangelicals and Catholics Together*, or for academics whose vocation is the study of theology, ecumenism tends to be a goal in itself. Nibbling at the edges of what divides us, or in other cases, putting out more substantive agreements, gets attention in periodicals such as *Christianity Today*, or *First Things*, but one wonders how far beyond these isolated environs these efforts carry. In the pews, the attitude is quite different, that is if ecumenism is even thought about. For those who do think about these things, anti-evangelicalism can sometimes be the posture of converts from evangelicalism to Rome, just as some former Catholics display palpable animus toward the Church they feel misled them. For both groups, their apprehension of truth is of first importance, and ecumenism takes second place to that.

Converts who proclaim they are making a statement of unity when they join a church with a hierarchical ecclesiology are at best naïve in this assumption. The announcement of Swedish Pentecostal pastor Ulf Elkman and his wife of their conversion to Catholicism is an example of this naïveté. (The Elkmans fit squarely into the McKnight paradigm of evangelical convert to Roman Catholicism we saw in Chapter 1.)

Elkman comments on the question of organizational unity and says,

This goes back to ecclesiology, to which view on the church you have...the church is the body of Christ, a structural unity. It's concrete; it's clearly defined; it's tangible. It isn't a cloud of gas but has both an outside and an inside, body and Spirit. And the body is visible. Jesus walked around for 30 years and was visible. In the same way, the church must have a concrete expression. And how was it in the beginning? We charismatics love to say we're going back to the Christianity of the book of Acts. And at that time, there was only one church...All Christians like unity, but we mean so many different things by it... It's great to have a good relation with people in other denominations, to surmount differences and stop bickering. And even if you can't agree, you can still have a conciliatory and objective attitude toward each other. This is a good and necessary effort—but it's not enough.[22]

The irony is that, in taking the step they have, the Elkmans are now in schism with all those who do not subscribe to the structural and tangible unity that they assert finds expression only in the Roman Catholic Church – schism not by evangelical definition, but by the definition of unity the Elkmans have now accepted. Their conversion is an adoption of an ecclesiology that says that unless we have visible unity there is not unity, that there must be one ecclesiastical communion which alone is the true body, and significantly, that *they can discern* which it is. They do so of course as individuals who have been convinced in their own minds. History has shown the folly of the claim that any particular hierarchical church is the only true expression of the body of Christ. Though both Catholicism and Orthodoxy make this claim, they may both be wrong, but they cannot both be right.

If we define unity not as submission to a hierarchy, or to membership in a particular group, but rather as embracing all who belong to Christ, we find a more biblical – and realistic – definition of unity. As Joe Rigney says, "Ephesians 4 tells us that Christian unity is something that we ought to maintain (4:3) and something that we ought to attain (4:13). It is both a given and a goal, something we possess and must protect, and something we

[22] Lukas Berggren, "Ulf Ekman Says Prophetic Word Confirmed His Catholic Conversion," *Charisma News*, March 14, 2014.

lack and must pursue."[23] By focusing almost exclusively on our failure to fully express unity, sacramentalism diminishes the unity that Jesus has already accomplished for the church. As it does with justification, sacramental doctrine affirms that we don't possess anything unless we do it ourselves. Unity is the birthright of every Christian, not because of our ecclesial or denominational associations, but because we belong to Christ. As Robert Webber has written, "No particular visible church entity has the right to lay exclusive claim to the nomenclature 'body of Christ' for herself. The whole church is much greater than the sum of her parts, and the multitudinous variety of the church shows her fullness more than any particular church. The church includes all who confess Jesus as Lord."[24]

---

23 Joe Rigney, "How to Weigh Doctrines for Christian Unity",
http://thegospelcoalition.org/article/weigh-doctrines-for-christian-unity.
24 Robert Webber, *Common Roots: The Original Call to an Ancient-Future Faith* (Grand Rapids, Zondervan, 1978), p. 86.

10
To Whom Shall We Go?

Evangelicals who choose to leave the "movement," dispersed and decentralized as it is, sometimes speak of gaining more without leaving behind what they learned and held as evangelicals. Francis Beckwith is an example when he says, "At the end of the day, I am an Evangelical Catholic because I believe in the Evangel, the Gospel, the Good News, and that it is a gift of God that ought to be embraced and lived by everyone. As an Evangelical, indeed as Christian, I have the obligation to spread the Good News of Jesus Christ. I am Catholic insofar as I believe that the Church is universal and that its continuity is maintained through history by the whole of its membership, the body of Christ, and not *merely* as a collection of isolated individuals in personal relationship with Jesus."[1] But this is to engage in wishful thinking at best and self-delusion at worst. Making the move away from evangelicalism and into sacramentalism is, especially for converts, a package deal.

Former evangelical David Currie illustrates this as well when he says, "Indulgences were the hardest issue for me to resolve in my reconciliation with Catholicism. For that reason, it was one of the last with which I made peace."[2] But why must he "make peace" with this issue at all? Because of the paradigm shift required, and because ecclesiology, as the wellspring of sacramentalism, means that whatever the Church defines to be essential is what one must believe. Regardless of whether there is a scriptural basis for it, it is still part of the package. Once you cross this Rubicon (or in this case, the Tiber), you can't bring anything

---

[1] Francis J. Beckwith, *Return to Rome: Confessions of an Evangelical Catholic* (Grand Rapids, Brazos Press, 2009), p. 128.

[2] David B. Currie, *Born Fundamentalist, Born Again Catholic* (San Francisco, Ignatius Press, 1996), p. 129.

with you that conflicts with official dogma.

Recalling David Bebbington's "Evangelical Quadrilateral," at least three of the four corners cannot describe sacramental faith. Biblicism, with the scriptures as final authority for what a person believes, how one worships, and how one grows into Christlikeness, is set aside in sacramentalism for a model of authority that places the Church in the position of mediating and interpreting the Scriptures. Despite attempts to nuance this, it is axiomatic to sacramentalism that no true understanding of the Bible is possible outside of the church hierarchy. Evangelicals agree, but as they believe that all who know Jesus are part of the church, the definition of what constitutes the church is the crux of the matter. It can credibly be argued that evangelicals are more catholic than sacramentalists in their approach to scripture. Many evangelicals read Augustine or Tertullian for their views. But do sacramentalists consult a Charles Spurgeon or a Martyn Lloyd-Jones? It is not simply a question of placing the Church as the arbiter of *meaning* when we look at the Scriptures, but also in assigning the place of *authority* to be other than the Bible as the source of doctrine. *Lex Orandi, Lex Credendi* is the logical end of this. By insisting on the mediation of the Church in every aspect of the believer's interaction with God, sacramentalism replaces the role of the Holy Spirit in the life of a Christian. It is a promise that the believer will have the guidance of the Spirit. Every Christian needs to ask this, will the Spirit guide us in ways that are directly contrary to what he inspired to be written in Scripture? To embrace sacramentalism is an implicit yes to this.

Crucicentrism as well is no part of sacramental doctrine. With the liturgical focus on the Eucharist, it may at first seem that the death of Christ is valued, but the finality and complete sufficiency of his death as the sole basis for the believer's justification – this biblical distinctive is completely absent from sacramental teaching. In other words, a wholly different meaning is assigned to the death of Christ and what it accomplishes for the believer.

Here, too, in rejecting the view of Christ's *imputed* righteousness to the Christian, and instead embracing the Catholic dogma of *infused* righteousness via the sacraments and good works, Beckwith must accept the entire package of sacramentalism. He cannot hold to both righteousness by infusion and righteousness by imputation at the same time.

When people are born again, their standing with God is entirely changed. They are now in Christ, and their righteousness is that of Christ himself. Their state is a different matter entirely. It may fluctuate from day to day. I may sin, and my fellowship with God is broken. I lose my joy, and indeed become unfruitful, but I do not cease to be an adopted child of God. In short, my state cannot change my standing. The latter rests on the sure and finished work of Christ. Sacramentalism turns this on its head, and makes one's standing dependent on state. As I do more, as my state improves, God pours more righteousness into me. This is the essence of infused righteousness, but it is not the gospel.

Conversionism is also impossible to hold to while embracing sacramental doctrine. Converts from evangelicalism uniformly affirm that they were Christians prior to becoming Roman Catholic or Orthodox. But nearly all converts from Catholicism or Orthodoxy to evangelicalism have testified that they previously did not know God; they were not converted. This, too, is why, upon coming to understand what conversion is and what it is based on, these converts almost always undergo believers' baptism, acknowledging the biblical necessity of personal faith. The proxy baptism they may have undergone as infants involved no personal faith of their own. In sacramental teaching, it is taught that divine life is given entirely apart from personal faith. A baptized infant is considered part of God's family, part of the Church. Whether sacramental doctrine views infant baptism to be a conversion, it is certainly not the type that Bebbington describes as personal faith in Jesus, that is, the new birth. Every conversion in the book of Acts demonstrates a clear crossing over from death to life. Upon expressing faith in Jesus, a person was instantly made a member of his body. Far from requiring any sacrament, the new birth for these individuals happened spontaneously as they saw Jesus to be the Son of God, and the Savior who could redeem them from their sins. In short, justification was not infused into them; it was imputed to them at that moment of faith.

The *Catechism of the Catholic Church* states unequivocally, "The Church affirms that for believers the sacraments of the New Covenant are *necessary for salvation*"[3] (italics original). This summarizes the sacramental view of grace and salvation I have repeatedly examined throughout the previous chapters. There is no experience of God, no conversion, and indeed no final salvation apart from engaging in the ritual acts defined by the Church. This is diametrically opposed to justification by faith in Christ alone. It is the system, rather than the Savior that assumes the importance in sacramentalism.

Theologian D. Jeffrey Bingham is not encouraged by evangelical prospects: "Allow me to be perfectly clear. I believe the future of evangelicalism is in jeopardy. My belief is linked directly to what I perceive as the subculture's movement away from, even rejection of, baptismal catechesis, particularly in the dizzying Free Church varieties. Such departures from baptismal catechesis, I believe, are at least in part responsible for recent concerns expressed about doctrinal weakness among evangelicals, the drift of 'post-evangelicals' from such basic faith commitments as inerrancy and the unity of the Hebrew Bible and New Testament, and a growing openness among perhaps half of evangelicals to flirt with the idea that several religions, other that Christianity, could be salvific."[4] As I've made clear, I share many of these concerns of doctrinal weakness in the church today.

---

[3] *Catechism of the Catholic Church*, p. 319.

[4] D. Jeffrey Bingham, "Evangelicals and the Rule of Faith, Irenaeus on Rome and Reading Christianly," in *Evangelicals and The Early Church: Recovery, Reform, Renewal* (Eugene, Cascade Books, 2012), p. 159.

Bingham is joined by the scholars I referenced earlier, such as D.H. Williams and Thomas Oden, in urging that the recovery of orthodoxy can only be accomplished by a recovery of the Great Tradition. However, I do not share these scholars' belief that any real recovery of orthodoxy and doctrinal fidelity will come through an embrace of creeds or tradition, much less from sacramentalism.

In his 2012 book, *Bad Religion: How We Became a Nation of Heretics*, New York Times columnist Ross Douthat chronicles the decades-long decay of mainline Protestantism, not only in numbers, but also in a shift away from exclusive truth claims. But he also traces a similar decline in the Catholic Church. Douthat discusses the "accommodation" that occurred with Vatican II, and indeed was accelerated by it, leading to a turn away from traditional theology. As Douthat writes, "From seminaries to parishes, theology departments to church bureaucracies, accomodationism became ubiquitous without always being made explicit. Still, it *was* ubiquitous."[5] This decline in orthodoxy occurred exactly where the Great Tradition was affirmed. These were the churches that recited the Apostles' Creed weekly, where the liturgical calendar was kept, where worship was strictly liturgical (in the case of Catholicism), or quasi-liturgical (in the case of mainline Protestantism). In short, these faith communions held to the Great Tradition, but this did nothing to prevent their departure from truth.

I am not suggesting that nothing can be learned by the engagement with history. By all means, read the church fathers, acquaint yourself with history, but understand that the fathers are men who could and did sin and make mistakes, and are therefore sometimes unreliable guides. They may have helpful insights into Scripture, but they may likewise lead us down the wrong path. Their temporal proximity as closer to the beginning of the church may count for little in what they are able to impart. They did not

---

[5] Ross Douthat, *Bad Religion: How We Became a Nation of Heretics* (New York, Free Press, 2012), p. 100.

live to see the fruition of some of the doctrines that were set in motion in earlier centuries. Those who urge us to "Read the Bible with the dead" must recognize that death alone does not confer upon the writings of the fathers a helpfulness or orthodoxy if they did not previously possess these. As George Weigel has said, "That something is antique in the Church, however, does not mean it is necessarily good, or true, or an aid to mission."[6]

Evangelicalism and the truth that has characterized it is not a protest against the hierarchical Church. It is rather an embrace of the incarnate Word as he is revealed to us through the written Word. The eyewitnesses of his glory are long gone from the earth. What God has left us is the record of Scripture; a record that puts before our eyes a Savior, Jesus, who fully atoned for our sins, and in whom we stand completely justified. He is a Savior who has made us children of God by faith, who sanctified us, and continues to sanctify us. There is no need to manufacture mystery, for the truth of Scripture gives the Christian all that is needed for life and godliness and for growing into Christlikeness. All of these truths of justification, of life in Christ, of abiding in him, and of bearing fruit for God – in short, what it means to be a member of the body of Christ – all of these are conveyed to us not by anything sacramental, but through the Spirit applying the Bible to our hearts.

It is perhaps in this area where sacramentalism may be most damaging: inserting the Church where the Holy Spirit himself belongs. Imparting understanding and comprehension of God's promises and blessings to the believer is the Spirit's work. Paul affirms this in 1 Cor. 2:12: "Now we have received not the spirit of the world, but the Spirit who is from God, *that we might understand the things freely given us by God.*"

Contemporary faith maintains the truest link with the apostolic and biblical faith when it affirms and conforms to this apostolic

---

[6] George Weigel, *Evangelical Catholicism: Deep Reform in the 21st Century Church* (New York, Basic Books, 2013), p. 100.

message. Paul begins his letter to the Romans avowing that the gospel, which he calls the power of God unto salvation, was promised beforehand by God through his prophets in the holy Scriptures (Rom. 1:2). Peter likewise affirms that we "have been born again, not of perishable seed but of imperishable, through the living and abiding word of God" (1 Peter 1:23). James also says that God brought us forth by the word of truth (James 1:18). Not only is our birth into God's family accomplished through the agency of the Word, but also our growth in him. Paul counsels the Colossians to "let the word of Christ dwell in you richly" (Col. 3:16). And the sole offensive weapon in the armor of God is the "sword of the Spirit, which is the word of God" (Eph. 6:17).

I agree with those who claim that instruction is needed within contemporary evangelicalism, but the Rule of Faith is no substitute for the Bible, and catechesis according to the Rule or tradition will do nothing to stem the tide of theological dereliction. To blame evangelical problems on a lack of awareness of tradition is but a distraction from the core issue. The irony is that evangelicals have found themselves in trouble by too often diminishing Scripture and its use. Whether through reverting to topical preaching, superficial interaction with the Bible, or in not considering that the Scriptures really are the final authority for their lives, evangelicals have not availed themselves of God's Word.

My appeal in these pages to fellow evangelicals has been to recover, and perhaps for some to newly recognize the incredible wealth that is ours in the written Word of God. Every problem, every shortcoming, every doctrinal aberration within evangelicalism, and indeed within any branch of the church, is solved only by an *intentional and sustained engagement with scripture*. Yet the Bible is not merely a corrective for our failures, but a prescription for a joyful, fruitful life in Christ. Embracing sacramentalism will only lead believers further away from the truth that a *relationship*, not *ritual*, is the scripturally ordained way of growth in Christ. Those who are adrift can only regain their moorings by once again submitting to the Bible for everything in their Christian lives. Evangelicals may have read it too little, valued it too little, and too infrequently put in the work of implanting into their lives these very words of God that tell us of Jesus the Word. David wrote in Psalm 138:2, "For you have exalted above all things your name and *your word*." It is imperative for evangelicals to once again say "Amen" to that.

Index of Modern Authors

Select Bibliography

Ådna, Jostein, *The Formation of the Early Church*. Tübingen: Mohr Siebeck, 2005.

Afonsky, Gregory. *Christ and the Church: In Orthodox Teaching and Tradition*. Crestwood: St. Vladimir's Seminary Press, 2001.

Aland, Kurt. *Did the Early Church Baptize Infants?* New York: SCM Press, 1964.

Allert, Craig. *A High View of Scripture?* Grand Rapids: Baker Academic, 2005.

Altaner, Berthold., Hilda C. Graef, trans. *Patrology*. New York: Herder And Herder, 1961.

Anastos, Milton V. "Nestorius Was Orthodox." *Dumbarton Oaks Papers*, *Vol. 16*, 1962.

Audisio, Gabriel, Claire Davison, trans. *The Waldensian Dissent: Persecution and Survival, c. 1170-c.1570*. Cambridge: Cambridge Univ. Press, 1999.

Barnes, T.D. *Tertullian: A Historical and Literary Study*. Oxford [Oxfordshire]: Clarendon Press; New York : Oxford University Press, 1985, 1971.

Barth, Karl., G.W. Bromiley and T.F. Torrance, trans. Church Dogmatics, 2nd ed. Edinburgh: T&T Clark, 1975.

Barton, John. *Holy Writings, Sacred Text: The Canon in Early Christianity*. Louisville: Westminster John Knox Press, 1997.

Baus, Karl., and Jedin, Hubert. Hubert Jedin & John Dolan, eds. *From the Apostolic Community to Constantine*. New York: Herder and Herder, 1965.

Baus, Karl., et. al. *The Imperial Church from Constantine to the Early Middle Ages*. New York: Seabury Press, 1980.

Bebbington, David. *Evangelicalism in Modern Britain: A History from the 1730s to the 1980s*. London: Unwin Hyman, 1989.

Beckwith, Francis J. *Return to Rome: Confessions of an Evangelical Catholic*. Grand Rapids: Brazos Press, 2009.

Beckwith, Roger T. *Elders in Every City, The Origin and Role of the Ordained Ministry*. Carlisle, Cumbria: PaterNoster Press, 2003.

_____. *The Old Testament Canon of the New Testament Church and its Background in Early Judaism*. Grand Rapids: Eerdmans, 1985.

Bell, Rob. *Love Wins: A Book About Heaven, Hell, and the Fate of Every Person Who Ever Lived*. New York: HarperOne, 2011.

Bennett, Richard Peter. *Far from Rome, Near to God: The Testimonies of Fifty Converted Roman Catholic Priests*. Carlisle: Banner of Truth, 2009.

Bergler, Thomas. *The Juvenalization of American Christianity*. Grand Rapids: Eerdmans, 2012.

Blosser, Philip. "What are the Philosophical and Practical Problems of

Sola Scriptura?" *Not By Scripture Alone: A Catholic Critique of the Protestant Doctrine of Sola Scriptura.* Robert A Sungenis, ed. Santa Barbara: Queenship Publishing, 1997.

Bradshaw, Paul F. *The Search for the Origins of Christian Worship* New York: Oxford University Press, 1992.

Broadbent, E.H. *The Pilgrim Church.* London: Pickering & Inglis, 1931.

Brown, Peter. *Augustine of Hippo.* Berkeley: Univ. of California Press, 1967.

Brown, Raymond E. *Priest and Bishop: Biblical Reflections.* Paramus: Paulist Press, 1970.

_____. *Priest and Bishop: Biblical Reflections.* Paramus: Paulist Press, 1970.

_____., Donfried, Karl P., Fitzmyer, Joseph A., Reumann, John., eds. *Mary in the New Testament.* Philadelphia: Fortress Press, 1978.

Bruce. F.F. *The Canon of Scripture.* Downers Grove: Inter-Varsity Press, 1988.

_____. *The Growing Day: The Progress and Growth of Christianity from the Fall of Jerusalem to the Accession of Constantine (A.D. 70-313).*Grand Rapids: Wm. B. Eerdmans, 1954.

_____. *The New Testament Documents, Are They Reliable? 5th* ed. Grand Rapids, Wm. B. Eerdmans, 1960.

_____. *New Testament History.* Garden City: Anchor Books, 1972.

Bulgakov, Sergius. "The Virgin and the Saints in Orthodoxy." *Eastern Orthodox Theology: A Reader.* Daniel Clendenin, ed. Grand Rapids: Baker, 1995.

Campenhausen, H. von. *Ecclesiastical Authority and Spiritual Power in the Church of the First Three Centuries.* Stanford: Stanford University Press, 1969.

Carroll, Colleen. *The New Faithful: Why Young Adults are Embracing Christian Orthodoxy.* Chicago: Loyola Press, 2002.

Carson, D. A. *The Gagging of God.* Grand Rapids: Zondervan Publishing, 1996.

Catechism of the Catholic Church. New York: Image Books, 1995.

Chadwick, Henry. *The Penguin History of the Church, Volume 1: The Early Church.*, Rev. Ed., London: Penguin Books, 1993.

Chafer, Lewis Sperry. *Systematic Theology, Volume 4: Ecclesiology - Eschatology.* Dallas: Dallas Seminary Press, 1948.

Childs, Brevard S. *Old Testament Theology in a Canonical Context.* Philadelphia: Fortress Press, 1985.

Cirlot, Felix L. *The Early Eucharist.* London: Society for Promoting Christian Knowledge, 1939.

Colson, Charles and Neuhaus, Richard John, eds. *Evangelicals and Catholics Together: Toward a Common Mission.* Dallas: Word, 1995.

Congar, Yves. Paul Philibert, O.P., trans. *True and False Reform in the Church.* Collegeville: Liturgical Press, 2011.

Cullmann, Oscar. *The Early Church*. London, SCM Press, Ltd., 1956.

Currie, David. *Born Fundamentalist, Born Again Catholic*. San Francisco: Ignatius Press, 1996.

Davis, Leo Donald. S.J. *The First Seven Ecumenical Councils (325-787)*. Collegeville: The Liturgical Press, 1983.

De Lubac, Henri., trans. Michael Mason. *The Splendor of the Church*. San Francisco: Ignatius Press, 1956.

De Margerie, Bernard., trans. Leonard Maluf. *An Introduction to the History of Exegesis, vol. 1: The Greek Fathers*. Petersham: Saint Bede's Publications, MA, 1994)

Demsky, Aaron. "Writing in Ancient Israel." *Mikra, Text, Translation, Reading and Interpretation of the Hebrew Bible in Ancient Judaism & Early Christianity*. Martin J. Mulder and Harry Sysling, eds. Peabody: Hendrickson, 2004.

Dever, Mark. *The Church: The Gospel Made Visible*. Nashville: B&H Publishing Group, 2012.

Dockery, David S. *Biblical Interpretation Then and Now: Contemporary Hermeneutics In Light of the Early Church*. Grand Rapids: Baker, 1992.

Douthat, Ross. *Bad Religion: How We Became a Nation of Heretics*. New York: The Free Press, 2012.

Dulles, Avery. *Models of the Church*. New York: Image Books, 1987.

_____. *Models of Revelation*, Garden City: Double Day, 1983.

Dunn, James D. G. *Unity and Diversity in the New Testament. An Enquiry into the Character of Earliest Christianity*. London: SCM Press, 1990.

Edersheim, Alfred. *The Life and Times of Jesus the Messiah*. Grand Rapids: Wm. B. Eerdmans, 1962.

Faber, G.S. *The History of the Ancient Vallenses and Albigenses*. Kindle Edition: Delmarva Publications, 2014.

Faivre, Alexandre, David Smith, trans., *The Emergence of the Laity in the Early Church*. Mahwah, NJ: Paulist Press, 1990.

Farksasfalvy, Denis, O. Cist. *Inspiration and Interpretation: A Theological Introduction to Sacred Scripture*. Washington: The Catholic University of America Press, 2010.

Ferguson, Everett. *The Church of Christ, a Biblical Ecclesiology for Today*. Grand Rapids: Wm. B. Eerdmans, 1996.

Foster, Paul. "The Epistles of Ignatius of Antioch and the Writings that later formed the New Testament." *The Reception of the New Testament in the Apostolic Fathers*. Andrew F. Gregory, Christopher M. Tuckett, eds. Oxford: Oxford University Press, 2005.

Franke, John R. "Scripture, Tradition, and Authority, Reconstructing the Evangelical Conception of Sola Scriptura." *Evangelicals & Scripture: Tradition, Authority, and Hermeneutics*. Vincent E. Bacote, Laura C. Miguélez, Dennis L. Okholm, eds. Downers Grove: IVP Academic, 2004.

Frassetto, Michael. *The Great Medieval Heretics: Five Centuries of*

Religious Dissent. New York: BlueBridge, 2008.

Frend, W.H.C. *The Early Church.* Minneapolis: Fortress Press, 1982.

Froehlich, Karlfried. *Biblical Interpretation in the Early Church.* Philadelphia: Fortress Press, 1984.

Ganoczy, Alexandre., William Thomas, Anthony Sherman, trans. *An Introduction to Catholic Sacramental Theology.* New York: Paulist Press, 1984.

Gillquist, Peter E. *Becoming Orthodox: A Journey to the Ancient Christian Faith.* Ben Lomond: Conciliar Press, 1992.

Gooding, David. *According to Luke: A New Exposition of the Third Gospel.* Grand Rapids: Wm. B. Eerdmans, 1987.

Graef, Hilda C. *Mary: A History of Doctrine and Devotion.* Notre Dame, IN: Ave Maria Press, 2009.

Grant, Robert M. *The Formation of the New Testament.* New York: Harper and Row, 1965.

_____., Tracey, David. *A Short History of Interpretation of the Bible.* Philadelphia: Fortress Press, 1984.

Gratsch, Edward J. *Where Peter Is: A survey of Ecclesiology.* New York: Alba House, 1975.

Gregory, Brad S. "A Response to Evangelicalism." *Journeys of Faith: Evangelicalism, Eastern Orthodoxy, Catholicism, and Anglicanism.* Robert L. Plummer, ed. Grand Rapids: Zondervan, 2012.

Grudem, Wayne. *Systematic Theology, An Introduction to Biblical Doctrine.* Grand Rapids: Zondervan, 1994.

Guthrie, Donald. *New Testament Theology.* Downers Grove: Inter-Varsity Press, 1981.

_____. *The Pastoral Epistles, an Introduction and Commentary.* Grand Rapids: Eerdmans, 1957.

Hall, Christopher. "Tradition, Authority, Magesterium" *Ancient Faith for the Church's Future.* Mark Husbands, Jeffrey P. Greenman, eds. Downers Grove: IVP Academic, 2007.

Hall, Stuart G. *Doctrine and Practice in the Early Church.* Grand Rapids: Eerdmans, 1991.

Hahn, Scott. *Lord Have Mercy: The Healing Power of Confession.* New York: Doubleday, 2003.

_____. *Scripture Matters: Essays on Reading the Bible from the Heart of the Church.* Steubenville: Emmaus Road Publishing, 1991.

_____. *Swear to God: The Promise and Power of the Sacraments.* New York: Doubleday, 2004.

_____., Hahn, Kimberley. *Rome Sweet Home: Our Journey to Catholicism.* San Francisco: Ignatius Press, 1993.

Hansen, Collin. "Not All Evangelicals and Catholics Together." Christianity Today. Oct. 29, 2009.

_____. "Why Johnny Can't Read the Bible". Christianity Today, May 24, 2010.

Hanson, R.P.C. "Basil's Doctrine of Tradition in Relation to the Holy

Spirit." *Vigiliae Christianae*, Vol. 22, No. 4. Dec. 1968.

_____. *Tradition in the Early Church*. Philadephia: The Westminster Press, 1962.

Hanson, Richard, Fuller, Reginald. *The Church of Rome: A Dissuasive*. London: SCM Press, 1950.

Hart, Darryl G. "The Use and Abuse of the Christian Past. Mercersburg, the Ancient Church, and American Evangelicalism." *Evangelicals and the Early Church: Recovery, Reform, Renewal*. George Kalantzis, Andrew Tooley, eds., Eugence: Cascade Books, 2012.

Hartog, Paul. *Polycarp and the New Testament*. Tübingen: Mohr Siebeck, 2002.

_____. "The Complexity and Variety of Contemporary Church – Early Church Engagements." *The Contemporary Church and the Early Church: Case studies in Ressourcement*. Paul Hartog, ed., Eugene: Wipf & Stock, 2010.

Hertel, Mary, Bennett, Richard eds. *The Truth Set Us Free: Twenty Former Nuns Tell Their Stories*. N.p.: WinePress Publishing, 1997.

Houlden, J.L., ed. *The Interpretation of the Bible in the Church* (Pontifical Bible Institute). London: SCM Press, Ltd., 1995.

Kaiser, Walter C. Jr. "Legitimate Hermeneutics". *A Guide to Contemporary Hermeneutics: Major Trends in Biblical Interpretation*. Donald K. McKim, ed. Grand Rapids: Wm. B. Eerdmans, 1986.

Kannengieser, Charles. *Handbook of Patristic Exegesis, Vol. 1*.Leiden: Brill, 2004.

_____. "Augustine and Tyconius: A Conflict of Christian Hermeneutics in Roman Africa". *Augustine and the Bible*. Pamela Bright, ed. and trans. Notre Dame: University of Notre Dame Press, 1999.

Kelley, J.N.D. *Early Christian Doctrines*. Rev. ed. San Francisco: HarperSanFrancisco, 1978.

Kennedy, John W. *The Torch of the Testimony*. Beaumont: The Seed Sowers, 1965.

Köstenberger, Andreas and Kruger, Michael. *The Heresy of Orthodoxy: How Contemporary Culture's Fascination with Diversity has Reshaped Our Understanding of Early Christianity*. Wheaton: Crossway, 2010.

Kraftchick, Steven J. *Jude, 2 Peter*. Nashville: Abingdon Press, 2002.

Kreeft, Peter. *Catholic Christianity*. San Francisco: Ignatius Press, 2001.

_____. "Ecumenical Jihad." *Reclaiming the Great Tradition: Evangelicals, Catholics & Orthodox in Dialogue*. James S. Cutsinger, ed. (Downers Grove, InterVarsity Press, 1997.

Kruger, Michael J. *The Question of Canon: Challenging the Status Quo In the New Testament Debate*. Kindle Edition: Intervarsity Press, 2013.

_____. *Canon Revisited: Establishing the Origins and Authority of the New Testament Books*. Good News Publishers. Kindle Edition, 2012.

Leiman, Sid. Z. *The Canonization of Hebrew Scripture, the Talmudic and Midrashic Evidence*. Hamden: Archon Books, 1976.

Lenski, R.C.H. *The Interpretation of St. Luke's Gospel*. Minneapolis: Augsburg Publishing House, 1946.

Lietzmann, Hans, trans. Bertram Lee Wolf. *A History of the Early Church, vol.II*. Cleveland: World Publishing Co., 1938.

Lightfoot, Neil R. *How We Got The Bible*, 3· ed., New York, MJF Books, 2003.

Litfin, Bryan M. *Getting to Know the Church Fathers: An Evangelical Introduction*. Grand Rapids: Brazos Press, 2007.

_____. "Learning from the Patristic Use of the Rule of Faith." *The Contemporary Church and the Early Church: Case Studies in Ressourcement*. Paul A Hartog, ed. Eugene: Pickwick, Publications, 2010.

Lockyer, Herbert. *All the Doctrines of the Bible*. Grand Rapids: Zondervan, 1964.

Longenecker, Dwight. *More Christianity*. Huntington: Our Sunday Visitor, Inc., 2002.

_____., Gustafson, David. *Mary: A Catholic-Evangelical Debate*. Eastborne: Brazos Press, 2003.

Lossky, Vladimir. *The Mystical Theology of the Eastern Church*. Crestwood: St. Vladimir's Seminary Press, 1976.

Lössl, Josef. *The Early Church: History and Memory*. London;New York: T & T Clark, 2010.

MacCulloch, Diarmaid. *The Reformation: A History*. New York: Penguin Books, 2003.

MacMullen, Ramsay. *Christianizing the Roman Empire (A.D. 100-400)*. New Haven: Yale University Press, 1984.

_____. *Voting About God in Early Church Councils*. New Haven: Yale Univ. Press, 2006.

Mango, Cyril. *Byzantium, The Empire of New Rome*. New York: Charles Scribners & Sons., 1980.

Markus, R.A. *Christianity in the Roman World*. New York: Charles Scribner's Sons, 1974.

Madrid, Patrick. *Surprised By Truth 2*. Manchester: Sophia Institute Press, 2000.

_____. *Surprised By Truth 3*. Manchester: Sophia Institute Press, 2007.

Marshall, I. Howard. *Last Supper and Lord's Supper*. Grand Rapids: Wm. B. Eerdmans, 1980.

Martin, Ralph P. *Worship in the Early Church*. Grand Rapids: Eerdmans, 1964.

McCallum, J. Ramsay. *Abelard's Christian Theology*. Merrick: Richwood Publishing Co., 1976.

McDonald, Lee Martin. *The Biblical Canon: Its Origin, Transmission, and Authority.*, 3· ed. Peabody, Hendrickson, 2007.

_____. *Forgotten Scriptures: The Selection and Rejection of Early*

Religious Writings. Louisville: Westminster John Knox Press, 2009.

McGinn, Bernard. *The Presence of God: A History of Western Christian Mysticism, vol. 1: Foundations of Mysticism: Origins to the Fifth Century*. New York: Crossroad Publishing Co., 1994.

McKnight, Scot. *The Real Mary: Why Evangelical Christians Can Embrace the Mother of Jesus*. Brewster, Paraclete Press, 2007.

_____. "From Wheaton to Rome: Why Evangelicals Convert to Roman Catholicism." *Journal of the Evangelical Theological Society*, September, 2002.

_____., and Ondrey, Hauna. *Finding Faith, Losing Faith: Stories of Conversion and Apostasy*. Waco: Baylor Univ. Press, 2008.

McLaren, Brian D. *The Church on the Other Side*. Grand Rapids: Zondervan, 2000.

McMichael, Ralph N. *Eucharist: A Guide for the Perplexed*. London: T&T Clark, 2010.

Merkle, Benjamin. *The Elder and Overseer, One Office in the Early Church*. New York: Peter Lang, 2003.

Metzger, Bruce M. *The Canon of the New Testament, Its Origin, Development, And Significance*. Oxford: Clarendon Press, 1987.

_____. *An Introduction to the Apochrypha*. New York: Oxford University Press, 1957.

_____. *The New Testament, Its Background, Growth, and Content*, 2nd ed. Nashville: Abingdon, 1983.

Meyendorff, John. *The Orthodox Church, Its Past and its Role in the World Today*. New York: Pantheon Books, 1962.

Meyer, Charles R. *Man of God: A Study of the Priesthood*. Eugene: Wipf and Stock, 2002.

Miller, Donald E. *Reinventing American Protestantism: Christianity in the New Millennium*. Berkeley: Univ. of California Press, 1997.

Mitros, Joseph, S.J. "The Norm of Faith in the Patristic Age." *Theological Studies*, 29.3, 1968.

Montague, George T., S.M. *First and Second Timothy, Titus*. Grand Rapids: Baker Academic, 2008.

Morrison, John Douglas. *Has God Said? Scripture, The Word of God, And the Crisis of Theological Authority*. Eugene: Pickwick Publications, 2006.

Morrison, Karl F. *Tradition and Authority in the Western Church 300-1140*. Princeton: Princeton University Press, 1969.

Mounce, Robert H. *The Book of Revelation*. Grand Rapids: Wm. B. Eerdmans, 1977.

Newman, John Henry. *An Essay on the Development of Christian Doctrine*. N.p.: Amazon Digital Services, 2011.

Noll, Mark A. and Nystrom, Carolyn. *Is the Reformation Over? An Evangelical Assessment of Contemporary Roman Catholicism*. Grand Rapids: Baker Academic, 2005.

Norris, Richard A. Jr. "Augustine and the Close of the Ancient Period". *A*

History of Biblical Interpretation, vol.1. Alan J. Hauser, Duane F. Watson, eds. Grand Rapids: Eerdmans, 2003.

Norwich, John Julius. *A Short History of Byzantium*. New York: Vintage Books, 1999.

Oberman, Heiko A. *Forerunners of the Reformation: The Shape of Late Medieval Thought*. New York: Holt, Rinehart and Winston, 1996.

O'Donnell, James J. *Augustine: A New Biography*. New York: Harper Collins, 2005.

O'Malley, John W. *Trent: What Happened at the Council*. Cambridge: The Belknap Press of Harvard University, 2013.

O'Rourke, David K. *A Process Called Conversion*. Garden City: Doubleday, 1985.

Ott, Ludwig, Patrick Lynch, trans., James Bastible, ed., *Fundamentals Of Catholic Dogma*. Rockford: Tan Books and Publishers, 1955.

Patzia, Arthur G. *The Making of the New Testament*. Downers Grove: Inter-Varsity Press, 1995.

Pelikan, Jaroslav. *The Christian Tradition: A History of the Development of Doctrine, vol.1: The Emergence of the Catholic Tradition (100-600)*. Chicago: University of Chicago Press, 1971.

_____. *The Christian Tradition: A History of the Development of Doctrine, vol. 2: The Spirit of Eastern Christendom (600-1700)* Chicago: University of Chicago Press, 1974.

_____. *The Christian Tradition: A History of the Development of Doctrine, vol. 3: The Growth of Medieval Theology (600-1300)* Chicago: University of Chicago Press, 1978

_____. *Historical Theology: Continuity and Change in Christian Doctrine*. New York: Corpus, 1971.

_____. *Mary Through the Centuries: Her Place in the History of Culture*. New York: History Book Club, 2005.

_____. ed., *Sacred Writings, Vol. 2, Christianity: The New Testament and Apochrypha*. New York: Book of the Month Club, 1992.

_____. *Whose Bible Is It? A History of the Scriptures Through the Ages*. New York: Viking, 2005.

Perry, Tim. *Mary for Evangelicals: Toward an Understanding of the Mother of Our Lord*. Downers Grove, Intervarsity Press, 2006.

Peters, George N.H. *The Theocratic Kingdom*. Grand Rapids: Kregel Publications, 1988.

Prestige, G.L. *Fathers and Heretics*. London, SPCK, 1968.

Preston, Geoffrey, Aidan Nichols, ed., *Faces of the Church: Meditations on a Mystery and Its Images*. Grand Rapids: Eerdmans, 1997.

Pritchard, G.A. *Willow Creek Seeker Services, Evaluating A New Way Of Doing Church*. Grand Rapids: Baker, 1996.

Rahner, Karl., Edward Quinn, trans. *The Priesthood*. New York: Seabury Press, 1973.

Rankin, David. *Tertullian and the Church*. Cambridge: Cambridge University Press, 1995.

Ray, Stephen K. *Crossing the Tiber: Evangelical Protestants Discover the Historical Church*. San Francisco: Ignatius Press, 1997.

Reese, Ruth Anne. *2 Peter and Jude*. Grand Rapids: Eerdmans, 2007.

Reventlow, Henning Graf., Leo G. Purdue, trans. *History of Biblical Interpretation, Vol. 1: From The Old Testament to Origen*. Atlanta: Society of Biblical Literature, 2009.

_____., James O. Duke, trans. *History of Biblical Interpretation, Vol. 2: From Late Antiquity to the End of the Middle Ages*. Atlanta: Society of Biblical Literature, 2009.

Rowley, H.H. *The Faith of Israel*. London: SCM Press, Ltd., 1956.

Saucy, Robert L. *The Church in God's Program*. Chicago: Moody Press, 1972.

Schmemann, Alexander. *For The Life of the World: Sacraments and Orthodoxy*. Crestwood: St. Vladimir's Seminary Press, 1973.

_____. *The Historical Road of Eastern Orthodoxy*. Crestwood: St. Vladimir's Seminary Press, 1977.

_____. "Moment of Truth for Orthodoxy." *Eastern Orthodox Theology: A Contemporary Reader.*, Daniel Clendenin, ed. Grand Rapids: Baker, 1995.

Schreiner, Thomas. "Baptism in the Epistles: An Initiation Rite for Believers." *Believer's Baptism*. Shawn D. Wright, Thomas Schreiner, eds. B&H Publishing, Kindle Edition, 2007.

Schmithals, Walter, O.C. Dean, Jr., trans., *The Theology of the First Christians*. Louisville: Westminster John Knox Press, 1997.

Slagle, Amy. *The Eastern Church in the Spiritual Marketplace: American Conversions to Orthodox Christianity*. Dekalb, IL: NIU Press, 2011.

Smalley, Stephen S. *The Revelation of John: A Commentary on the Greek Text of the Apocalypse*. Downers Grove: InterVarsity Press, 2005.

Smidt, Corwin E. *American Evangelicals Today*. Lanham, MD: Rowman & Littlefield, Publications, 2013.

Smith, Christian. *How to Go From Being A Good Evangelical to A Committed Catholic in Ninety-Five Difficult Steps*. Eugene: Cascade Books, 2011.

_____. *The Bible Made Impossible: Why Biblicism Is Not a Truly Evangelical Reading of Scripture*. Grand Rapids: Brazos Press, 2011.

Smith, Warren Cole. *A Lover's Quarrel with the Evangelical Church*. Colorado Springs: Authentic Publishing, 2008.

Snyder, Graydon F. *Ante-Pacem: Archaeological Evidence of Church Life Before Constantine*. Macon: Mercer University Press, 1985.

Soulen, Richard N. *Sacred Scripture: A Short History of Interpretation*. Louisville: Westminster John Knox Press, 2009.

Southern, R.W. *The Penguin History of the Church, Volume 2: Western Society and the Church in the Middle Ages*. London: Penguin Books, 1970.

Stevenson, J. ed., *Creeds, Councils, And Controversies: Documents illustrating the history of the Church, AD 337-461*. London: SPCK,

1966.

Strayer, Joseph R. *The Albigensian Crusades.* New York: The Dial Press, 1971.

Stuhmacher, Peter. Roy A Harrisville, trans. *Historical Criticism and Theological Interpretation of Scripture.* Philadelphia: Fortress Press, 1977.

Sullivan, Francis A. S.J., *Magesterium: The Teaching Authority in the Catholic Church.* Ramsey: Paulist Press, 1983.

_____. *From Apostles to Bishops: The Development of the Episcopacy in the Early Church.* Mahwah: The Newman Press, 2001.

Sweeney, Jon M. *Strange Heaven: The Virgin Mary as Woman, Mother, Disciple, and Advocate.* Brewster, MA: Paraclete Press, 2006.

Tavard, George H. "Tradition in Theology: A Problematic Approach." *Perspectives on Scripture and tradition: Essays.* Robert M. Grant, Robert E. McNally, George H. Tavard. Notre Dame: Fides Publishers, 1976.

Thiel, John E. *Senses of Tradition: Continuity and Development in Catholic Faith.* Oxford: Oxford University Press, 2000.

Tierney, Brian. *Origins of Papal Infallibility, 1150-1350.* Leiden, E.J. Brill, 1972.

Tilley, Maureen. *The Bible In Christian North Africa: The Donatist World.* Minneapolis: Augsburg Fortress Press, 1997.

Trigg, Joseph W. *Biblical Interpretation.* Wilmington, Del.: Michael Glazier, 1988.

Verduin, Leonard. *The Reformers and Their Stepchildren.* Grand Rapids: Wm. B. Eerdmans, 1964.

Vila, Manuel Perez. *I Found the Ancient Way.* Chicago: Moody Press, 1958.

Webber, Robert. *Common Roots: A Call to Evangelical Maturity,* Grand Rapids: Zondervan, 1978.

Weigel, George. *Evangelical Catholicism: Deep Reform in the 21st Century Church.* New York: Basic Books, 2013.

Wells, David F. *No Place for Truth: Whatever Happened To Evangelical Theology?,* Grand Rapids: Wm. B. Eerdmans, 1993.

_____. *Turning To God: Reclaiming Christian Conversion as Unique, Necessary, and Supernatural.* Grand Rapids: Baker Books, 1989-2012.

Welsh, Frank. *The Battle for Christendom: The Council of Constance, The East-West Conflict, and the Dawn of Modern Europe.* Woodstock: The Overlook Press, 2008.

Westcott, Brooke Foss. *A General Survey of the History of the Canon of the New Testament,* 5 ed. Cambridge: Macmillan and co., 1881.

Wilken, Robert Louis. *The First Thousand Years: A Global History of Christianity.* New Haven: Yale University Press, 2012.

_____. *The Myth of Christian Beginnings: History's Impact on Belief.* Garden City: Doubleday & Co., 1971.

Williams, D.H. *Evangelicals and Tradition: The Formative Influence of the*

Early Church. Grand Rapids: Baker Academic, 2005.

_____. *Retrieving the Tradition and Renewing Evangelicalism: A Primer for Suspicious Protestants*. Grand Rapids: Wm. B. Eerdmans, 1999.

_____. "Similis Et Dissimilis: Gauging Our Expectations of the Early Fathers." *Ancient Faith for the Church's Future*. Mark Husbands and Jeffrey P. Greenman, eds. Downers Grove: IVP Academic, 2007.

Witherington, Ben. *Making A Meal Of It: Rethinking the Theology of the Lord's Supper*. Waco: Baylor University Press, 2007.

Wright, David F. *What Has Infant Baptism Done to Baptism? An Enquiry at the End of Christendom*. London: Paternoster, 2005.

_____. *Infant Baptism in Historical Perspective*. Eugene: Wipf & Stock, 2007.

Wylie, J.A. *The History of the Albigensian Crusades*. N.p.: Amazon Digital Services, 2011.

Worthen, Molly. *Apostles of Reason: The Crisis of Authority in American Evangelicalism*. Oxford University Press. Kindle Edition, 2013.

Young, Frances M. *From Nicaea to Chalcedon: A Guide to the Literature and Its Background*. Philadelphia: Fortress Press, 1983.

_____. "Alexandrian and Antiochene Exegesis". *A History of Biblical Interpretation, vol. 1., The Ancient Period*. Alan J. Hauser, Duane F. Watson, eds. Grand Rapids: Eerdmans, 2003.

Subject Index

Abelard, Peter, 110, 131

Adversus Haereses (Ignatius), 32, 73, 121

Alexandrian School, 90, 141ff.

allegorical interpretation of Scripture, 90, 141ff.; contrasted with typology, 144; subjective nature of, 90, 144; basis for sacramental view of Eucharist, 172;legacy in sacramental Church, 147ff.; rejection by modern scholars, 150

Ambrose, 129, 147, 163

Antiochene School, 144ff.; contrasted with Alexandrian, 146

Apocalypse of Peter, 100

apophatic theology, 157

apostasy, 51; warned of by apostles, 31, 51; warned of by apostles, 31, 51; originating in the church, 31, 51

Apostles' Creed, 200, 226

apostolicity, distinct from men, 31; Paul's denial of privilege, 32; unique character of, 31

apostolic succession, 35-36; Orthodox affirmation of, 31; residing in doctrine, 32-33

Athanasius, 67, 94, 95, 97, 100, 111

Aquinas, 44, 69, 131

Arius, 111

Assumption of Mary, 88

Augustine, 9,10, 58, 69, 96, 100, 108; and baptism, 164; and Canon of Scripture, 96-97; endorsement of extra-ecclesial sources, 150-152; exegesis of Good Samaritan, 147ff.; heir of Alexandrian school of hermeneutics, 148

baptism, effecting conversion, 160; following personal faith, 161, 165; importance in apostolic church, 160; reduction of meaning, 167ff., 211; symbol of death, burial, resurrection, 159;

baptism (continued), of infants not found in early church, 10, 163ff.

Baptists, 1

Barnabas, Epistle of, 98

Barna Group, 17

Basil of Caesarea, 88, 131,144

Benedict XVI, 89

Bible, authoritative in Israel, 78-79; authority for Evangelicals, 6, 23; Counter-Reformation attitude toward, 93; derivative authority of in sacramentalism, 86-87, 104; illiteracy among Evangelicals, 17-18; importance in corporate worship, 93; inerrancy of, 6-8, 225; in training for the RC priesthood, 112; interpretation of permitted to the Church alone, 86, 103-104, 137-138.

biblicism, 115-117

bishop(s) - see also elders, elected by congregation, 38; as institutional administrators, 40-41; untraceable as successors to the Twelve, 35

Boniface VIII, 210n.

Bonaventura, 131

Canon of Scripture, 94ff; assembled without hierarchical act, 96-97; criteria of, 97ff; early evidence for, 98; extrinsic model of, 94-96, 101, 104; authority precedes, 95, 104; intrinsic model of, 101-102

Carthage, Council of (397), 95

celibacy, 107

certainty, basis of, 113ff; crisis of, 6

Chafer, Lewis Sperry, 16

Chalcedon, council of (451), 66, 67, 128

Chicago Statement on Biblical Inerrancy, 7

Chrysostom, 145ff, 163

Church, authority of, 7, 17, 29, 35, 64, 74, 131, 138, 152;

Church (continued), clergy/laity division, 41-42, 62, 85-86, 178; distinct from Kingdom, 52; diversity of views within early church, 10, 109; doctrine of, 16, 42; founding of, 27-28; hierarchical view of in sacramentalism, 29-31; infallibility of in sacramentalism, 31-32, 55-56, 68, 103, 134; mediator of grace, 21, 55, 74; necessary for salvation, 53-55; officers of, 33ff.; organization of in NT, 33, 36, 39; organization of in sacramentalism, 30ff.; Orthodox view of, 28; Roman Catholic view of, 28, 30ff.

Clement VI, 108

clergy, 1, 45, 57, 60, 62, 63, 86, 178; title for all believers, 41-42; sacramental office not found in NT, 41, 86, 179;

Communion of Saints, 201ff.; vicarious atonement through, 202ff.

Conciliarism, 64ff

confession, condition of receiving forgiveness, 179; undermining the gospel, 183-184

Constance, Council of (1415), 70, 71, 72

Constantine (Emperor), 49, 51, 64, 65, 133

Constantine (Paulician leader), 60-61

Constantinian Fall, 50-52

Constantinople, Council of (381), 67

Constantinople, Council of (553), 145

Constantia's, 67

councils, authority of, 64ff.; definition of ecumenical, 64; differences between Catholic and Orthodox, 64-65; infallibility of, 68

creeds, 7, 106

curia, 10

Cyprian of Carthage, 39, 53-54, 55, 110; adherent of rigorism, 54, 109; rejection of ex opere operato, 60; opposition to hierarchy, 39; views on baptism, 109

Cyril of Alexandria, 65-66

Cyril of Jerusalem, 72-73

deacons, 33-34, 36

Dialogue with Trypho, 99

Didache, 109

Diodorus of Tarsus, 144ff

Dioscurus, 68

documents, expected with New Covenant, 81-82; growing preference for in early Church, 98-100

ecclesiology, 16, 27, 46, 53ff, 132, 135, 210, 220, 223; fundamental difference in views, 16; importance in sacramentalism, 27, 46, 55, 132, 138, 220

ecumenism, 14, 212, 219ff

elder(s), qualifications of, 40; synonymous with presbyter, 33-34; pastoral nature of, 41; plurality of, 36-37; local nature of, 39

Emergent church, 13-14, 219

Ephesus, council of, 66

Epiphanius of Salamis, 198

ERC (Evangelical Convert to Roman Catholicism), 5

eschatology, Amillennial view of Catholic and Orthodox Churches, 109; Premillennial view of in early Church, 108

Eucharist, diminishment in Evangelicalism, 171; establishment of, 170; Judaizing of, 172, 175; real presence view, 172ff.; transition away from memorial view, 171ff.

Eusebius of Caesarea, 132, 133

Evangelicals and Catholics Together, 213, 219

Evangelicalism, anti-clericalism of, 1; challenge of conversion away from, 4; decentralized nature of, 2; distinctives of, 3; populism of, 1; sectarianism within, 15

Evangelical(s), loss of meaning as descriptive term, 3

Execrabilis, 71

exegesis, 89, 112, 124-125, 141, 142ff.

filioque, 107, 131